Progress Chart

This chart lists the topics in the book. Once you have completed each page, stick a star in the correct box below.

Page	Topic	Star	Page	Topic	Star	Page	Topic	Star
2	Multiplying by 10, 100, and 1000	⭐	15	Decimal subtraction	⭐	28	Interpreting circle graphs	⭐
3	The simplest form of fractions	⭐	16	Decimal subtraction	⭐	29	Probability scale 0 to 1	⭐
4	Changing improper fractions to mixed numbers	⭐	17	Multiplying larger numbers by ones	⭐	30	Likely outcomes	⭐
5	Rounding decimals	⭐	18	Multiplying larger numbers by ones	⭐	31	Naming quadrilaterals	⭐
6	Adding with different numbers of digits	⭐	19	Real-life multiplication problems	⭐	32	Speed trials	⭐
7	Adding with different numbers of digits	⭐	20	Comparing and ordering decimals	⭐	33	All the 3s	⭐
8	Subtracting one number from another	⭐	21	Converting units of measure	⭐	34	All the 3s again	⭐
9	Subtracting one number from another	⭐	22	Converting units of measure	⭐	35	All the 4s	⭐
10	Real-life problems	⭐	23	Areas of rectangles and squares	⭐	36	All the 4s again	⭐
11	Everyday problems	⭐	24	Perimeter of shapes	⭐	37	Speed trials	⭐
12	Everyday problems	⭐	25	Decimal place value	⭐	38	Some of the 6s	⭐
13	Decimal addition	⭐	26	Speed problems	⭐	39	The rest of the 6s	⭐
14	Decimal addition	⭐	27	Conversion table	⭐	40	Practise the 6s	⭐

0	1	2	3	4	5	6	7	8	9	10
zero	one	two	three	four	five	six	seven	eight	nine	ten

Extra Practice Section

Page	Topic	Star	Page	Topic	Star
180	Choosing the operation	★	191	Graphs	★
181	Real-life problems	★	192	Using data	★
182	Adding decimals	★	193	Perimeters	★
183	Subtracting decimals	★	194	Square numbers	★
184	Money problems	★	195	Areas	★
185	Real-life problems	★	196	Recognizing angles	★
186	Keeping skills sharp	★	197	Measuring angles	★
187	Keeping skills sharp	★	198	3-D shapes	★
188	Reading schedules	★	199	Sorting 3-D shapes	★
189	Time problems	★	200	Keeping skills sharp	★
190	Coordinates	★	201	Keeping skills sharp	★

When you have completed the progress chart
in this book, fill in the certificate on page 202.

Ages 10-11
Grade 5
Math Workbook

Math Made Easy

Expanded Canadian Edition

Author Sean McArdle
Canadian math consultant Marilyn Wilson

Multiplying by 10, 100, and 1000

Write the answers in the boxes.

472 x 10 = [4720]   324 x 100 = [32 400]   57 x 1000 = [57 000]

Write the answers in the boxes.

426 x 10 =   319 x 10 =   584 x 10 =

740 x 10 =   985 x 10 =   612 x 10 =

102 x 100 =   725 x 100 =   383 x 100 =

909 x 100 =   651 x 100 =   737 x 100 =

4000 x 10 =   5649 x 10 =   8714 x 10 =

6302 x 100 =   9711 x 100 =   4826 x 100 =

Find the number that has been multiplied by 100.

[   ] x 100 = 163 100   [   ] x 100 = 562 300

[   ] x 100 = 841 300   [   ] x 100 = 864 700

[   ] x 100 = 636 500   [   ] x 100 = 839 100

[   ] x 100 = 521 000   [   ] x 100 = 537 000

Write the answers in the boxes.

4732 x 1000 =   9105 x 1000 =

6211 x 1000 =   4711 x 1000 =

11 264 x 1000 =   84 322 x 1000 =

47 544 x 1000 =   75 543 x 1000 =

59 223 x 1000 =   84 326 x 1000 =

Find the number that has been multiplied by 1000.

[   ] x 1000 =   764 000   [   ] x 1000 = 9 810 000

[   ] x 1000 = 5 372 000   [   ] x 1000 = 6 141 000

[   ] x 1000 = 4 169 000   [   ] x 1000 = 8 399 000

The simplest form of fractions

Make these fractions equivalent by putting a number in the box.

$$\frac{70}{100} = \frac{\boxed{7}}{10} \qquad \frac{4}{12} = \frac{1}{\boxed{3}}$$

Make these fractions equivalent by putting a number in each box.

$$\frac{30}{100} = \frac{\square}{10} \qquad \frac{8}{100} = \frac{\square}{25} \qquad \frac{40}{100} = \frac{\square}{10} \qquad \frac{15}{100} = \frac{\square}{20}$$

$$\frac{5}{20} = \frac{\square}{4} \qquad \frac{25}{100} = \frac{\square}{4} \qquad \frac{12}{60} = \frac{\square}{5} \qquad \frac{8}{20} = \frac{\square}{5}$$

$$\frac{16}{40} = \frac{\square}{5} \qquad \frac{2}{6} = \frac{\square}{3} \qquad \frac{10}{60} = \frac{\square}{6} \qquad \frac{2}{12} = \frac{\square}{6}$$

$$\frac{9}{18} = \frac{\square}{2} \qquad \frac{10}{18} = \frac{\square}{9} \qquad \frac{4}{24} = \frac{\square}{6} \qquad \frac{7}{28} = \frac{\square}{4}$$

$$\frac{4}{6} = \frac{2}{\square} \qquad \frac{6}{10} = \frac{3}{\square} \qquad \frac{9}{15} = \frac{3}{\square} \qquad \frac{8}{12} = \frac{2}{\square}$$

$$\frac{18}{20} = \frac{9}{\square} \qquad \frac{21}{28} = \frac{3}{\square} \qquad \frac{6}{8} = \frac{3}{\square} \qquad \frac{5}{50} = \frac{1}{\square}$$

$$\frac{15}{25} = \frac{3}{\square} \qquad \frac{4}{16} = \frac{1}{\square} \qquad \frac{12}{20} = \frac{3}{\square} \qquad \frac{12}{18} = \frac{2}{\square}$$

$$\frac{3}{15} = \frac{1}{\square} \qquad \frac{9}{36} = \frac{1}{\square} \qquad \frac{9}{27} = \frac{1}{\square} \qquad \frac{30}{50} = \frac{3}{\square}$$

Make these rows of fractions equivalent by putting a number in each box.

$$\frac{1}{9} = \frac{\square}{18} = \frac{3}{\square} = \frac{\square}{36} = \frac{\square}{45} = \frac{6}{\square}$$

$$\frac{1}{10} = \frac{\square}{20} = \frac{3}{\square} = \frac{4}{\square} = \frac{\square}{50} = \frac{\square}{60}$$

$$\frac{3}{5} = \frac{12}{\square} = \frac{\square}{25} = \frac{18}{\square} = \frac{\square}{35} = \frac{24}{\square}$$

$$\frac{5}{6} = \frac{\square}{12} = \frac{15}{\square} = \frac{20}{\square} = \frac{25}{\square} = \frac{30}{\square}$$

$$\frac{1}{7} = \frac{\square}{14} = \frac{\square}{21} = \frac{\square}{28} = \frac{5}{\square} = \frac{\square}{42}$$

$$\frac{3}{11} = \frac{\square}{44} = \frac{\square}{77} = \frac{27}{\square} = \frac{\square}{110} = \frac{33}{\square}$$

3

Changing improper fractions to mixed numbers

Change this improper fraction to a mixed number.
(Remember you may need to cancel.)

$$\frac{27}{12} = 2\frac{\cancel{3}^{\ 1}}{\cancel{12}_{\ 4}} = 2\frac{1}{4}$$

Change these mixed numbers to improper fractions.

$$2\frac{3}{4} = \frac{11}{4} \qquad\qquad 4\frac{1}{2} = \frac{9}{2}$$

Change these improper fractions to mixed numbers.

$\dfrac{25}{3} =$ $\qquad\qquad$ $\dfrac{15}{12} =$ $\qquad\qquad$ $\dfrac{40}{7} =$

$\dfrac{17}{6} =$ $\qquad\qquad$ $\dfrac{11}{9} =$ $\qquad\qquad$ $\dfrac{12}{5} =$

$\dfrac{27}{5} =$ $\qquad\qquad$ $\dfrac{26}{3} =$ $\qquad\qquad$ $\dfrac{32}{5} =$

$\dfrac{9}{2} =$ $\qquad\qquad$ $\dfrac{19}{2} =$ $\qquad\qquad$ $\dfrac{15}{4} =$

$\dfrac{30}{4} =$ $\qquad\qquad$ $\dfrac{26}{8} =$ $\qquad\qquad$ $\dfrac{42}{9} =$

Change these mixed numbers to improper fractions.

$4\dfrac{3}{4} =$ $\qquad\qquad$ $9\dfrac{1}{2} =$ $\qquad\qquad$ $12\dfrac{1}{4} =$

$3\dfrac{2}{3} =$ $\qquad\qquad$ $6\dfrac{3}{4} =$ $\qquad\qquad$ $3\dfrac{9}{10} =$

$5\dfrac{1}{8} =$ $\qquad\qquad$ $3\dfrac{2}{5} =$ $\qquad\qquad$ $2\dfrac{5}{6} =$

$5\dfrac{1}{4} =$ $\qquad\qquad$ $3\dfrac{3}{8} =$ $\qquad\qquad$ $2\dfrac{11}{12} =$

$2\dfrac{7}{10} =$ $\qquad\qquad$ $4\dfrac{3}{10} =$ $\qquad\qquad$ $4\dfrac{1}{8} =$

$7\dfrac{3}{4} =$ $\qquad\qquad$ $8\dfrac{1}{2} =$ $\qquad\qquad$ $1\dfrac{5}{12} =$

Rounding decimals

Write these decimals to the nearest tenth.

6.23 is 6.2   6.27 is 6.3

If the second decimal place is a 5, we round up the first decimal place to the next larger number.

6.25 is 6.3

Write these decimals to the nearest tenth.

9.21 is [ ]   4.38 is [ ]   2.47 is [ ]

3.48 is [ ]   8.17 is [ ]   6.28 is [ ]

7.14 is [ ]   3.91 is [ ]   2.56 is [ ]

8.41 is [ ]   2.36 is [ ]   1.53 is [ ]

Write these decimals to the nearest tenth.

9.35 is [ ]   8.71 is [ ]   6.05 is [ ]

1.19 is [ ]   3.65 is [ ]   4.21 is [ ]

8.55 is [ ]   7.35 is [ ]   9.14 is [ ]

6.83 is [ ]   2.15 is [ ]   6.34 is [ ]

Write these decimals to the nearest tenth.

25.61 is [ ]   14.35 is [ ]   11.24 is [ ]

16.85 is [ ]   24.34 is [ ]   71.36 is [ ]

26.85 is [ ]   11.54 is [ ]   37.25 is [ ]

92.42 is [ ]   95.65 is [ ]   27.36 is [ ]

45.17 is [ ]   36.75 is [ ]   22.05 is [ ]

Adding with different numbers of digits

Find the total for each problem.

```
  432          ¹¹176
+  43          +  97
  475             273
```

Remember to regroup if you need to.

Find the total for each problem.

```
  148          271          371          938
+  31        +  17        +  24        +  31
```

```
  942          747          633          101
+  26        +  34        +  43        +  75
```

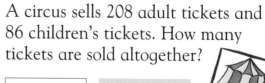

Write the answer in the box.

47 + 320 =

26 + 251 =

273 + 97 =

849 + 38 =

Write in the missing numbers in these problems.

```
  2 4 2          9 3▯          8 ▯5          6▯4
+   2 7        +  3 8        + 1 2        + 6 3
  2 ▯9            9 7 7          8 3 7          6 8 7
```

Find the answer to these problems. Use the space for working them out.

Tommy has saved $238. For his birthday he is given another $52. How much does he have now?

A circus sells 208 adult tickets and 86 children's tickets. How many tickets are sold altogether?

6

Adding with different numbers of digits

Work out the answer to each problem.

```
  1 11
   987
+ 423 123
───────────
  424 110
```

```
  1 11
  2 767
+ 12 844
─────────
  15 611
```

Remember to regroup if you need to.

Work out the answer to each problem.

```
   3 587
+ 17 628
─────────
```

```
  8 537 227
+    86 518
───────────
```

```
      27
+ 9964
────────
```

```
    436
+ 12 844
─────────
```

```
  387 177
+   8 381
──────────
```

```
    6 770
+ 772 142
──────────
```

Write the answer in the box.

$$6\ 437\ 501 + 913\ 548 =$$

$$101\ 876\ +\ 62\ 725 =$$

Write in the missing numbers in these sums.

```
  5 8
+   849
────────
  6 2 3 6
```

```
     2 1
+ 8 1 8 9
─────────
   8 5 1
```

```
   6 7 5
+   9 0 9
─────────
   7 6 6 1
```

Work out the answer to the problem. Use the space for working it out.

Jennifer has 1342 stamps in her collection. Dennis has 742.
How many do they have altogether?

Subtracting one number from another

Find the difference for each problem.

$$\begin{array}{r} \scriptstyle 7\,13 \\ \cancel{8}\cancel{3}4 \\ -\ \ 44 \\ \hline 790 \end{array}$$
$$\begin{array}{r} \scriptstyle 3\,12\,11 \\ \cancel{4}\cancel{3}\cancel{1} \\ -\ \ 84 \\ \hline 347 \end{array}$$

Find the difference for each problem.

835	490	175	428
− 23	− 70	− 54	− 67

587	674	389	270
− 43	− 62	− 58	− 30

483	951	746	234
− 35	− 28	− 17	− 16

Write the answer in the box.

491 − 31 =

654 − 22 =

874 − 63 =

577 − 26 =

Find the difference for each problem.

There are 565 children in a school. If 36 children are on a field trip, how many children are still at school?

A hardware store has 247 cans of paint. If they sell 29 cans, how many will they have left?

Subtracting one number from another

Work out the answer to each problem.

```
  1 16 16 7 15          3 12
  27 685             47 423
 –  8 726            –  5 351
   18 959              42 072
```

Work out the answer to each problem.

```
   68 231          62 411          11 684          37 481
 –  3 846        – 47 566        –  2 845        – 19 804


     7965          92 112          67 444            8818
 –   3976        – 46 489        – 29 545        –  7465


   52 812            2522            8529            6387
 – 37 341        –   1176        –  5892        –  2798
```

Write the answer in the box.

$$55\ 562 - 24\ 871 = \boxed{}$$

$$9118 - 8467 = \boxed{}$$

Work out the answer to the problem. Use the space for working it out.

2826 people went to see a rock concert. 135 had to leave early to catch their train. How many were left at the end?

Real-life problems

Toby has $525.95 in the bank and he spends $146.37 on his vacation. How much does he have left?

> Toby has $379.58 left.

```
     4 11 15  8 15
   $5̶2̶5̶.9̶5̶
 − $146.37
   $379.58
```

A rally driver drives 183 km on the first day of a race and 147 km on the second day. How many kilometres does he travel in the two days?

> He drives 330 kilometres.

```
    1 1
   183 km
 + 147 km
   330 km
```

Mia spends $1525 on a new computer and $146 on a printer. How much does she spend altogether?

Derek has a board that is 3.46 m long to make a shelf to fit an alcove 2.63 m long. How much must he cut off his board in order for it to fit?

A family is on a vacation. If they travel 358 km in the first week and 388 km in the second week, how many kilometres have they travelled altogether?

If their car had already gone 17 028 km before the vacation, how many kilometres will it have gone by the end?

Two boxers are weighed before a boxing match. If the first has a mass of $84\frac{1}{2}$ kg and the second has a mass of 83 kg, what is the difference between their masses?

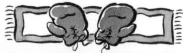

Everyday problems

An electrician buys 415 m of cable. If he uses 234 m, how much does he have left?

He has 181 m of cable left.

```
  3 11
  4̸1̸5 m
− 234 m
  181 m
```

Simon travels by train for 110 km, by bus for 56 km and then walks the final 5 km. How far does he travel?

Simon travels 171 km.

```
    1
  110 km
   56 km
+   5 km
  171 km
```

Mr. Hindley works 185 hours a month. His wife works 73 hours a month. How many hours do they work altogether in a month?

A school collects money for the local shelter. If the pupils collect $275 in the first month, $210 in the second month, and $136 in the third month, how much do they collect altogether?

Danny's car finishes the race in 12.75 seconds, Rachelle's car finishes in 14.83 seconds. Whose car won the race?

How much faster was the winning car?

A builder buys 8755 kg of sand, but uses only 6916 kg. How much does he have left?

Everyday problems

Rudy, Andrew, and Rachelle want to put their money together to buy a present for their brother. If Rudy gives $12.50, Andrew gives $14.75, and Rachelle gives $15.25, how much will they have to spend?

```
  11 1
  $12.50
  $14.75
+ $15.25
  $42.50
```

They will have $42.50 to spend.

A store has 130 kg of potatoes and sells 80 kg. How much does it have left?

```
    13
   1̶3̶0 kg
 −  80 kg
    50 kg
```

The store has 50 kg left.

A bakery orders 145 kg of sugar, 565 kg of salt, and 926 kg of butter. What is the total mass of the order?

Mr. Jean-Paul travelled in a limo to the airport. After he paid a fare of $65, he had $125 left. How much money did he start with?

A vacation in Florida costs $394. A vacation in Majorca costs $876. How much cheaper is the Florida vacation?

Chamique is saving up to buy a guitar that costs $159.99. If she already has $65.37, how much more does she need?

Mr. Lorenzo's garden is 10 m long and 8 m wide. How much fence does he need to surround all four sides?

Decimal addition

Write in the answers to these problems.

$$\begin{array}{r} \overset{1}{4}7.\overset{1}{1}5 \\ +19.36 \\ \hline 66.51 \end{array}$$
$$\begin{array}{r} 4\overset{1}{3}.\overset{1}{9}9 \\ +12.76 \\ \hline 56.75 \end{array}$$

Write the answer to each problem.

53.72	84.17	29.36	23.56	62.49
+77.92	+68.21	+66.84	+79.14	+18.75

35.67	29.88	67.39	49.32	27.22
+12.99	+43.02	+81.70	+14.95	+38.84

Write the answer to each problem.

76.30	44.29	81.97	29.86	68.25
+22.97	+11.04	+69.14	+76.33	+84.36

83.90	45.83	52.17	84.93	72.83
+30.24	+45.71	+90.21	+29.37	+41.16

Write the answer to each problem.

37.89 + 82.15 =   32.44 + 21.88 =   37.19 + 28.24 =

68.67 + 29.82 =   21.99 + 79.32 =   52.45 + 34.58 =

84.77 + 39.12 =   63.84 + 29.81 =   34.43 + 25.64 =

33.97 + 24.62 =   76.39 + 43.78 =   52.38 + 38.43 =

Decimal addition

Write the sum for each problem.

```
  1   1
  296.48        1 1
+ 131.70        73.00
  ------      + 269.23
  428.18        ------
                342.23
```

Write the sum for each problem.

```
   91.83        64.71       32.045        306
 + 37.84      + 21.2      +  4.99      + 44.24
 -------      -------     -------      -------
```

```
   71.932       842.01      675.82        37.82
 +  55.26     + 11.842    +105        + 399.71
 --------     --------    -------      -------
```

```
   65.24       178.935      184.70       443.27
 + 605.27     +599.41     + 372.81     +  75
 --------     --------    --------     -------
```

```
   563          703.95      825.36       529.3
 +413.98      +  85.11    + 249.857    + 482.56
 -------      --------    ---------    -------
```

Write the sum for each problem.

421 + 136.25 =

92.31 + 241.73 =

501.8 + 361.93 =

558.32 + 137.945 =

27 + 142.07 =

75.31 + 293.33 =

153.3 + 182.02 =

491.445 + 105.37 =

253.71+ 62 =

829.2 + 63.74 =

14

Decimal subtraction

Write the difference for each problem.

$$\begin{array}{r} 59.\overset{6\ 16}{\cancel{76}} \\ -\ 21.47 \\ \hline 38.29 \end{array}$$ $$\begin{array}{r} 57.\overset{0\ 18}{\cancel{18}} \\ -\ 22.09 \\ \hline 35.09 \end{array}$$

Write the difference for each problem.

$$\begin{array}{r} 64.92 \\ -\ 26.35 \\ \hline \end{array}$$ $$\begin{array}{r} 64.21 \\ -\ 16.02 \\ \hline \end{array}$$ $$\begin{array}{r} 73.71 \\ -\ 19.24 \\ \hline \end{array}$$ $$\begin{array}{r} 92.63 \\ -\ 67.14 \\ \hline \end{array}$$

$$\begin{array}{r} 45.76 \\ -\ 16.18 \\ \hline \end{array}$$ $$\begin{array}{r} 73.52 \\ -\ 39.27 \\ \hline \end{array}$$ $$\begin{array}{r} 98.98 \\ -\ 39.19 \\ \hline \end{array}$$ $$\begin{array}{r} 53.58 \\ -\ 14.39 \\ \hline \end{array}$$

$$\begin{array}{r} 94.87 \\ -\ 65.28 \\ \hline \end{array}$$ $$\begin{array}{r} 21.74 \\ -\ 12.1 \\ \hline \end{array}$$ $$\begin{array}{r} 62.35 \\ -\ 13.16 \\ \hline \end{array}$$ $$\begin{array}{r} 81.94 \\ -\ 28.15 \\ \hline \end{array}$$

$$\begin{array}{r} 62.95 \\ -\ 33.37 \\ \hline \end{array}$$ $$\begin{array}{r} 81.42 \\ -\ 25.04 \\ \hline \end{array}$$ $$\begin{array}{r} 48.52 \\ -\ 14.49 \\ \hline \end{array}$$ $$\begin{array}{r} 61.55 \\ -\ 13.26 \\ \hline \end{array}$$

Write the difference for each problem.

$51.52 - 12.13 =$ $72.41 - 23.18 =$

$91.91 - 22.22 =$ $53.84 - 19.65 =$

$41.82 - 18.13 =$ $51.61 - 23.14 =$

$83.91 - 14.73 =$ $64.65 - 37.26 =$

$53.21 - 35.12 =$ $77.31 - 28.15 =$

Decimal subtraction

Write the difference for each problem.

$$\begin{array}{r} {\scriptstyle 7\ 11} \\ 68.\cancel{1}7 \\ -11.40 \\ \hline \boxed{56.77} \end{array} \qquad \begin{array}{r} {\scriptstyle 1\ 10} \\ 39.2\cancel{0} \\ -13.15 \\ \hline \boxed{26.05} \end{array}$$

Work out the difference for each problem.

87.23 – 24.4	95.15 – 31.356	66.37 – 21.9	85 – 26.32
72.28 – 1.3	63.14 – 32	99.235 – 33.70	62.1 – 29.34
77.3 – 24.42	55.492 – 27.66	68 – 31.5	35.612 – 13.207
82.35 – 23.40	63.20 – 15.36	53.64 – 23	35.612 – 26.19

Write the difference for each problem.

63.4 – 24.51 =

91.3 – 33 =

52.251 – 22.42 =

92.84 – 23 =

81.815 – 55.90 =

92.197 – 63.28 =

41.24 – 14.306 =

72.6 – 53.71 =

61.16 – 24.4 =

94.31 – 27.406 =

Multiplying larger numbers by ones

Write the product for each problem.

¹³
529
x   4
2116

¹³¹
1273
x   5
6365

Write the product for each problem.

724	831	126	455
x 2	x 3	x 3	x 4

161	282	349	253
x 4	x 5	x 5	x 6

328	465	105	562
x 6	x 6	x 4	x 4

Write the product for each problem.

4261	1582	3612	4284
x 3	x 3	x 4	x 4

5907	1263	1303	1467
x 5	x 5	x 6	x 6

6521	8436	1599	3761
x 6	x 6	x 6	x 6

5837	6394	8124	3914
x 4	x 5	x 6	x 6

Multiplying larger numbers by ones

Write the answer to each problem.

```
    14              174
   417            2185
 ×    7          ×    9
  2919           19 665
```

Write the answer to each problem.

```
   419        604        715        327
 ×   7      ×   7      ×   8      ×   7
```

```
   425        171        682        246
 ×   8      ×   9      ×   8      ×   8
```

```
   436        999        319        581
 ×   8      ×   9      ×   9      ×   9
```

Work out the answer to each problem.

```
  4331       2816       1439       2617
 ×   7      ×   7      ×   8      ×   8
```

```
  3104       4022       3212       2591
 ×   8      ×   8      ×   9      ×   9
```

```
  1710       3002       2468       1514
 ×   9      ×   8      ×   7      ×   8
```

```
  4624       2993       3894       4361
 ×   7      ×   8      ×   8      ×   9
```

Real-life multiplication problems

There are 157 apples in a box.
How many will there be in three boxes?

471 apples

$$\begin{array}{r} 12 \\ 157 \\ \times \quad 3 \\ \hline 471 \end{array}$$

A stamp album can hold 550 stamps.
How many stamps will 5 albums hold?

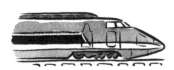
A train can take 425 passengers.
How many can it take in four trips?

Mr Jenkins puts $256 a month into the bank.
How much will he have put in after six months?

A theatre can seat 5524 people. If a play runs for 7 days, what is
the maximum number of people who will be able to see it?

A car costs $19 956. How much will it cost a
company to buy nine cars for its salespeople?

Installing a new window for a house costs $435. How
much will it cost to install 8 windows of the same size?

An airplane flies at a steady speed of 550 km/h.
How far will it travel in 7 hours?

Comparing and ordering decimals

Compare the decimals. Which decimal is greater?

| 2.2 and 3.1 | 0.45 and 0.6 |

Line them up vertically.

| 2.2 | 0.45 |
| 3.1 | 0.60 |

3>2, so 3.1>2.2   6>4, so 0.6>0.45

Compare the decimals. Which decimal is greater?

7.9 and 8.1   0.5 and 0.62   3.6 and 0.94   0.4 and 0.67

1.6 and 1.9   0.31 and 3.10   8.5 and 6.9   6.75 and 6.71

Find the greatest decimal.

2.9 and 2.75 and 2.6   0.97 and 1.09 and 1.3   4.9 and 3.87 and 4.75

Write the decimals in order from greatest to least.

0.33   3.1   0.3   24.95   23.9   24.5   7.5   6.95   7.58

Find the answer to each problem.

The Weather Bureau reported 5.18 centimetres of rain in March, 6.74 centimetres in April, and 5.23 centimetres in May. Which month had the least rainfall?

A postal worker walked 4.5 kilometres on Wednesday, 3.75 kilometres on Thursday, and 4.25 kilometres on Friday. Which day did she walk the farthest?

Converting units of measure

Convert 25 centimetres to millimetres.

$25 \times 10 =$ 250 mm

Convert 200¢ to dollars.

$200 \div 100 =$ $2

Convert these centimetres to millimetres.

40 cm		15 cm		9 cm	
12 cm		34 cm		62 cm	
43 cm		96 cm		105 cm	
92 cm		20 cm		426 cm	

Convert these millimetres to centimetres.

30 mm		100 mm		120 mm	
60 mm		90 mm		200 mm	
130 mm		10 mm		400 mm	

Convert these dollars to cents.

$35		$600		$15	
$12		$36		$95	
$72		$4		$250	

Convert these cents to dollars.

450¢		900¢		6000¢	
250¢		400¢		150¢	
100¢		300¢		750¢	

Converting units of measure

Convert these centimetres to metres.

500 cm	900 cm	400 cm
8000 cm	3000 cm	4000 cm
9800 cm	8300 cm	6200 cm
36 800 cm	94 200 cm	73 500 cm

Convert these metres to centimetres.

47 m	29 m	84 m
69 m	24 m	38 m
146 m	237 m	921 m

Convert these metres to kilometres.

5000 m	6000 m	9000 m
15 000 m	27 000 m	71 000 m
19 000 m	86 000 m	42 000 m

Convert these kilometres to metres.

7 km	9 km	4 km
23 km	46 km	87 km
12 km	96 km	39 km

Area of rectangles and squares

Find the area of this rectangle.

To find the area of a rectangle or square, we multiply length (l) by width (w).

Area = 800 cm²

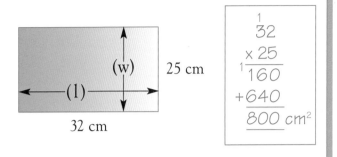

(w)   25 cm

(1)

32 cm

```
  1
  32
x 25
 1
 160
+640
 800 cm²
```

Find the area of these rectangles and squares.
You may need to do your work on a separate sheet.

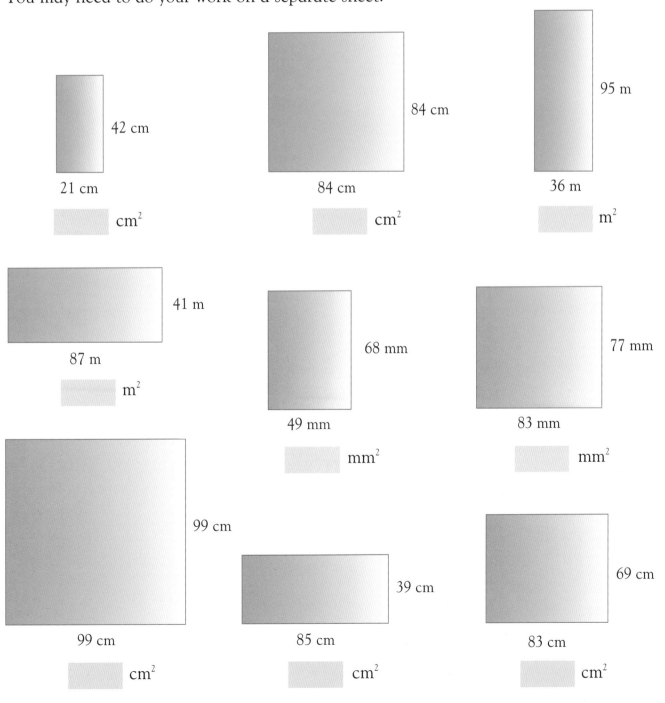

42 cm

21 cm

☐ cm²

84 cm

84 cm

☐ cm²

95 m

36 m

☐ m²

41 m

87 m

☐ m²

68 mm

49 mm

☐ mm²

77 mm

83 mm

☐ mm²

99 cm

99 cm

☐ cm²

39 cm

85 cm

☐ cm²

69 cm

83 cm

☐ cm²

Perimeter of shapes

Find the perimeter of this rectangle.

To find the perimeter of a rectangle or square, we add the two lengths and the two widths together.

12.4 cm

27.3 cm

```
  1 1
  27.3 cm
  27.3 cm
  12.4 cm
+ 12.4 cm
  79.4  cm
```

79.4 cm

Find the perimeter of these rectangles and squares.
You may need to do your work on a separate sheet.

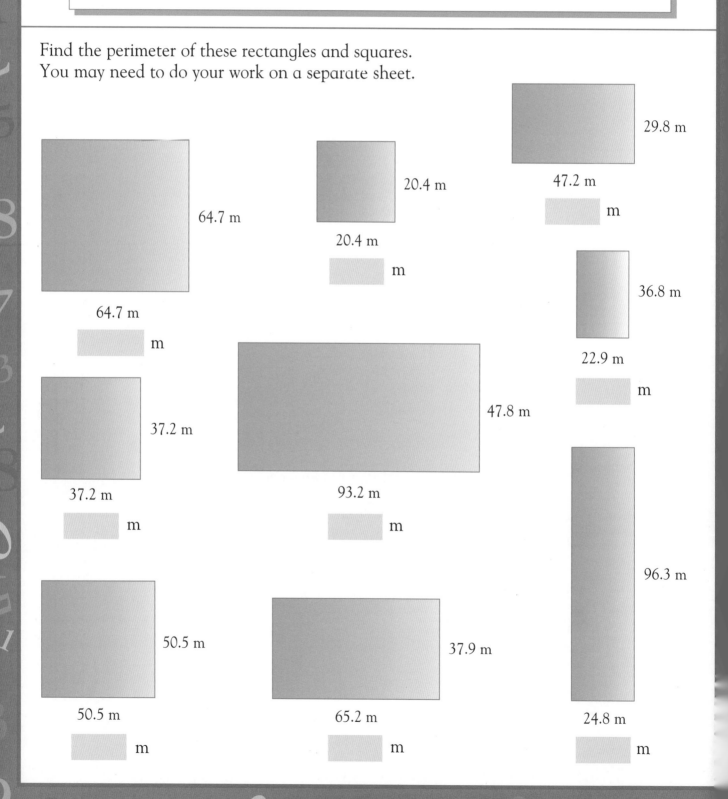

29.8 m

47.2 m

_____ m

64.7 m

64.7 m

_____ m

20.4 m

20.4 m

_____ m

36.8 m

22.9 m

_____ m

37.2 m

37.2 m

_____ m

47.8 m

93.2 m

_____ m

50.5 m

50.5 m

_____ m

37.9 m

65.2 m

_____ m

96.3 m

24.8 m

_____ m

Decimal place value

Work out the answer to the problem.

2.	3	8	5	0
Ones	Tenths	Hundredths	Thousandths	Ten-thousandths

2.385
What is the value of the digit 8?

2.3850
8 is in the hundredths place,
so, its value is 8 hundredths.

Name the place of the digit 8 in each of the problems.

0.387	3.87	4.82	8.11

Name the value of the highlighted digit.

6.5937	5.371	7.403	0.42

6.24	3.611	1.062

Which number has a digit with the value 6 tenths?

Which number has a digit with the value 6 hundredths?

Which number has a digit with the value 6 ones?

How much greater is the second decimal than the first?

7.46 7.56	3.27 3.67	0.82 0.85
one tenth more		

Speed problems

How long will it take a bike rider to travel 36 km at a constant speed of 9 kilometres per hour?

$$\boxed{4\ hours}$$
$$9\overline{)36}$$
Time = Distance ÷ Speed

If a car travelled 150 km at a constant speed in 5 hours, at what speed was it travelling?

$$\boxed{30\ km/h}$$
$$5\overline{)150}$$
Speed = Distance ÷ Time

If a bus travels for 5 hours at 40 km/h, how far does it travel?

$$5 \times 40 = \boxed{200\ km}$$
Distance = Speed × Time

A car travels along a road at a steady speed of 60 km/h. How far will it travel in 6 hours?

A train covers a distance of 480 km in 8 hours. If it travels at a constant speed, how fast is it travelling?

John walks at a steady speed of 3 km/h. How long will it take him to travel 24 kilometres?

A car travels at a constant speed of 65 km/h. How far will it have travelled in 4 hours?

Melanie completes a long distance run at an average speed of 6 km/h. If it takes her 3 hours, how far did she run?

Sarah cycles 30 km to her grandmother's house at a steady speed of 10 km/h. If she leaves home at 2:00 P.M., what time will she arrive?

Conversion table

This is part of a conversion table that shows how to change dollars to pesos when 10 Mexican pesos (10MN) equal $1.

Canadian Dollars	Mexican Pesos
1	10
2	20
3	30

How many pesos would you get for $2? **20MN**

How much is 25 pesos worth in dollars? **$2.50**

How many dollars would you get for 40MN?

How many dollars would you get for 85MN?

How much is 1MN worth?

Change $65 into pesos.

What is $3.50 in pesos?

Change 250MN into dollars.

How many pesos could you get for $0.40?

Canadian Dollars	Mexican Pesos
1	10
2	20
3	30
4	40
5	50
6	60
7	70
8	80
9	90
10	100

The rate then changes to 8MN to the dollar.
The conversion chart now looks like the one shown here.

How many pesos are worth $4?

How many dollars can you get for 56MN?

How many pesos are worth $9.50?

How many pesos can you get for $20?

How many dollars would you get for 120MN?

What is the value of 4MN?

Canadian Dollars	Mexican Pesos
1	8
2	16
3	24
4	32
5	40
6	48
7	56
8	64
9	72
10	80

Interpreting circle graphs

32 children voted for their favourite ice-cream flavours.

How many children voted for chocolate?

$\frac{3}{8}$ of 32 is 12

12 children voted for chocolate.

12 children

How many children voted for fudge?

$\frac{1}{8}$ of 32 is 4

4 children voted for fudge.

4 children

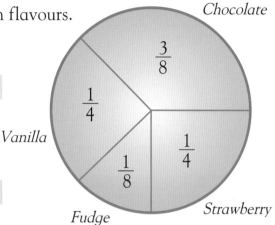

A class of 30 children voted for their favourite actor who has played James Bond.

How many voted for Sean Connery?

How many did not vote for George Lazenby?

How many more children voted for Pierce Brosnan than Roger Moore?

How many children altogether voted for Sean Connery and Roger Moore?

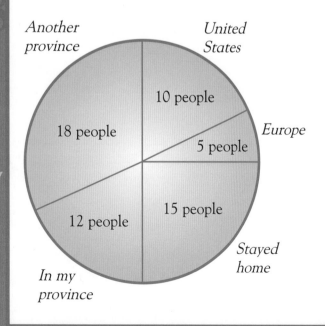

60 people were asked where they went on vacation last year. The circle graph shows the results.

What fraction of people vacationed in another province?

What fraction of people vacationed in the United States, or in Europe?

What fraction of people did not stay at home?

What fraction of people vacationed in their province or another province?

Probability scale 0 to 1

Look at this probability line.

Impossible = 0
Poor chance = 0.25
Fair = 0.5
Good chance = 0.75
Certain = 1

Write each letter in the correct place on the probability line.

a. It will be daylight in New Orleans at midnight.
b. The sun will come up tomorrow.
c. If I toss a coin it will come down heads.

a		c		b
0	0.25	0.5	0.75	1

0	0.25	0.5	0.75	1

Write each letter in the correct place on the probability line.

a. If I cut a pack of cards I will get a red card.

b. If I cut a pack of cards I will get a diamond.

c. If I cut a pack of cards I will get a diamond, a spade, or a club.

d. If I cut a pack of cards I will get a diamond, a spade, a club, or a heart.

e. If I cut a pack of cards it will be a 15.

0	0.25	0.5	0.75	1

Write each letter in the correct place on the probability line.

a. Next week, Wednesday will be the day after Tuesday.

b. There will be 33 days in February next year.

c. It will snow in Vancouver in May.

d. It will snow in Newfoundland in January.

e. The next person to knock on the door will be a woman.

Likely outcomes

Throw one coin 20 times.

Keep a tally.

H	⊮ ||||
T	⊮ ⊮	

Put your results on a bar graph.

What do you notice?

Heads and tails come up roughly the same number of times because there are only two possible outcomes and they are equally likely.

Predict what you think the outcome will be if you tossed two coins 48 times.

2 heads [   ] times   2 tails [   ] times   1 of each [   ] times

Now actually throw two coins 48 times and record your results on this tally chart.

2 Heads	
2 Tails	
1 of each	

Draw a bar graph to show your results.

Which result comes up the most often?

Can you explain why some results are more probable than others?

Naming quadrilaterals

Name this shape.

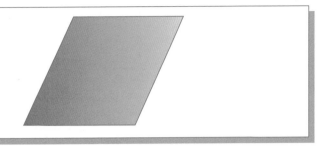

Rhombus

Name these shapes.

Sketch these shapes.

Parallelogram

Rectangle

Rhombus

Trapezoid

Speed trials

Write the answers as fast as you can, but get them right!

4 x 10 = 40   8 x 2 = 16   6 x 5 = 30

Write the answers as fast as you can, but get them right!

3 x 2 =	0 x 5 =	3 x 10 =	0 x 3 =
5 x 2 =	10 x 5 =	5 x 10 =	10 x 3 =
1 x 2 =	8 x 5 =	1 x 10 =	8 x 3 =
4 x 2 =	6 x 5 =	4 x 10 =	6 x 3 =
7 x 2 =	2 x 5 =	7 x 10 =	2 x 3 =
2 x 2 =	7 x 5 =	2 x 10 =	7 x 3 =
6 x 2 =	4 x 5 =	6 x 10 =	4 x 3 =
8 x 2 =	1 x 5 =	8 x 10 =	1 x 3 =
10 x 2 =	5 x 5 =	10 x 10 =	5 x 3 =
0 x 2 =	3 x 5 =	0 x 10 =	3 x 3 =
9 x 2 =	5 x 3 =	9 x 10 =	6 x 4 =
2 x 7 =	5 x 8 =	10 x 7 =	3 x 4 =
2 x 1 =	5 x 6 =	10 x 1 =	7 x 4 =
2 x 4 =	5 x 9 =	10 x 4 =	4 x 4 =
3 x 7 =	5 x 7 =	10 x 7 =	10 x 4 =
2 x 5 =	5 x 4 =	10 x 5 =	8 x 4 =
2 x 9 =	5 x 1 =	10 x 9 =	0 x 4 =
2 x 6 =	4 x 7 =	10 x 6 =	9 x 4 =
2 x 8 =	5 x 10 =	10 x 8 =	5 x 4 =
2 x 3 =	5 x 2 =	10 x 3 =	2 x 4 =

All the 3s

You will need to know these:

1 x 3 = 3   2 x 3 = 6   3 x 3 = 9   4 x 3 = 12   5 x 3 = 15   10 x 3 = 30

How many altogether?

6 sets of three are _____   six threes are _____   6 x 3 = _____

How many altogether?

7 sets of three are _____   seven threes are _____   7 x 3 = _____

How many altogether?

8 sets of three are _____   eight threes are _____   8 x 3 = _____

How many altogether?

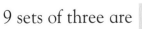

9 sets of three are _____   nine threes are _____   9 x 3 = _____

All the 3s again

Cover the three times table with a sheet of paper so you can't see the numbers.
Write the answers. Be as fast as you can, but get them right!

1 x 3 =	5 x 3 =	6 x 3 =
2 x 3 =	7 x 3 =	9 x 3 =
3 x 3 =	9 x 3 =	4 x 3 =
4 x 3 =	4 x 3 =	5 x 3 =
5 x 3 =	6 x 3 =	3 x 7 =
6 x 3 =	8 x 3 =	3 x 4 =
7 x 3 =	10 x 3 =	2 x 3 =
8 x 3 =	1 x 3 =	10 x 3 =
9 x 3 =	3 x 3 =	3 x 9 =
10 x 3 =	2 x 3 =	3 x 6 =
3 x 1 =	3 x 5 =	3 x 5 =
3 x 2 =	3 x 7 =	3 x 8 =
3 x 3 =	3 x 9 =	7 x 3 =
3 x 4 =	3 x 4 =	3 x 2 =
3 x 5 =	3 x 6 =	3 x 10 =
3 x 6 =	3 x 8 =	8 x 3 =
3 x 7 =	3 x 10 =	3 x 0 =
3 x 8 =	3 x 1 =	1 x 3 =
3 x 9 =	3 x 0 =	3 x 3 =
3 x 10 =	3 x 2 =	3 x 9 =

All the 4s

You should know these:

$1 \times 4 = 4$ $2 \times 4 = 8$ $3 \times 4 = 12$ $4 \times 4 = 16$ $5 \times 4 = 20$ $10 \times 4 = 40$

How many altogether?

6 sets of four are ▢   six fours are ▢ $6 \times 4 =$ ▢

How many altogether?

7 sets of four are ▢   seven fours are ▢ $7 \times 4 =$ ▢

How many altogether?

8 sets of four are ▢   eight fours are ▢ $8 \times 4 =$ ▢

How many altogether?

9 sets of four are ▢   nine fours are ▢ $9 \times 4 =$ ▢

All the 4s again

You should know all of the four times table by now.

1 x 4 = 4	2 x 4 = 8	3 x 4 = 12	4 x 4 = 16	5 x 4 = 20
6 x 4 = 24	7 x 4 = 28	8 x 4 = 32	9 x 4 = 36	10 x 4 = 40

Say these to yourself a few times.

Cover the four times table with a sheet of paper so you can't see the numbers.
Write the answers. Be as fast as you can, but get them right!

1 x 4 =	5 x 4 =	6 x 4 =
2 x 4 =	7 x 4 =	9 x 4 =
3 x 4 =	9 x 4 =	4 x 1 =
4 x 4 =	3 x 4 =	5 x 4 =
5 x 4 =	6 x 4 =	4 x 7 =
6 x 4 =	8 x 4 =	3 x 4 =
7 x 4 =	10 x 4 =	2 x 4 =
8 x 4 =	1 x 4 =	10 x 4 =
9 x 4 =	4 x 4 =	4 x 3 =
10 x 4 =	2 x 4 =	4 x 6 =
4 x 1 =	4 x 5 =	4 x 5 =
4 x 2 =	4 x 7 =	4 x 8 =
4 x 3 =	4 x 9 =	7 x 4 =
4 x 4 =	4 x 4 =	4 x 2 =
4 x 5 =	4 x 6 =	4 x 10 =
4 x 6 =	4 x 8 =	8 x 4 =
4 x 7 =	4 x 10 =	4 x 0 =
4 x 8 =	4 x 1 =	1 x 4 =
4 x 9 =	4 x 0 =	4 x 4 =
4 x 10 =	4 x 2 =	4 x 9 =

Speed trials

You should know all of the 1, 2, 3, 4, 5, and 10 times tables by now, but how quickly can you do them?
Ask someone to time you as you do this page.
Remember, you must be fast but also correct.

4 x 2 =	6 x 3 =	9 x 5 =
8 x 3 =	3 x 4 =	8 x 10 =
7 x 4 =	7 x 5 =	7 x 2 =
6 x 5 =	3 x 10 =	6 x 3 =
8 x 10 =	1 x 2 =	5 x 4 =
8 x 2 =	7 x 3 =	4 x 5 =
5 x 3 =	4 x 4 =	3 x 10 =
9 x 4 =	6 x 5 =	2 x 2 =
5 x 5 =	4 x 10 =	1 x 3 =
7 x 10 =	6 x 2 =	0 x 4 =
0 x 2 =	5 x 3 =	10 x 5 =
4 x 3 =	8 x 4 =	9 x 2 =
6 x 4 =	0 x 5 =	8 x 3 =
3 x 5 =	2 x 10 =	7 x 4 =
4 x 10 =	7 x 2 =	6 x 5 =
7 x 2 =	8 x 3 =	5 x 10 =
3 x 3 =	9 x 4 =	4 x 0 =
2 x 4 =	5 x 5 =	3 x 2 =
7 x 5 =	7 x 10 =	2 x 8 =
9 x 10 =	5 x 2 =	1 x 9 =

Some of the 6s

You should already know parts of the 6 times table because they are parts of the 1, 2, 3, 4, 5, and 10 times tables.

1 x 6 = 6   2 x 6 = 12   3 x 6 = 18

4 x 6 = 24   5 x 6 = 30   10 x 6 = 60

Find out if you can remember them quickly and correctly.

Cover the six times table with paper so you can't see the numbers.
Write the answers as quickly as you can.

What is three sixes?   What is ten sixes?

What is two sixes?   What is four sixes?

What is one six?   What is five sixes?

Write the answers as quickly as you can.

How many sixes make 12?   How many sixes make 6?

How many sixes make 30?   How many sixes make 18?

How many sixes make 24?   How many sixes make 60?

Write the answers as quickly as you can.

Multiply six by three.   Multiply six by ten.

Multiply six by two.   Multiply six by five.

Multiply six by one.   Multiply six by four.

Write the answers as quickly as you can.

4 x 6 =   2 x 6 =   10 x 6 =

5 x 6 =   1 x 6 =   3 x 6 =

Write the answers as quickly as you can.

A box contains six eggs. A man buys five boxes. How many eggs does he have?

A pack contains six sticks of gum.
How many sticks will there be in 10 packs?

The rest of the 6s

You need to learn these:

6 x 6 = 36   7 x 6 = 42   8 x 6 = 48   9 x 6 = 54

This work will help you remember the 6 times table.

Complete these sequences.

6   12   18   24   30

5 x 6 = 30   so   6 x 6 = 30 plus another 6 =

18   24   30

6 x 6 = 36   so   7 x 6 = 36 plus another 6 =

6   12   18   48   60

7 x 6 = 42   so   8 x 6 = 42 plus another 6 =

6   18   24   30

8 x 6 = 48   so   9 x 6 = 48 plus another 6 =

                        24   42   60

Test yourself on the rest of the 6 times table.
Cover the above part of the page with a sheet of paper.

What is six sixes?   What is seven sixes?

What is eight sixes?   What is nine sixes?

8 x 6 =   7 x 6 =   6 x 6 =   9 x 6 =

Practise the 6s

You should know all of the 6 times table now, but how quickly can you remember it?
Ask someone to time you as you do this page.
Remember, you must be fast but also correct.

1 x 6 =	2 x 6 =	7 x 6 =
2 x 6 =	4 x 6 =	3 x 6 =
3 x 6 =	6 x 6 =	9 x 6 =
4 x 6 =	8 x 6 =	6 x 4 =
5 x 6 =	10 x 6 =	1 x 6 =
6 x 6 =	1 x 6 =	6 x 2 =
7 x 6 =	3 x 6 =	6 x 8 =
8 x 6 =	5 x 6 =	0 x 6 =
9 x 6 =	7 x 6 =	6 x 3 =
10 x 6 =	9 x 6 =	5 x 6 =
6 x 1 =	6 x 3 =	6 x 7 =
6 x 2 =	6 x 5 =	2 x 6 =
6 x 3 =	6 x 7 =	6 x 9 =
6 x 4 =	6 x 9 =	4 x 6 =
6 x 5 =	6 x 2 =	8 x 6 =
6 x 6 =	6 x 4 =	10 x 6 =
6 x 7 =	6 x 6 =	6 x 5 =
6 x 8 =	6 x 8 =	6 x 0 =
6 x 9 =	6 x 10 =	6 x 1 =
6 x 10 =	6 x 0 =	6 x 6 =

Speed trials

You should know all of the 1, 2, 3, 4, 5, 6, and 10 times tables by now,
but how quickly can you remember them?
Ask someone to time you as you do this page.
Remember, you must be fast but also correct.

4 x 6 =	6 x 3 =	9 x 6 =
5 x 3 =	8 x 6 =	8 x 6 =
7 x 3 =	6 x 6 =	7 x 3 =
6 x 5 =	3 x 10 =	6 x 6 =
6 x 10 =	6 x 2 =	5 x 4 =
8 x 2 =	7 x 3 =	4 x 6 =
5 x 3 =	4 x 6 =	3 x 6 =
9 x 6 =	6 x 5 =	2 x 6 =
5 x 5 =	6 x 10 =	6 x 3 =
7 x 6 =	6 x 2 =	0 x 6 =
0 x 2 =	5 x 3 =	10 x 5 =
6 x 3 =	8 x 4 =	6 x 2 =
6 x 6 =	0 x 6 =	8 x 3 =
3 x 5 =	5 x 10 =	7 x 6 =
4 x 10 =	7 x 6 =	6 x 5 =
7 x 10 =	8 x 3 =	5 x 10 =
3 x 6 =	9 x 6 =	6 x 0 =
2 x 4 =	5 x 5 =	3 x 10 =
6 x 9 =	7 x 10 =	2 x 8 =
9 x 10 =	5 x 6 =	1 x 8 =

Some of the 7s

You should already know parts of the 7 times table because they are parts of the 1, 2, 3, 4, 5, 6 and 10 times tables.

1 x 7 = 7   2 x 7 = 14   3 x 7 = 21   4 x 7 = 28
5 x 7 = 35   6 x 7 = 42   10 x 7 = 70

Find out if you can remember them quickly and correctly.

Cover the seven times table with paper and write the answers to these questions as quickly as you can.

What is three sevens?   What is ten sevens?

What is two sevens?   What is four sevens?

What is six sevens?   What is five sevens?

Write the answers as quickly as you can.

How many sevens make 14?   How many sevens make 42?

How many sevens make 35?   How many sevens make 21?

How many sevens make 28?   How many sevens make 70?

Write the answers as quickly as you can.

Multiply seven by three.   Multiply seven by ten.

Multiply seven by two.   Multiply seven by five.

Multiply seven by six.   Multiply seven by four.

Write the answers as quickly as you can.

4 x 7 =   2 x 7 =   10 x 7 =

5 x 7 =   1 x 7 =   3 x 7 =

Write the answers as quickly as you can.

A bag has seven candies. Ann buys five bags. How many candies does she have?

How many days are there in six weeks?

The rest of the 7s

You should now know all of the 1, 2, 3, 4, 5, 6, and 10 times tables.

You need to learn only these parts of the seven times table.
7 x 7 = 49   8 x 7 = 56   9 x 7 = 63

This work will help you remember the 7 times table.

Complete these sequences.

7   14   21   28   35   42

6 x 7 = 42   so   7 x 7 = 42 plus another 7 =

21   28   35

7 x 7 = 49   so   8 x 7 = 49 plus another 7 =

7   14   21   56   70

8 x 7 = 56   so   9 x 7 = 56 plus another 7 =

7   21   28   35

Test yourself on the rest of the 7 times table.
Cover the section above with a sheet of paper.

What is seven sevens?   What is eight sevens?

What is nine sevens?   What is ten sevens?

8 x 7 =   7 x 7 =    9 x 7 =   10 x 7 =

How many days are there in eight weeks?

A package contains seven pens.
How many pens will there be in nine packets?

How many sevens make 56?

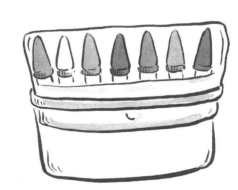

43

Practise the 7s

You should know all of the 7 times table now, but how quickly can you remember it?
Ask someone to time you as you do this page.
Remember, you must be fast but also correct.

1 x 7 =

2 x 7 =

3 x 7 =

4 x 7 =

5 x 7 =

6 x 7 =

7 x 7 =

8 x 7 =

9 x 7 =

10 x 7 =

7 x 1 =

7 x 2 =

7 x 3 =

7 x 4 =

7 x 5 =

7 x 6 =

7 x 7 =

7 x 8 =

7 x 9 =

7 x 10 =

2 x 7 =

4 x 7 =

6 x 7 =

8 x 7 =

10 x 7 =

1 x 7 =

3 x 7 =

5 x 7 =

7 x 7 =

9 x 7 =

7 x 3 =

7 x 5 =

7 x 7 =

7 x 9 =

7 x 2 =

7 x 4 =

7 x 6 =

7 x 8 =

7 x 10 =

7 x 0 =

7 x 6 =

3 x 7 =

9 x 7 =

7 x 4 =

1 x 7 =

7 x 2 =

7 x 8 =

0 x 7 =

7 x 3 =

5 x 7 =

7 x 7 =

2 x 7 =

7 x 9 =

4 x 7 =

8 x 7 =

10 x 7 =

7 x 5 =

7 x 0 =

7 x 1 =

6 x 7 =

Speed trials

You should know all of the 1, 2, 3, 4, 5, 6, 7, and 10 times tables by now, but how quickly can you remember them?
Ask someone to time you as you do this page.
Remember, you must be fast but also correct.

4 x 7 =	7 x 3 =	9 x 7 =
5 x 10 =	8 x 7 =	7 x 6 =
7 x 5 =	6 x 6 =	8 x 3 =
6 x 5 =	5 x 10 =	6 x 6 =
6 x 10 =	6 x 3 =	7 x 4 =
8 x 7 =	7 x 5 =	4 x 6 =
5 x 8 =	4 x 6 =	3 x 7 =
9 x 6 =	6 x 5 =	2 x 8 =
5 x 7 =	7 x 10 =	7 x 3 =
7 x 6 =	6 x 7 =	0 x 6 =
0 x 5 =	5 x 7 =	10 x 7 =
6 x 3 =	8 x 4 =	6 x 2 =
6 x 7 =	0 x 7 =	8 x 7 =
3 x 5 =	5 x 8 =	7 x 7 =
4 x 7 =	7 x 6 =	6 x 5 =
7 x 10 =	8 x 3 =	5 x 10 =
7 x 8 =	9 x 6 =	7 x 0 =
2 x 7 =	7 x 7 =	3 x 10 =
4 x 9 =	9 x 10 =	2 x 7 =
9 x 10 =	5 x 6 =	7 x 8 =

Some of the 8s

You should already know some of the 8 times table because it is part of the 1, 2, 3, 4, 5, 6, 7, and 10 times tables.

1 x 8 = 8   2 x 8 = 16   3 x 8 = 24   4 x 8 = 32
5 x 8 = 40   6 x 8 = 48   7 x 8 = 56   10 x 8 = 80

Find out if you can remember them quickly and correctly.

Cover the 8 times table with paper so you can't see the numbers.
Write the answers as quickly as you can.

What is three eights?   What is ten eights?

What is two eights?   What is four eights?

What is six eights?   What is five eights?

Write the answers as quickly as you can.

How many eights equal 16?   How many eights equal 40?

How many eights equal 32?   How many eights equal 24?

How many eights equal 56?   How many eights equal 48?

Write the answers as quickly as you can.

Multiply eight by three.   Multiply eight by ten.

Multiply eight by two.   Multiply eight by five.

Multiply eight by six.   Multiply eight by four.

Write the answers as quickly as you can.

6 x 8 =   2 x 8 =   10 x 8 =

5 x 8 =   7 x 8 =   3 x 8 =

Write the answers as quickly as you can.

A pizza has eight slices. John buys six pizzas.

How many slices does he have?

Which number multiplied by 8 gives the answer 56?

The rest of the 8s

You need to learn only these parts of the eight times table.
8 x 8 = 64   9 x 8 = 72

This work will help you remember the 8 times table.

Complete these sequences.

| 8 | 16 | 24 | 32 | 40 | 48 | | | | |

7 x 8 = 56   so   8 x 8 = 56 plus another 8 =

| 24 | 32 | 40 | | | | | |

8 x 8 = 64   so   9 x 8 = 64 plus another 8 =

| 8 | 16 | 24 | | | | 64 | | 80 |

| 8 | | 24 | | 40 | | | | |

Test yourself on the rest of the 8 times table.
Cover the section above with a sheet of paper.

What is seven eights?   What is eight eights?

What is nine eights?   What is eight nines?

8 x 8 =   9 x 8 =   8 x 9 =   10 x 8 =

What number multiplied by 8 gives the answer 72?

A number multiplied by 8 gives the answer 80. What is the number?

David puts out building bricks in piles of 8.
How many bricks will there be in 10 piles?

What number multiplied by 5 gives the answer 40?

How many 8s make 72?

Practise the 8s

You should know all of the 8 times table now, but how quickly can you remember it?
Ask someone to time you as you do this page.
Be fast but also correct.

1 x 8 =	2 x 8 =	8 x 6 =
2 x 8 =	4 x 8 =	3 x 8 =
3 x 8 =	6 x 8 =	9 x 8 =
4 x 8 =	8 x 8 =	8 x 4 =
5 x 8 =	10 x 8 =	1 x 8 =
6 x 8 =	1 x 8 =	8 x 2 =
7 x 8 =	3 x 8 =	7 x 8 =
8 x 8 =	5 x 8 =	0 x 8 =
9 x 8 =	7 x 8 =	8 x 3 =
10 x 8 =	9 x 8 =	5 x 8 =
8 x 1 =	8 x 3 =	8 x 8 =
8 x 2 =	8 x 5 =	2 x 8 =
8 x 3 =	8 x 8 =	8 x 9 =
8 x 4 =	8 x 9 =	4 x 8 =
8 x 5 =	8 x 2 =	8 x 6 =
8 x 6 =	8 x 4 =	10 x 8 =
8 x 7 =	8 x 6 =	8 x 5 =
8 x 8 =	8 x 8 =	8 x 0 =
8 x 9 =	8 x 10 =	8 x 1 =
8 x 10 =	8 x 0 =	6 x 8 =

Speed trials

You should know all of the 1, 2, 3, 4, 5, 6, 7, 8, and 10 times tables now, but how quickly can you remember them?
Ask someone to time you as you do this page.
Be fast but also correct.

4 x 8 =	7 x 8 =	9 x 8 =
5 x 10 =	8 x 7 =	7 x 6 =
7 x 8 =	6 x 8 =	8 x 3 =
8 x 5 =	8 x 10 =	8 x 8 =
6 x 10 =	6 x 3 =	7 x 4 =
8 x 7 =	7 x 7 =	4 x 8 =
5 x 8 =	5 x 6 =	3 x 7 =
9 x 8 =	6 x 7 =	2 x 8 =
8 x 8 =	7 x 10 =	7 x 3 =
7 x 6 =	6 x 9 =	0 x 8 =
7 x 5 =	5 x 8 =	10 x 8 =
6 x 8 =	8 x 4 =	6 x 2 =
6 x 7 =	0 x 8 =	8 x 6 =
5 x 7 =	5 x 9 =	7 x 8 =
8 x 4 =	7 x 6 =	6 x 5 =
7 x 10 =	8 x 3 =	8 x 10 =
2 x 8 =	9 x 6 =	8 x 7 =
4 x 7 =	8 x 6 =	5 x 10 =
6 x 9 =	9 x 10 =	8 x 2 =
9 x 10 =	6 x 6 =	8 x 9 =

49

Some of the 9s

You should already know nearly all of the 9 times table because it is part of the 1, 2, 3, 4, 5, 6, 7, 8, and 10 times tables.

1 x 9 = 9	2 x 9 = 18	3 x 9 = 27	4 x 9 = 36	5 x 9 = 45
6 x 9 = 54	7 x 9 = 63	8 x 9 = 72	10 x 9 = 90	

Find out if you can remember them quickly and correctly.

Cover the nine times table so you can't see the numbers.
Write the answers as quickly as you can.

What is three nines?

What is ten nines?

What is two nines?

What is four nines?

What is six nines?

What is five nines?

What is seven nines?

What is eight nines?

Write the answers as quickly as you can.

How many nines equal 18?

How many nines equal 54?

How many nines equal 90?

How many nines equal 27?

How many nines equal 72?

How many nines equal 36?

How many nines equal 45?

How many nines equal 63?

Write the answers as quickly as you can.

Multiply nine by seven.

Multiply nine by ten.

Multiply nine by two.

Multiply nine by five.

Multiply nine by six.

Multiply nine by four.

Multiply nine by three.

Multiply nine by eight.

Write the answers as quickly as you can.

6 x 9 =

2 x 9 =

10 x 9 =

5 x 9 =

3 x 9 =

8 x 9 =

0 x 9 =

7 x 9 =

4 x 9 =

The rest of the 9s

You need to learn only this part of the nine times table.

$$9 \times 9 = 81$$

This work will help you remember the 9 times table.

Complete these sequences.

9   18   27   36   45   54

$8 \times 9 = 72$ so $9 \times 9 = 72$ plus another 9 =

27   36   45

9   18   27   72   90

9   27   45

Look for a pattern in the nine times table.

1	x	9	=	09
2	x	9	=	18
3	x	9	=	27
4	x	9	=	36
5	x	9	=	45
6	x	9	=	54
7	x	9	=	63
8	x	9	=	72
9	x	9	=	81
10	x	9	=	90

Write down any patterns you can see. (There is more than one.)

_____

_____

_____

_____

_____

_____

_____

Practise the 9s

You should know all of the 9 times table now, but how quickly can you remember it?
Ask someone to time you as you do this page.
Be fast and correct.

1 x 9 =   2 x 9 =   9 x 6 =

2 x 9 =   4 x 9 =   3 x 9 =

3 x 9 =   6 x 9 =   9 x 9 =

4 x 9 =   9 x 7 =   9 x 4 =

5 x 9 =   10 x 9 =   1 x 9 =

6 x 9 =   1 x 9 =   9 x 2 =

7 x 9 =   3 x 9 =   7 x 9 =

8 x 9 =   5 x 9 =   0 x 9 =

9 x 9 =   7 x 9 =   9 x 3 =

10 x 9 =   9 x 9 =   5 x 9 =

9 x 1 =   9 x 3 =   9 x 9 =

9 x 2 =   9 x 5 =   2 x 9 =

9 x 3 =   0 x 9 =   8 x 9 =

9 x 4 =   9 x 1 =   4 x 9 =

9 x 5 =   9 x 2 =   9 x 7 =

9 x 6 =   9 x 4 =   10 x 9 =

9 x 7 =   9 x 6 =   9 x 5 =

9 x 8 =   9 x 8 =   9 x 0 =

9 x 9 =   9 x 10 =   9 x 1 =

9 x 10 =   9 x 0 =   6 x 9 =

Speed trials

You should know all of the times tables by now, but how quickly can you remember them?
Ask someone to time you as you do this page.
Be fast and correct.

6 x 8 =	4 x 8 =	8 x 10 =
9 x 10 =	9 x 8 =	7 x 9 =
5 x 8 =	6 x 6 =	8 x 5 =
7 x 5 =	8 x 9 =	8 x 7 =
6 x 4 =	6 x 4 =	7 x 4 =
8 x 8 =	7 x 3 =	4 x 9 =
5 x 10 =	5 x 9 =	6 x 7 =
9 x 8 =	6 x 8 =	4 x 6 =
8 x 3 =	7 x 7 =	7 x 8 =
7 x 7 =	6 x 9 =	6 x 9 =
9 x 5 =	7 x 8 =	10 x 8 =
4 x 8 =	8 x 4 =	6 x 5 =
6 x 7 =	0 x 9 =	8 x 8 =
2 x 9 =	10 x 10 =	7 x 6 =
8 x 4 =	7 x 6 =	6 x 8 =
7 x 10 =	8 x 7 =	9 x 10 =
2 x 8 =	9 x 6 =	8 x 4 =
4 x 7 =	8 x 6 =	7 x 10 =
6 x 9 =	9 x 9 =	5 x 8 =
9 x 9 =	6 x 7 =	8 x 9 =

Times tables for division

Knowing the times tables can also help with division problems. Look at these examples.
$3 \times 6 = 18$ which means that $18 \div 3 = 6$ and that $18 \div 6 = 3$
$4 \times 5 = 20$ which means that $20 \div 4 = 5$ and that $20 \div 5 = 4$
$9 \times 3 = 27$ which means that $27 \div 3 = 9$ and that $27 \div 9 = 3$

Use your knowledge of the times tables to work these division problems.

$3 \times 8 = 24$ which means that $24 \div 3 = $ [ ] and that $24 \div 8 = $ [ ]

$4 \times 7 = 28$ which means that $28 \div 4 = $ [ ] and that $28 \div 7 = $ [ ]

$3 \times 5 = 15$ which means that $15 \div 3 = $ [ ] and that $15 \div 5 = $ [ ]

$4 \times 3 = 12$ which means that $12 \div 3 = $ [ ] and that $12 \div 4 = $ [ ]

$3 \times 10 = 30$ which means that $30 \div 3 = $ [ ] and that $30 \div 10 = $ [ ]

$4 \times 8 = 32$ which means that $32 \div 4 = $ [ ] and that $32 \div 8 = $ [ ]

$3 \times 9 = 27$ which means that $27 \div 3 = $ [ ] and that $27 \div 9 = $ [ ]

$4 \times 10 = 40$ which means that $40 \div 4 = $ [ ] and that $40 \div 10 = $ [ ]

These division problems help practise the 3 and 4 times tables.

$20 \div 4 = $ [ ] $15 \div 3 = $ [ ] $16 \div 4 = $ [ ]

$24 \div 4 = $ [ ] $27 \div 3 = $ [ ] $30 \div 3 = $ [ ]

$12 \div 3 = $ [ ] $18 \div 3 = $ [ ] $28 \div 4 = $ [ ]

$24 \div 3 = $ [ ] $32 \div 4 = $ [ ] $21 \div 3 = $ [ ]

How many fours in 36? [ ]   Divide 27 by three. [ ]

Divide 28 by 4. [ ]   How many threes in 21? [ ]

How many fives in 35? [ ]   Divide 40 by 5. [ ]

Divide 15 by 3. [ ]   How many eights in 48? [ ]

Times tables for division

This page will help you remember times tables by dividing by 2, 3, 4, 5, and 10.

20 ÷ 5 = 4   18 ÷ 3 = 6   60 ÷ 10 = 6

Complete the problems.

40 ÷ 10 =   14 ÷ 2 =   32 ÷ 4 =

25 ÷ 5 =   21 ÷ 3 =   16 ÷ 4 =

24 ÷ 4 =   28 ÷ 4 =   12 ÷ 2 =

45 ÷ 5 =   35 ÷ 5 =   12 ÷ 3 =

10 ÷ 2 =   40 ÷ 10 =   12 ÷ 4 =

20 ÷ 10 =   20 ÷ 2 =   20 ÷ 2 =

6 ÷ 2 =   18 ÷ 3 =   20 ÷ 4 =

24 ÷ 3 =   32 ÷ 4 =   20 ÷ 5 =

30 ÷ 5 =   40 ÷ 5 =   20 ÷ 10 =

30 ÷ 10 =   80 ÷ 10 =   18 ÷ 2 =

40 ÷ 5 =   6 ÷ 2 =   18 ÷ 3 =

21 ÷ 3 =   15 ÷ 3 =   15 ÷ 3 =

14 ÷ 2 =   24 ÷ 4 =   15 ÷ 5 =

27 ÷ 3 =   15 ÷ 5 =   24 ÷ 3 =

90 ÷ 10 =   10 ÷ 10 =   24 ÷ 4 =

15 ÷ 5 =   4 ÷ 2 =   50 ÷ 5 =

15 ÷ 3 =   9 ÷ 3 =   50 ÷ 10 =

20 ÷ 5 =   4 ÷ 4 =   30 ÷ 3 =

20 ÷ 4 =   10 ÷ 5 =   30 ÷ 5 =

16 ÷ 2 =   100 ÷ 10 =   30 ÷ 10 =

Times tables for division

This page will help you remember times tables by dividing by 2, 3, 4, 5, 6, and 10.

$30 \div 6 =$ 5 $\qquad$ $12 \div 6 =$ 2 $\qquad$ $60 \div 10 =$ 6

Complete the problems.

$18 \div 6 =$	$27 \div 3 =$	$48 \div 6 =$
$30 \div 10 =$	$18 \div 6 =$	$35 \div 5 =$
$14 \div 2 =$	$20 \div 2 =$	$36 \div 4 =$
$18 \div 3 =$	$24 \div 6 =$	$24 \div 3 =$
$20 \div 4 =$	$24 \div 3 =$	$20 \div 2 =$
$15 \div 5 =$	$24 \div 4 =$	$30 \div 6 =$
$36 \div 6 =$	$30 \div 10 =$	$25 \div 5 =$
$50 \div 10 =$	$18 \div 2 =$	$32 \div 4 =$
$8 \div 2 =$	$18 \div 3 =$	$27 \div 3 =$
$15 \div 3 =$	$36 \div 4 =$	$16 \div 2 =$
$16 \div 4 =$	$36 \div 6 =$	$42 \div 6 =$
$25 \div 5 =$	$40 \div 5 =$	$5 \div 5 =$
$6 \div 6 =$	$100 \div 10 =$	$4 \div 4 =$
$10 \div 10 =$	$16 \div 4 =$	$28 \div 4 =$
$42 \div 6 =$	$42 \div 6 =$	$14 \div 2 =$
$24 \div 4 =$	$48 \div 6 =$	$24 \div 6 =$
$54 \div 6 =$	$54 \div 6 =$	$18 \div 6 =$
$90 \div 10 =$	$60 \div 6 =$	$54 \div 6 =$
$30 \div 6 =$	$60 \div 10 =$	$60 \div 6 =$
$30 \div 5 =$	$30 \div 6 =$	$40 \div 5 =$

Times tables for division

This page will help you remember times tables by dividing by 2, 3, 4, 5, 6, and 7.

$14 \div 7 = $ 2 $\qquad$ $28 \div 7 = $ 4 $\qquad$ $70 \div 7 = $ 10

Complete the problems.

$21 \div 7 =$	$18 \div 6 =$	$49 \div 7 =$
$35 \div 5 =$	$28 \div 7 =$	$35 \div 5 =$
$14 \div 2 =$	$24 \div 6 =$	$35 \div 7 =$
$18 \div 6 =$	$24 \div 4 =$	$24 \div 6 =$
$20 \div 5 =$	$24 \div 2 =$	$21 \div 3 =$
$15 \div 3 =$	$21 \div 7 =$	$70 \div 7 =$
$36 \div 4 =$	$42 \div 7 =$	$42 \div 7 =$
$56 \div 7 =$	$18 \div 3 =$	$32 \div 4 =$
$18 \div 2 =$	$49 \div 7 =$	$27 \div 3 =$
$15 \div 5 =$	$36 \div 4 =$	$16 \div 4 =$
$49 \div 7 =$	$36 \div 6 =$	$42 \div 6 =$
$25 \div 5 =$	$40 \div 5 =$	$45 \div 5 =$
$7 \div 7 =$	$70 \div 7 =$	$40 \div 4 =$
$63 \div 7 =$	$24 \div 3 =$	$24 \div 3 =$
$42 \div 7 =$	$42 \div 6 =$	$14 \div 7 =$
$24 \div 6 =$	$48 \div 6 =$	$24 \div 4 =$
$54 \div 6 =$	$54 \div 6 =$	$18 \div 3 =$
$28 \div 7 =$	$60 \div 6 =$	$56 \div 7 =$
$30 \div 6 =$	$63 \div 7 =$	$63 \div 7 =$
$35 \div 7 =$	$25 \div 5 =$	$48 \div 6 =$

Times tables for division

This page will help you remember times tables by dividing by 2, 3, 4, 5, 6, 7, 8, and 9.

$16 \div 8 =$ 2 $\qquad 35 \div 7 =$ 5 $\qquad 27 \div 9 =$ 3

Complete the problems.

$42 \div 6 =$	$81 \div 9 =$	$56 \div 7 =$
$32 \div 8 =$	$56 \div 7 =$	$45 \div 5 =$
$14 \div 7 =$	$72 \div 9 =$	$35 \div 7 =$
$18 \div 9 =$	$24 \div 8 =$	$18 \div 9 =$
$63 \div 7 =$	$27 \div 9 =$	$21 \div 3 =$
$72 \div 9 =$	$72 \div 9 =$	$28 \div 7 =$
$72 \div 8 =$	$42 \div 6 =$	$64 \div 8 =$
$56 \div 7 =$	$27 \div 3 =$	$32 \div 8 =$
$18 \div 6 =$	$14 \div 7 =$	$27 \div 9 =$
$81 \div 9 =$	$36 \div 4 =$	$16 \div 8 =$
$63 \div 9 =$	$36 \div 6 =$	$42 \div 6 =$
$45 \div 5 =$	$48 \div 8 =$	$45 \div 9 =$
$54 \div 9 =$	$21 \div 7 =$	$40 \div 4 =$
$70 \div 7 =$	$24 \div 3 =$	$24 \div 8 =$
$42 \div 7 =$	$40 \div 8 =$	$63 \div 7 =$
$30 \div 5 =$	$45 \div 9 =$	$24 \div 6 =$
$54 \div 6 =$	$54 \div 6 =$	$18 \div 6 =$
$56 \div 8 =$	$42 \div 7 =$	$56 \div 8 =$
$30 \div 5 =$	$63 \div 9 =$	$63 \div 9 =$
$35 \div 7 =$	$50 \div 5 =$	$48 \div 8 =$

Times tables practice grids

This is a times tables grid.

X	3	4	5
7	21	28	35
8	24	32	40

Complete each times tables grid.

X	1	3	5	7	9
2					
3					

X	4	6
6		
7		
8		

X	6	7	8	9	10
3					
4					
5					

X	10	7	8	4
3				
5				
7				

X	6	2	4	7
5				
10				

X	8	7	9	6
9				
7				

Times tables practice grids

Here are more times tables grids.

X	2	4	6
5			
7			

X	8	3	9	2
5				
6				
7				

X	2	3	4	5
8				
9				

X	10	9	8	7
6				
5				
4				

X	3	8
2		
3		
4		
5		
6		
7		

X	2	4	6	8
1				
3				
5				
7				
9				
0				

Times tables practice grids

Here are some other times tables grids.

X	8	9
7		
8		

X	9	8	7	6	5	4
9						
8						
7						

X	2	5	9
4			
7			
8			

X	2	3	4	5	7
4					
6					
8					

X	3	5	7
2			
8			
6			
0			
4			
7			

X	8	7	9	6
7				
9				
0				
10				
8				
6				

Speed trials

Try this final test.

27 ÷ 3 = ⬚   4 x 9 = ⬚   14 ÷ 2 = ⬚

7 x 9 = ⬚   18 ÷ 2 = ⬚   9 x 9 = ⬚

64 ÷ 8 = ⬚   6 x 8 = ⬚   15 ÷ 3 = ⬚

90 ÷ 10 = ⬚   21 ÷ 3 = ⬚   8 x 8 = ⬚

6 x 8 = ⬚   9 x 7 = ⬚   24 ÷ 4 = ⬚

45 ÷ 9 = ⬚   36 ÷ 4 = ⬚   7 x 8 = ⬚

3 x 7 = ⬚   4 x 6 = ⬚   30 ÷ 5 = ⬚

9 x 5 = ⬚   45 ÷ 5 = ⬚   6 x 6 = ⬚

48 ÷ 6 = ⬚   8 x 5 = ⬚   42 ÷ 6 = ⬚

7 x 7 = ⬚   42 ÷ 6 = ⬚   9 x 5 = ⬚

3 x 9 = ⬚   7 x 4 = ⬚   49 ÷ 7 = ⬚

56 ÷ 8 = ⬚   35 ÷ 7 = ⬚   8 x 6 = ⬚

36 ÷ 4 = ⬚   9 x 3 = ⬚   72 ÷ 8 = ⬚

24 ÷ 3 = ⬚   24 ÷ 8 = ⬚   9 x 7 = ⬚

36 ÷ 9 = ⬚   8 x 2 = ⬚   54 ÷ 9 = ⬚

6 x 7 = ⬚   36 ÷ 9 = ⬚   7 x 6 = ⬚

4 x 4 = ⬚   6 x 10 = ⬚   10 ÷ 10 = ⬚

32 ÷ 8 = ⬚   80 ÷ 10 = ⬚   7 x 7 = ⬚

49 ÷ 7 = ⬚   6 x 9 = ⬚   16 ÷ 8 = ⬚

25 ÷ 5 = ⬚   16 ÷ 2 = ⬚   7 x 9 = ⬚

56 ÷ 7 = ⬚   54 ÷ 9 = ⬚   63 ÷ 7 = ⬚

Line of symmetry

If a plane figure is cut into two equal parts, the line of the cut is called a line of symmetry.

Draw as many lines of symmetry as you can find on each of these shapes.

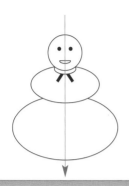

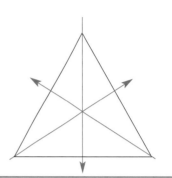

Draw a line of symmetry on each of these shapes.

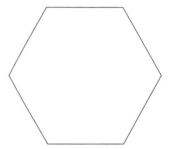

Draw as many lines of symmetry as you can find on each of these shapes.

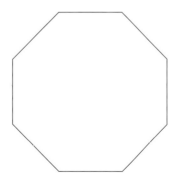

Ordering large numbers

Write these numbers in order, starting with the least.

256	654 327	39 214	147 243	9631
256	9631	39 214	147 243	654 327

Write these numbers in order, starting with the least.

72 463	730 241	261	5247	643 292

641 471	260 453	59 372	657 473	4290

327 914	647 212	47 900	3825	416

593 103	761	374 239	91 761	1425

600 200	500 200	5200	50 200	52 000

6437	643	64 370	6430	643 000

9900	999	900 200	920 200	9 200 000

In a country's election
O'Neil got 900 550 votes,
Schneider got 840 690 votes,
Rojas got 8 406 900 votes,
Marsalis got 7 964 201 votes and
Samperi got 859 999 votes.

Place the candidates in order.

1st _____

2nd _____

3rd _____

4th _____

5th _____

Rounding whole numbers

Write these numbers to the nearest hundred.

529   500   1687   1700

If the place to the right of the place we are rounding is 5, round to the number above.

652   700

Round to the nearest hundred.

873		295		7348		3561	
16 537		4855		569		1200	
22 851		227		782		452	

Round to the nearest ten-thousand.

23 478		418 700		58 397		351 899	
109 544		31 059		67 414		33 500	
89 388		801 821		134 800		45 010	

Round to the nearest ten.

87		397		52		65	
1392		15		12 489		2861	
75		715		34		18 149	

Round to the nearest thousand.

3284		112 810		10 518		83 477	
8499		225 500		4500		6112	
1059		93 606		6752		2550	

Choosing units of measure

Circle the units that are the closest estimate.

The amount of orange juice in a full glass.

6 millilitres   (350 millilitres)   2 litres

Circle the units that are the closest estimate.

The mass of a box of cereal	750 grams	3 kilograms	2 tonnes
The length of a football field	20 centimetres	100 metres	1 kilometre
The area of a rug	20 sq centimetres	30 sq metres	1 sq kilometre
The amount of cough medicine in a bottle	120 millilitres	6 litres	1 litre
The distance from home plate to first base	120 centimetres	30 metres	6 metres
The mass of a package of sugar	2 grams	10 kilograms	1/2 tonne
The length of an airport runway	2 kilometres	50 metres	500 centimetres
The amount of water in a full pail	8 millilitres	2 millilitres	3 litres
The area of a place mat	200 sq centimetres	6 sq metres	1 sq kilometre

Comparing fractions

 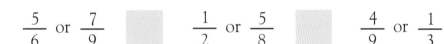

Which is greater, $\frac{2}{3}$ or $\frac{3}{4}$? $\boxed{\frac{3}{4}}$

The common denominator of 3 and 4 is 12.

So $\frac{2}{3} = \frac{8}{12}$ and $\frac{3}{4} = \frac{9}{12}$

$\frac{3}{4}$ is greater.

Which is greater?

$\frac{1}{4}$ or $\frac{1}{3}$	$\frac{5}{6}$ or $\frac{7}{9}$	$\frac{1}{2}$ or $\frac{5}{8}$	$\frac{4}{9}$ or $\frac{1}{3}$
$\frac{2}{5}$ or $\frac{3}{8}$	$\frac{7}{10}$ or $\frac{8}{9}$	$\frac{8}{10}$ or $\frac{7}{8}$	$\frac{7}{12}$ or $\frac{2}{3}$
$\frac{2}{3}$ or $\frac{5}{8}$	$\frac{4}{15}$ or $\frac{1}{3}$	$\frac{3}{5}$ or $\frac{2}{3}$	$\frac{3}{8}$ or $\frac{1}{4}$

Which two fractions in each row are equal?

$\frac{1}{4}$	$\frac{3}{8}$	$\frac{4}{12}$	$\frac{3}{12}$	$\frac{7}{8}$	$\frac{5}{8}$
$\frac{5}{8}$	$\frac{6}{9}$	$\frac{7}{10}$	$\frac{8}{12}$	$\frac{1}{2}$	$\frac{3}{4}$
$\frac{7}{12}$	$\frac{6}{14}$	$\frac{7}{14}$	$\frac{3}{8}$	$\frac{4}{8}$	$\frac{9}{12}$
$\frac{3}{8}$	$\frac{3}{9}$	$\frac{2}{6}$	$\frac{4}{7}$	$\frac{9}{10}$	$\frac{6}{7}$
$\frac{3}{10}$	$\frac{5}{15}$	$\frac{2}{10}$	$\frac{3}{15}$	$\frac{4}{10}$	$\frac{7}{15}$

Put these fractions in order starting with the least.

$\frac{1}{2}$	$\frac{5}{6}$	$\frac{2}{3}$
$\frac{5}{8}$	$\frac{3}{4}$	$\frac{11}{12}$
$\frac{2}{3}$	$\frac{8}{15}$	$\frac{3}{5}$

Converting fractions to decimals

Convert these fractions to decimals.

$\dfrac{3}{10}$ = 0.3

(because the three goes in the tenths column)

$\dfrac{7}{100}$ = 0.07

(because the seven goes in the hundredths column)

Convert these fractions to decimals.

$\dfrac{6}{10}$ = ⬚ $\dfrac{9}{100}$ = ⬚ $\dfrac{4}{100}$ = ⬚ $\dfrac{6}{100}$ = ⬚

$\dfrac{4}{10}$ = ⬚ $\dfrac{2}{10}$ = ⬚ $\dfrac{1}{10}$ = ⬚ $\dfrac{7}{100}$ = ⬚

$\dfrac{8}{100}$ = ⬚ $\dfrac{5}{10}$ = ⬚ $\dfrac{7}{10}$ = ⬚ $\dfrac{8}{10}$ = ⬚

$\dfrac{2}{100}$ = ⬚ $\dfrac{5}{100}$ = ⬚ $\dfrac{1}{100}$ = ⬚ $\dfrac{3}{10}$ = ⬚

Convert $\dfrac{1}{4}$ to a decimal.

To do this we have to divide the bottom number into the top.

When we run out of numbers we put in the decimal point and enough zeros to finish the sum.
Be careful to keep the decimal point in your answer above the decimal point in the sum.

```
      0.25
  4)1.00
     8
    20
    20
     0
```

Convert these fractions to decimals.

$\dfrac{1}{2}$ = ⬚ $\dfrac{3}{4}$ = ⬚ $\dfrac{2}{5}$ = ⬚ $\dfrac{1}{5}$ = ⬚

$\dfrac{4}{5}$ = ⬚ $\dfrac{3}{8}$ = ⬚ $\dfrac{3}{5}$ = ⬚ $\dfrac{1}{4}$ = ⬚

68

Adding fractions

Work out the answer to the problem.

$$\frac{1}{5} + \frac{3}{5} = \boxed{\frac{4}{5}} \qquad\qquad \frac{4}{9} + \frac{2}{9} = \boxed{\frac{^2\cancel{6}}{\cancel{9}_3}} = \boxed{\frac{2}{3}}$$

Remember to reduce to simplest form if you need to.

Work out the answer to each sum. Reduce to simplest form if you need to.

$$\frac{2}{7} + \frac{3}{7} = \frac{\boxed{}}{7} \qquad \frac{2}{9} + \frac{5}{9} = \frac{\boxed{}}{9} \qquad \frac{1}{3} + \frac{1}{3} = \frac{\boxed{}}{3}$$

$$\frac{3}{10} + \frac{4}{10} = \frac{\boxed{}}{10} \qquad \frac{1}{8} + \frac{2}{8} = \frac{\boxed{}}{8} \qquad \frac{2}{9} + \frac{3}{9} = \frac{\boxed{}}{9}$$

$$\frac{2}{5} + \frac{1}{5} = \boxed{} \qquad \frac{1}{7} + \frac{5}{7} = \boxed{} \qquad \frac{4}{9} + \frac{1}{9} = \frac{\boxed{}}{9}$$

$$\frac{3}{20} + \frac{4}{20} = \boxed{} \qquad \frac{3}{100} + \frac{8}{100} = \boxed{} \qquad \frac{7}{10} + \frac{2}{10} = \boxed{}$$

$$\frac{1}{6} + \frac{2}{6} = \boxed{} = \boxed{} \qquad \frac{31}{100} + \frac{19}{100} = \boxed{} = \boxed{} \qquad \frac{11}{20} + \frac{4}{20} = \boxed{} = \boxed{}$$

$$\frac{3}{10} + \frac{3}{10} = \boxed{} = \boxed{} \qquad \frac{1}{12} + \frac{5}{12} = \boxed{} = \boxed{} \qquad \frac{2}{6} + \frac{2}{6} = \boxed{} = \boxed{}$$

$$\frac{3}{8} + \frac{3}{8} = \boxed{} = \boxed{} \qquad \frac{3}{8} + \frac{1}{8} = \boxed{} = \boxed{} \qquad \frac{5}{12} + \frac{3}{12} = \boxed{} = \boxed{}$$

$$\frac{1}{4} + \frac{1}{4} = \boxed{} = \boxed{} \qquad \frac{3}{20} + \frac{2}{20} = \boxed{} = \boxed{} \qquad \frac{2}{6} + \frac{2}{6} = \boxed{} = \boxed{}$$

$$\frac{2}{7} + \frac{4}{7} = \boxed{} \qquad \frac{2}{9} + \frac{2}{9} = \boxed{} \qquad \frac{13}{20} + \frac{5}{20} = \boxed{} = \boxed{}$$

$$\frac{81}{100} + \frac{9}{100} = \boxed{} = \boxed{} \qquad \frac{7}{20} + \frac{6}{20} = \boxed{} \qquad \frac{3}{8} + \frac{2}{8} = \boxed{}$$

$$\frac{6}{10} + \frac{2}{10} = \boxed{} = \boxed{} \qquad \frac{29}{100} + \frac{46}{100} = \boxed{} = \boxed{} \qquad \frac{73}{100} + \frac{17}{100} = \boxed{} = \boxed{}$$

Subtracting fractions

Write the answer to each problem.

$$\frac{4}{5} - \frac{2}{5} = \boxed{\frac{2}{5}}$$

$$\frac{8}{9} - \frac{5}{9} = \frac{\cancel{3}}{\cancel{9}_3} = \boxed{\frac{1}{3}}$$

Reduce to simplest form if you need to.

Write the answer to each problem. Reduce to simplest form if you need to.

$$\frac{3}{5} - \frac{1}{5} = \frac{\boxed{}}{5}$$

$$\frac{6}{7} - \frac{3}{7} = \frac{\boxed{}}{7}$$

$$\frac{9}{10} - \frac{6}{10} = \frac{\boxed{}}{10}$$

$$\frac{7}{10} - \frac{4}{10} = \boxed{\underline{}}$$

$$\frac{5}{9} - \frac{4}{9} = \boxed{\underline{}}$$

$$\frac{2}{3} - \frac{1}{3} = \boxed{\underline{}}$$

$$\frac{7}{8} - \frac{3}{8} = \boxed{\underline{}} = \boxed{\underline{}}$$

$$\frac{14}{20} - \frac{10}{20} = \boxed{\underline{}} = \boxed{\underline{}}$$

$$\frac{5}{6} - \frac{1}{6} = \boxed{\underline{}} = \boxed{\underline{}}$$

$$\frac{11}{12} - \frac{5}{12} = \boxed{\underline{}} = \boxed{\underline{}}$$

$$\frac{17}{20} - \frac{12}{20} = \boxed{\underline{}} = \boxed{\underline{}}$$

$$\frac{9}{12} - \frac{3}{12} = \boxed{\underline{}} = \boxed{\underline{}}$$

$$\frac{8}{10} - \frac{6}{10} = \boxed{\underline{}} = \boxed{\underline{}}$$

$$\frac{12}{12} - \frac{2}{12} = \boxed{\underline{}} = \boxed{\underline{}}$$

$$\frac{9}{10} - \frac{3}{10} = \boxed{\underline{}} = \boxed{\underline{}}$$

$$\frac{8}{9} - \frac{2}{9} = \boxed{\underline{}} = \boxed{\underline{}}$$

$$\frac{7}{8} - \frac{1}{8} = \boxed{\underline{}} = \boxed{\underline{}}$$

$$\frac{9}{12} - \frac{5}{12} = \boxed{\underline{}} = \boxed{\underline{}}$$

$$\frac{3}{4} - \frac{2}{4} = \boxed{\underline{}}$$

$$\frac{6}{8} - \frac{3}{8} = \boxed{\underline{}}$$

$$\frac{18}{20} - \frac{8}{20} = \boxed{\underline{}} = \boxed{\underline{}}$$

$$\frac{4}{6} - \frac{2}{6} = \boxed{\underline{}} = \boxed{\underline{}}$$

$$\frac{5}{12} - \frac{4}{12} = \boxed{\underline{}}$$

$$\frac{3}{8} - \frac{2}{8} = \boxed{\underline{}}$$

$$\frac{5}{7} - \frac{1}{7} = \boxed{\underline{}}$$

$$\frac{5}{16} - \frac{1}{16} = \boxed{\underline{}} = \boxed{\underline{}}$$

$$\frac{90}{100} - \frac{80}{100} = \boxed{\underline{}} = \boxed{\underline{}}$$

Adding fractions

Write the answer to each problem.

$$\frac{3}{8} + \frac{5}{8} = \frac{8}{8} = 1 \qquad\qquad \frac{3}{4} + \frac{3}{4} = \frac{3\cancel{6}}{\cancel{4}2} = \frac{3}{2} = 1\frac{1}{2}$$

Write the answer to each problem.

$\dfrac{7}{10} + \dfrac{6}{10} = \dfrac{\ }{10} = 1\dfrac{\ }{10}$ $\qquad$ $\dfrac{6}{7} + \dfrac{5}{7} = \dfrac{\ }{7} = 1\dfrac{\ }{7}$ $\qquad$ $\dfrac{2}{3} + \dfrac{2}{3} = \dfrac{\ }{3} = 1\dfrac{\ }{3}$

$\dfrac{5}{10} + \dfrac{6}{10} = \dfrac{\ }{\ } = \ \dfrac{\ }{\ }$ $\qquad$ $\dfrac{8}{13} + \dfrac{5}{13} = \dfrac{\ }{\ } = \ $ $\qquad$ $\dfrac{7}{8} + \dfrac{4}{8} = \dfrac{\ }{\ } = \ \dfrac{\ }{\ }$

$\dfrac{7}{8} + \dfrac{5}{8} = \dfrac{\ }{\ } = \dfrac{\ }{\ } = \ \dfrac{\ }{\ }$ $\qquad$ $\dfrac{2}{5} + \dfrac{3}{5} = \dfrac{\ }{\ } = \ $ $\qquad$ $\dfrac{5}{8} + \dfrac{5}{8} = \dfrac{\ }{\ } = \dfrac{\ }{\ } = \ \dfrac{\ }{\ }$

$\dfrac{10}{20} + \dfrac{15}{20} = \dfrac{\ }{\ } = \dfrac{\ }{\ } = \ \dfrac{\ }{\ }$ $\qquad$ $\dfrac{2}{3} + \dfrac{1}{3} = \dfrac{\ }{\ } = \ $ $\qquad$ $\dfrac{5}{6} + \dfrac{5}{6} = \dfrac{\ }{\ } = \dfrac{\ }{\ } = \ \dfrac{\ }{\ }$

$\dfrac{5}{6} + \dfrac{3}{6} = \dfrac{\ }{\ } = \dfrac{\ }{\ } = \ \dfrac{\ }{\ }$ $\qquad$ $\dfrac{6}{12} + \dfrac{7}{12} = \dfrac{\ }{\ } = \ \dfrac{\ }{\ }$ $\qquad$ $\dfrac{8}{10} + \dfrac{6}{10} = \dfrac{\ }{\ } = \dfrac{\ }{\ } = \ \dfrac{\ }{\ }$

$\dfrac{12}{20} + \dfrac{10}{20} = \dfrac{\ }{\ } = \dfrac{\ }{\ } = \ \dfrac{\ }{\ }$ $\qquad$ $\dfrac{3}{10} + \dfrac{7}{10} = \dfrac{\ }{\ } = \ $ $\qquad$ $\dfrac{75}{100} + \dfrac{75}{100} = \dfrac{\ }{\ } = \dfrac{\ }{\ } = \ \dfrac{\ }{\ }$

$\dfrac{10}{20} + \dfrac{16}{20} = \dfrac{\ }{\ } = \dfrac{\ }{\ } = \ \dfrac{\ }{\ }$ $\qquad$ $\dfrac{4}{5} + \dfrac{4}{5} = \dfrac{\ }{\ } = \ \dfrac{\ }{\ }$ $\qquad$ $\dfrac{11}{21} + \dfrac{17}{21} = \dfrac{\ }{\ } = \dfrac{\ }{\ } = \ \dfrac{\ }{\ }$

Adding fractions

Write the answer to each problem.

$$\frac{2}{3} + \frac{1}{6} = \frac{4}{6} + \frac{1}{6} = \frac{5}{6}$$

$$\frac{3}{4} + \frac{5}{6} = \frac{9}{12} + \frac{10}{12} = \frac{19}{12} = 1\frac{7}{12}$$

Work out the answer to each problem. Rename as a mixed number if you need to.

$$\frac{2}{5} + \frac{7}{10} = \frac{\ }{\ } + \frac{\ }{\ } = \frac{\ }{\ } = \square \frac{\ }{\ }$$

$$\frac{3}{4} + \frac{7}{10} = \frac{\ }{\ } + \frac{\ }{\ } = \frac{\ }{\ } = \square \frac{\ }{\ }$$

$$\frac{1}{4} + \frac{5}{6} = \frac{\ }{\ } + \frac{\ }{\ } = \frac{\ }{\ } = \square \frac{\ }{\ }$$

$$\frac{3}{4} + \frac{7}{8} = \frac{\ }{\ } + \frac{\ }{\ } = \frac{\ }{\ } = \square \frac{\ }{\ }$$

$$\frac{2}{3} + \frac{1}{4} = \frac{\ }{\ } + \frac{\ }{\ } = \frac{\ }{\ }$$

$$\frac{5}{6} + \frac{11}{12} = \frac{\ }{\ } + \frac{\ }{\ } = \frac{\ }{\ } = \square \frac{\ }{\ }$$

$$\frac{5}{7} + \frac{3}{14} = \frac{\ }{\ } + \frac{\ }{\ } = \frac{\ }{\ }$$

$$\frac{5}{8} + \frac{7}{10} = \frac{\ }{\ } + \frac{\ }{\ } = \frac{\ }{\ } = \square \frac{\ }{\ }$$

$$\frac{3}{4} + \frac{3}{5} = \frac{\ }{\ } + \frac{\ }{\ } = \frac{\ }{\ } = \square \frac{\ }{\ }$$

$$\frac{1}{2} + \frac{5}{9} = \frac{\ }{\ } + \frac{\ }{\ } = \frac{\ }{\ } = \square \frac{\ }{\ }$$

$$\frac{2}{3} + \frac{7}{9} = \frac{\ }{\ } + \frac{\ }{\ } = \frac{\ }{\ } = \square \frac{\ }{\ }$$

$$\frac{1}{3} + \frac{7}{8} = \frac{\ }{\ } + \frac{\ }{\ } = \frac{\ }{\ } = \square \frac{\ }{\ }$$

$$\frac{3}{8} + \frac{1}{6} = \frac{\ }{\ } + \frac{\ }{\ } = \frac{\ }{\ }$$

$$\frac{2}{3} + \frac{4}{5} = \frac{\ }{\ } + \frac{\ }{\ } = \frac{\ }{\ } = \square \frac{\ }{\ }$$

$$\frac{4}{5} + \frac{5}{6} = \frac{\ }{\ } + \frac{\ }{\ } = \frac{\ }{\ } = \square \frac{\ }{\ }$$

$$\frac{2}{3} + \frac{3}{10} = \frac{\ }{\ } + \frac{\ }{\ } = \frac{\ }{\ }$$

Subtracting fractions

Work out the answer to the problems.

$$\frac{7}{9} - \frac{1}{3} = \frac{7}{9} - \frac{3}{9} = \frac{4}{9}$$

$$\frac{7}{10} - \frac{3}{8} = \frac{28}{40} - \frac{15}{40} = \frac{13}{40}$$

Work out the answer to each problem. Reduce to the simplest form if you need to.

$$\frac{5}{8} - \frac{1}{2} = \boxed{\ }\ -\ \boxed{\ }\ =\ \boxed{\ }$$

$$\frac{5}{6} - \frac{1}{4} = \boxed{\ }\ -\ \boxed{\ }\ =\ \boxed{\ }$$

$$\frac{9}{10} - \frac{3}{8} = \boxed{\ }\ -\ \boxed{\ }\ =\ \boxed{\ }$$

$$\frac{9}{10} - \frac{5}{8} = \boxed{\ }\ -\ \boxed{\ }\ =\ \boxed{\ }$$

$$\frac{6}{7} - \frac{2}{5} = \boxed{\ }\ -\ \boxed{\ }\ =\ \boxed{\ }$$

$$\frac{11}{12} - \frac{1}{6} = \boxed{\ }\ -\ \boxed{\ }\ =\ \boxed{\ }\ =\ \boxed{\ }$$

$$\frac{7}{12} - \frac{1}{6} = \boxed{\ }\ -\ \boxed{\ }\ =\ \boxed{\ }$$

$$\frac{7}{10} - \frac{1}{4} = \boxed{\ }\ -\ \boxed{\ }\ =\ \boxed{\ }\ =\ \boxed{\ }$$

$$\frac{5}{9} - \frac{1}{3} = \boxed{\ }\ -\ \boxed{\ }\ =\ \boxed{\ }$$

$$\frac{7}{9} - \frac{1}{4} = \boxed{\ }\ -\ \boxed{\ }\ =\ \boxed{\ }$$

$$\frac{7}{16} - \frac{1}{8} = \boxed{\ }\ -\ \boxed{\ }\ =\ \boxed{\ }$$

$$\frac{3}{7} - \frac{1}{5} = \boxed{\ }\ -\ \boxed{\ }\ =\ \boxed{\ }$$

$$\frac{3}{8} - \frac{1}{6} = \boxed{\ }\ -\ \boxed{\ }\ =\ \boxed{\ }$$

$$\frac{3}{5} - \frac{1}{4} = \boxed{\ }\ -\ \boxed{\ }\ =\ \boxed{\ }$$

$$\frac{2}{3} - \frac{1}{2} = \boxed{\ }\ -\ \boxed{\ }\ =\ \boxed{\ }$$

$$\frac{4}{5} - \frac{1}{4} = \boxed{\ }\ -\ \boxed{\ }\ =\ \boxed{\ }$$

Adding mixed numbers

Work out the answer to each problem.

$2\frac{1}{8} + 3\frac{3}{8} = \boxed{} = \boxed{}$

$3\frac{5}{6} + 1\frac{1}{8} = \boxed{} + \boxed{} = \boxed{}$

$3\frac{3}{4} + 2\frac{1}{16} = \boxed{} + \boxed{} = \boxed{}$

$1\frac{2}{3} + 3\frac{2}{7} = \boxed{} + \boxed{} = \boxed{}$

$4\frac{1}{4} + 2\frac{1}{6} = \boxed{} + \boxed{} = \boxed{}$

$6\frac{1}{6} + 3\frac{2}{9} = \boxed{} + \boxed{} = \boxed{}$

$7\frac{5}{6} + 2\frac{1}{10} = \boxed{} + \boxed{} = \boxed{} = \boxed{}$

$1\frac{7}{12} + 4\frac{1}{12} = \boxed{} = \boxed{}$

$5\frac{1}{4} + 3\frac{2}{5} = \boxed{} + \boxed{} = \boxed{} = \boxed{}$

$3\frac{3}{8} + 1\frac{1}{4} = \boxed{} + \boxed{} = \boxed{}$

$6\frac{1}{4} + 2\frac{1}{4} = \boxed{} = \boxed{}$

$6\frac{2}{3} + 3\frac{1}{10} = \boxed{} + \boxed{} = \boxed{}$

$7\frac{1}{3} + 1\frac{2}{9} = \boxed{} + \boxed{} = \boxed{}$

$2\frac{2}{5} + 1\frac{3}{10} = \boxed{} + \boxed{} = \boxed{}$

Subtracting mixed numbers

Work out the answer to the problems.

$$2\frac{7}{8} - 1\frac{5}{8} = \boxed{1\frac{2}{8}} = \boxed{1\frac{1}{4}}$$

$$9\frac{9}{10} - 6\frac{5}{8} = \boxed{9\frac{36}{40}} - \boxed{6\frac{25}{40}} = \boxed{3\frac{11}{40}}$$

Work out the answer to each problem.

$$7\frac{3}{8} - 3\frac{1}{8} = \boxed{} = \boxed{}$$

$$2\frac{14}{15} - 1\frac{4}{9} = \boxed{} - \boxed{} = \boxed{}$$

$$2\frac{2}{3} - 1\frac{1}{6} = \boxed{} - \boxed{} = \boxed{} = \boxed{}$$

$$6\frac{4}{5} - 2\frac{1}{2} = \boxed{} - \boxed{} = \boxed{}$$

$$5\frac{11}{20} - 2\frac{1}{8} = \boxed{} - \boxed{} = \boxed{}$$

$$8\frac{11}{12} - 5\frac{5}{12} = \boxed{} = \boxed{}$$

$$9\frac{7}{9} - 3\frac{4}{6} = \boxed{} - \boxed{} = \boxed{} = \boxed{}$$

$$4\frac{7}{8} - 2\frac{1}{4} = \boxed{} - \boxed{} = \boxed{}$$

$$8\frac{2}{5} - 4\frac{1}{4} = \boxed{} - \boxed{} = \boxed{}$$

$$4\frac{5}{6} - 3\frac{1}{4} = \boxed{} - \boxed{} = \boxed{}$$

$$4\frac{2}{3} - 1\frac{2}{3} = \boxed{} = \boxed{}$$

$$9\frac{8}{9} - 3\frac{3}{4} = \boxed{} - \boxed{} = \boxed{}$$

$$3\frac{8}{15} - 2\frac{2}{5} = \boxed{} - \boxed{} = \boxed{}$$

$$2\frac{7}{9} - 1\frac{1}{5} = \boxed{} - \boxed{} = \boxed{}$$

★ Adding mixed numbers and fractions

Work out the answer to the problems.

$4\frac{3}{4} + \frac{3}{4} = 4\frac{6}{4} = 5\frac{2}{4} = 5\frac{1}{2}$

$3\frac{1}{2} + \frac{2}{3} = 3\frac{3}{6} + \boxed{\frac{4}{6}} = 3\frac{7}{6} = 4\frac{1}{6}$

Work out the answer to each problem.

$6\frac{2}{3} + \frac{2}{3} = \boxed{} = \boxed{}$

$4\frac{1}{4} + \frac{7}{8} = \boxed{} + \boxed{} = \boxed{} = \boxed{}$

$4\frac{5}{8} + \frac{7}{8} = \boxed{} = \boxed{}$

$3\frac{7}{10} + \frac{1}{2} = \boxed{} + \boxed{} = \boxed{} = \boxed{}$

$2\frac{3}{7} + \frac{8}{7} = \boxed{} = \boxed{}$

$1\frac{1}{2} + \frac{3}{4} = \boxed{} + \boxed{} = \boxed{} = \boxed{}$

$3\frac{5}{6} + \frac{2}{3} = \boxed{} + \boxed{} = \boxed{} = \boxed{}$

$5\frac{3}{4} + \frac{4}{5} = \boxed{} + \boxed{} = \boxed{} = \boxed{}$

$3\frac{7}{8} + \frac{1}{4} = \boxed{} + \boxed{} = \boxed{} = \boxed{}$

$3\frac{6}{7} + \frac{3}{4} = \boxed{} + \boxed{} = \boxed{} = \boxed{}$

$7\frac{7}{8} + \frac{1}{4} = \boxed{} + \boxed{} = \boxed{} = \boxed{}$

$4\frac{2}{3} + \frac{5}{8} = \boxed{} + \boxed{} = \boxed{} = \boxed{}$

$1\frac{9}{10} + \frac{2}{5} = \boxed{} + \boxed{} = \boxed{} = \boxed{}$

$8\frac{5}{6} + \frac{3}{5} = \boxed{} + \boxed{} = \boxed{} = \boxed{}$

Simple use of parentheses

Work out these problems.

$(4 + 6) - (2 + 1) =$ 10 − 3 = 7

$(2 \times 5) + (10 - 4) =$ 10 + 6 = 16

Remember to work out the parentheses first.

Work out these problems.

$(5 + 3) + (6 - 2) =$

$(6 - 1) - (1 + 2) =$

$(8 + 3) + (12 - 2) =$

$(7 - 2) + (4 + 5) =$

$(3 - 1) + (12 - 1) =$

$(9 + 5) - (3 + 6) =$

$(14 + 12) - (9 + 4) =$

$(9 - 3) - (4 + 2) =$

Now try these longer problems.

$(5 + 9) + (12 - 2) - (4 + 3) =$

$(10 + 5) - (2 + 4) + (9 + 6) =$

$(19 + 4) - (3 + 2) - (2 + 1) =$

$(24 - 5) - (3 + 7) - (5 - 2) =$

$(15 + 3) + (7 - 2) - (5 + 7) =$

Now try these. Be careful, the parentheses now have multiplication problems.

$(2 \times 3) + (5 \times 2) =$

$(7 \times 2) + (3 \times 3) =$

$(6 \times 4) - (4 \times 3) =$

$(12 \times 4) - (8 \times 3) =$

$(3 \times 4) - (2 \times 2) =$

$(5 \times 4) - (3 \times 2) =$

$(9 \times 5) - (4 \times 6) =$

$(7 \times 4) - (8 \times 2) =$

If the answer is 24, which of these problems gives the correct answer? Write the correct letter.

a $(3 + 5) + (3 \times 1)$

b $(3 \times 5) + (3 \times 2)$

c $(3 \times 5) + (3 \times 3)$

d $(2 \times 5) + (2 \times 6)$

e $(5 \times 7) - (2 \times 5)$

f $(6 + 7) + (12 - 2)$

Simple use of parentheses

Work out these problems.

(7 + 3) x (8 − 4) =   (5 − 2) x (8 − 1) =

(9 + 5) ÷ (1 + 6) =   (14 − 6) x (4 + 3) =

(14 + 4) ÷ (12 − 6) =   (9 + 21) ÷ (8 − 5) =

(11 − 5) x (7 + 5) =   (8 + 20) ÷ (12 − 10) =

(6 + 9) ÷ (8 − 3) =   (14 − 3) x (6 + 1) =

(10 + 10) ÷ (2 + 3) =   (9 + 3) x (2 + 4) =

Now try these.

(4 x 3) ÷ (1 x 2) =   (5 x 4) ÷ (2 x 2) =

(8 x 5) ÷ (4 x 1) =   (6 x 4) ÷ (3 x 4) =

(2 x 4) x (2 x 3) =   (3 x 5) x (1 x 2) =

(8 x 4) ÷ (2 x 2) =   (6 x 4) ÷ (4 x 2) =

If the answer is 30, which of these problems gives the correct answer?

a   (3 x 5) x (2 x 2)   d   (20 ÷ 2) x (12 ÷ 3)

b   (4 x 5) x (5 x 2)   e   (5 x 12) ÷ (2 x 5)

c   (12 x 5) ÷ (8 ÷ 4)   f   (9 x 5) ÷ (10 ÷ 2)

If the answer is 8, which of these problems gives the correct answer?

a   (16 ÷ 2) ÷ (2 x 1)   d   (24 ÷ 6) x (8 ÷ 4)

b   (9 ÷ 3) x (3 x 2)   e   (8 ÷ 4) x (8 ÷ 1)

c   (12 x 4) ÷ (6 x 2)   f   (16 ÷ 4) x (20 ÷ 4)

Simple use of parentheses

Work out these problems.

(5 + 3) + (9 – 2) =   8 + 7 = 15
(5 + 2) – (4 – 1) =   7 – 3 = 4
(4 + 2) x (3 + 1) =   6 x 4 = 24
(3 x 5) ÷ (9 – 6) =   15 ÷ 3 = 5

Remember to work out the parentheses first.

Work out these problems.

(5 + 4) + (7 – 3) =   (9 – 2) + (6 + 4) =

(7 + 3) – (9 – 7) =   (15 – 5) + (2 + 3) =

(11 x 2) – (3 x 2) =   (15 ÷ 3) + (9 x 2) =

(12 x 2) – (3 x 3) =   (6 ÷ 2) + (8 x 2) =

(9 x 3) – (7 x 3) =   (15 ÷ 5) + (3 x 4) =

(20 ÷ 5) – (8 ÷ 2) =   (5 x 10) – (12 x 4) =

Now try these.

(4 + 8) ÷ (3 x 2) =   (6 x 4) ÷ (3 x 2) =

(9 + 5) ÷ (2 x 1) =   (7 x 4) ÷ (3 + 4) =

(3 + 6) x (3 x 3) =   (5 x 5) ÷ (10 ÷ 2) =

(24 ÷ 2) x (3 x 2) =   (8 x 6) ÷ (2 x 12) =

Write down the letters of all the problems that make 25.
a   (2 x 5) x (3 x 2)   d   (40 ÷ 2) + (10 ÷ 2)
b   (5 x 5) + (7 – 2)   e   (10 x 5) – (5 x 5)
c   (6 x 5) – (10 ÷ 2)   f   (10 x 10) ÷ (10 – 6)

Write down the letters of all the problems that make 20.
a   (10 ÷ 2) x (4 ÷ 4)   d   (20 ÷ 4) x (8 + 2)
b   (7 x 3) – (3 ÷ 3)   e   (10 ÷ 2) + (20 ÷ 2)
c   (8 x 4) – (6 x 2)   f   (14 ÷ 2) + (2 x 7)

Multiplying decimals

Work out these problems.

	1		4		3
	4.6		3.9		8.4
x	3	x	5	x	8
	13.8		19.5		67.2

Work out these problems.

4.7	9.1	5.8	1.7	5.1
x 3	x 3	x 3	x 2	x 2

| 7.4 | 3.6 | 6.5 | 4.2 | 3.8 |
| x 2 | x 4 | x 4 | x 2 | x 2 |

| 4.2 | 4.7 | 1.8 | 3.4 | 3.7 |
| x 4 | x 4 | x 5 | x 5 | x 5 |

| 2.5 | 2.4 | 5.3 | 7.2 | 5.1 |
| x 5 | x 6 | x 7 | x 8 | x 9 |

| 7.9 | 8.6 | 8.8 | 7.5 | 9.9 |
| x 9 | x 9 | x 8 | x 8 | x 6 |

| 6.8 | 5.7 | 6.9 | 7.5 | 8.4 |
| x 7 | x 6 | x 7 | x 9 | x 9 |

| 7.3 | 2.8 | 3.8 | 7.7 | 9.4 |
| x 8 | x 7 | x 8 | x 7 | x 9 |

Multiplying decimals

Work out these problems.

|
37.5
x   2
75.0 |
26.2
x   5
131.0 |
65.3
x   9
587.7 |

Work out these problems.

53.3 x 2	93.2 x 2	51.4 x 2	34.6 x 3	35.2 x 3
46.5 x 4	25.8 x 4	16.4 x 3	47.1 x 5	37.4 x 5
12.4 x 5	46.3 x 5	17.5 x 6	36.5 x 6	72.4 x 7
37.5 x 7	20.3 x 7	73.4 x 7	92.6 x 6	47.9 x 6
53.9 x 8	75.6 x 8	28.8 x 8	79.4 x 8	99.9 x 9
37.9 x 9	14.8 x 9	35.4 x 9	46.8 x 8	27.2 x 7
39.5 x 6	84.2 x 9	68.5 x 8	73.2 x 9	47.6 x 6

Real-life problems

Carlos earns $3.50 a day on his paper route. How much does he earn per week?

$24.50

$$\begin{array}{r} {\scriptstyle 3}\\ \$3.50 \\ \times \quad 7 \\ \hline \$24.50 \end{array}$$

When Chanté subtracts the width of her closet from the length of her bedroom wall she finds she has 3.65 m of wall space left. If the closet is 0.87 m wide, what is the length of her bedroom wall?

4.52 m

$$\begin{array}{r} {\scriptstyle 1\ 1}\\ 3.65 \\ + \quad 0.87 \\ \hline 4.52 \end{array}$$

Sophie buys her mother a bunch of flowers for $12.95 and her brothers some candy for $2.76. If she has $7.83 left, how much did she start with?

If Pedro were 7.5 cm taller, he would be twice as tall as Ian. Ian is 74.25 cm tall, so how tall is Pedro?

Sasha is making some shelves which are 75.5 cm long. If the wood she is using is 180 cm long, how many pieces will she need to make six shelves?

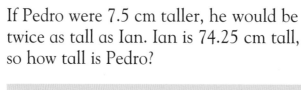

A café uses 27.5 litres of milk a day. If they have a weekly delivery of 180 litres, how much will they have left after six days?

Charles has 12.5 m of railway track. Gavin has 8.6 m and Kristy has 4.8 m. If they put their track together how long will their layout be?

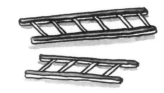

Real-life problems

A novelist writes 9.5 pages of his book a day.
How many pages will he write in nine days?

85.5 pages

```
      4
     9.5
  ×    9
  ──────
    85.5
```

After driving 147.7 km a driver stops at a service
station. If he has another 115.4 km to go, how long
will his trip be?

263.1 km

```
      11
   147.7
 + 115.4
 ───────
   263.1
```

Mr. Mayfield divides his money equally
among four separate banks. If he has $98.65
in each bank, what is the total of his savings?

Mrs. Eldon buys two bottles of perfume; one contains
48.5 ml and the other contains 150.5 ml. How much
more perfume is in the larger of the two bottles?

A teacher spends 5.75 minutes grading
each story. How long would it take to
grade eight stories?

Eight tiles, each 15.75 cm wide, fit exactly
across the width of the bathroom wall. How
wide is the bathroom wall?

Terry has $8.50. If he spends $1.05 a day
over the next seven days, how much will he
have left at the end of the seven days?

A shop sells 427.56 kg of loose peanuts the
first week and 246.94 kg the second week.
How much did they sell over the two weeks?

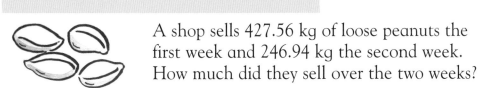

Real-life problems

In a class of 30 children, 6 children are painting. What percent of children are painting?

$\frac{6}{30}$ of the children are painting and to change a fraction to a percent we multiply by 100.

20%

$$\frac{\cancel{6}^{1}}{\cancel{30}_{1}} \times \cancel{100}^{20} = 20$$

40% of a class is made up of girls. If there are 12 girls, how many children are in the class?

If 12 girls are 40% of the class, we divide 12 by 40 to find 1%. Then we multiply by 100 to find 100%.

30 children

$$\frac{\cancel{12}^{3}}{\cancel{40}_{10}} \times \cancel{100}^{10} = 30$$

A shop has 60 books by a new author. If the shop sells 45 books, what percent does it sell?

A school disco sells 65% of its tickets. If it had 120 tickets to start with, how many has it sold?

200 people go on a school trip. If 14% are adults, how many children go on the trip?

A shop sells 150 T-shirts but 12 are returned because they are faulty. What percent of the T-shirts was faulty?

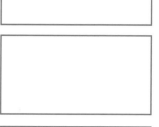

A group of 120 children are asked their favourite colours.

15% like red. How many children like red?

20% like green. How many children like green?

30% like yellow. How many children like yellow?

35% like blue. How many children like blue?

Conversions: length

Units of length	
10 millimetres	1 centimetre
1000 millimetres	1 metre
100 centimetres	1 metre
1000 metres	1 kilometre

This conversion table shows how to convert millimetres, centimetres, metres, and kilometres.

Brian's rope is 600 centimetres long. How many metres long is it?

$$600 \div 100 = 6 \qquad 6 \text{ metres}$$

Neilika's rope is 3 metres long. How many millimetres long is it?

$$3 \times 100 = 300 \qquad 300 \text{ centimetres long}$$
$$300 \times 10 = 3000 \qquad 3000 \text{ millimetres long}$$

Convert each measurement to centimetres.

10 millimetres	200 millimetres	48 millimetres	72 millimetres

Convert each measurement to metres.

600 centimetres	1200 centimetres	270 centimetres	3600 centimetres

Convert each measurement to millimetres.

4 centimetres	12 centimetres	8 centimetres	5 centimetres

Convert each measurement to centimetres.

6 metres	2 metres	7 metres	5 metres

Convert each measurement.

4 metres	5 kilometres	4 metres	1 kilometre
centimetres	metres	centimetres	centimetres

5840 centimetres	31 680 centimetres	1760 metres	352 metres
metres	kilometres	kilometres	kilometres

Conversions: capacity

Units of capacity	
1000 millilitres	1 litre

This conversion table shows how to convert millilitres and litres.

Katya's thermos holds 8 litres. How many millilitres does it hold?

8 x 1000 = 8000   8000 millilitres

Hannah's thermos holds 60 000 millilitres. How many litres does it hold?

60 000 ÷ 1000 = 60   60 litres

Convert each measurement to litres.

32 000 millilitres	16 000 millilitres	9600 millilitres	8000 millilitres

Convert each measurement to millilitres.

6 litres	12 litres	36 litres	50 litres

4 litres	12 litres	30 litres	16 litres

Convert each measurement to litres.

14 000 millilitres	32 000 millilitres	100 000 millilitres	20 000 millilitres

Convert each measurement.

3000 millilitres	5 litres	36 000 millilitres	72 litres
litres	millilitres	litres	millilitres

1 litre	24 000 millilitres	7 litres	11 000 millilitres
millilitres	litres	millilitres	litres

Fraction of a number

Work out to find the fraction of the number. Write the answer in the box.

$\frac{1}{6}$ of 42

$\frac{1}{6}$ x 42 = $\frac{42}{6}$ = 7

1 x 7 = 7

So, $\frac{1}{6}$ of 42 = 7

$\frac{3}{5}$ of 35

$\frac{1}{5}$ x 35 = $\frac{35}{5}$ = 7

3 x 7 = 21

So, $\frac{3}{5}$ of 35 = 21

$\frac{1}{4}$ of 100 = $\frac{100}{4}$ = 25

$\frac{1}{3}$ of 69 = $\frac{69}{3}$ = 23

Work out to find the fraction of the number. Write the answer in the box.

$\frac{1}{8}$ of 72

$\frac{1}{9}$ of 54

$\frac{1}{4}$ of 52

$\frac{1}{5}$ of 175

$\frac{1}{6}$ of 300

$\frac{1}{10}$ of 100

$\frac{3}{4}$ of 100

$\frac{2}{5}$ of 25

$\frac{5}{9}$ of 36

$\frac{3}{4}$ of 56

$\frac{4}{5}$ of 100

$\frac{2}{3}$ of 210

$\frac{1}{5}$ of 250

$\frac{1}{2}$ of 84

$\frac{1}{7}$ of 140

$\frac{1}{8}$ of 64

$\frac{1}{9}$ of 81

$\frac{1}{5}$ of 55

$\frac{2}{3}$ of 75

$\frac{5}{8}$ of 40

$\frac{2}{3}$ of 225

$\frac{5}{7}$ of 133

$\frac{2}{10}$ of 100

$\frac{4}{9}$ of 90

$\frac{1}{2}$ of 38

$\frac{1}{6}$ of 72

$\frac{1}{3}$ of 36

$\frac{1}{4}$ of 100

$\frac{1}{2}$ of 114

$\frac{1}{7}$ of 140

$\frac{4}{7}$ of 42

$\frac{2}{3}$ of 27

$\frac{5}{6}$ of 120

$\frac{2}{3}$ of 180

$\frac{3}{8}$ of 64

$\frac{7}{8}$ of 72

Showing decimals

Write the decimals on the number line.

0.4, 0.5, 0.6, 0.8, 0.9, 0.25, 0.45, 0.63

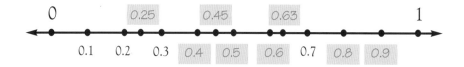

Write the decimals on the number line.

0.56, 0.2, 0.87, 0.45, 0.98, 0.6, 0.1

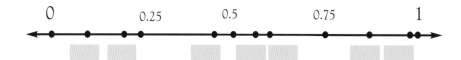

Write the decimals on the number line.

1.41, 1.8, 1.3, 1.98, 1.68, 1.2

Write these decimals on the number line.

2.5, 3.75, 2.25, 3.1, 3.68, 4.2

Area of right-angled triangles

Find the area of this right-angled triangle.

Because the area of this triangle is
half the area of the rectangle shown,
we can find the area of the rectangle and
then divide it by two to find the area
of the triangle.
So the area = (8 cm x 4 cm) ÷ 2
= 32 cm² ÷ 2 = 16 cm²

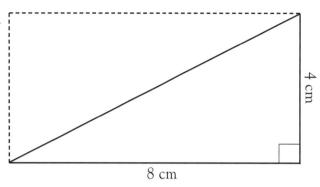

Area = 16 cm²

Find the area of these right-angled triangles.

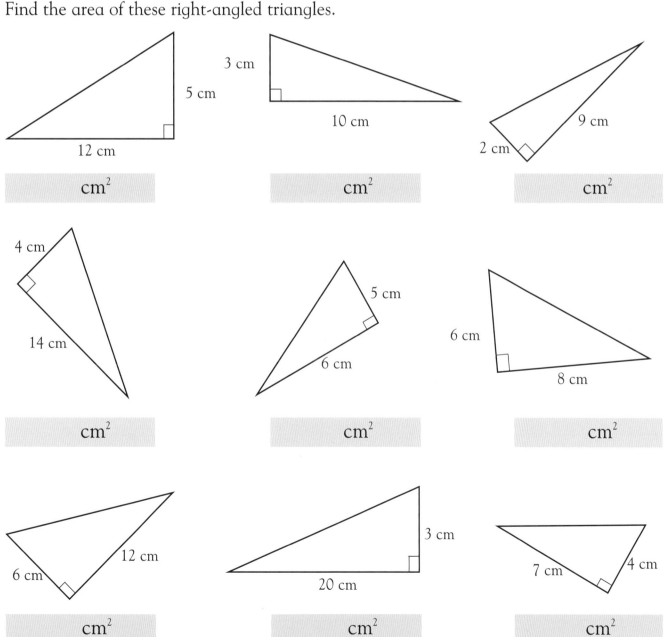

5 cm
3 cm
12 cm
10 cm
9 cm
2 cm

_____ cm²   _____ cm²   _____ cm²

4 cm
14 cm
5 cm
6 cm
6 cm
8 cm

_____ cm²   _____ cm²   _____ cm²

12 cm
6 cm
20 cm
3 cm
7 cm
4 cm

_____ cm²   _____ cm²   _____ cm²

Speed problems

How long would it take to travel
120 km at 8 km/h?
(Time = Distance ÷ Speed)

15 hours

$$\begin{array}{r} 15 \\ 8\overline{)120} \end{array}$$

If a bus takes 3 hours to travel 150 km,
how fast is it going?
(Speed = Distance ÷ Time)

50 km/h

$$\begin{array}{r} 50 \\ 3\overline{)150} \end{array}$$

If a car travels at 60 km/h for 2 hours,
how far has it gone?
(Distance = Speed × Time)

120 km

$$\begin{array}{r} 60 \\ \times\ 2 \\ \hline 120 \end{array}$$

If a man walks for 6 kilometres at a
steady speed of 3 km/h, how long will
it take him?

A truck driver travels 120 km in 3 hours.
If he drove at a steady speed, how fast
was he going?

A car travels at a steady speed of 40 km/h.
How far will it travel in 4 hours?

Shane walks 10 km at 4 km/h. Damien
walks 12 km at 5 km/h. Which of them will
take the longest?

Courtney drives for 30 minutes at 50 km/h
and for 1 hour at 40 km/h. How far has he
travelled altogether?

A racing car travels 340 km in 120
minutes. What speed is it travelling at?

Conversion tables

Draw a table to convert dollars to cents.

$	cents
1	100
2	200
3	300

Complete the conversion chart below.

Weeks	Days
1	7
2	
	28
10	70

If there are 60 minutes in 1 hour, make a conversion chart for up to 10 hours.

Hours	Minutes

Reading bar graphs

Look at this graph.

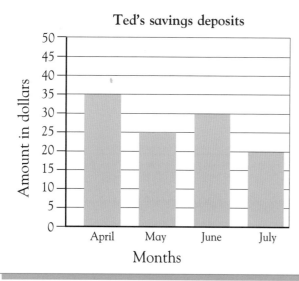

Ted's savings deposits

In which month did Ted save $25?

May

How much more money did Ted save in June than in July?

$10

Look at this graph.

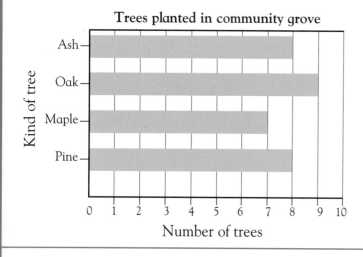

Trees planted in community grove

How many maple trees were planted?

The same number of ash trees were planted as what other kind of tree?

How many more oak trees were planted than maple trees?

Look at this graph.

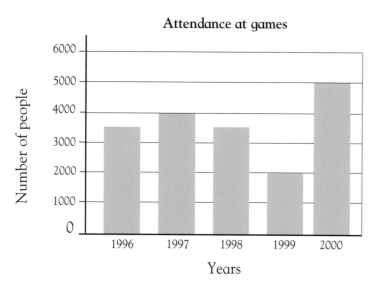

Attendance at games

In which year did 4000 people attend the games?

How many more people attend the games in 2000 than in 1997?

The biggest increase in attendance was between which years?

Expanded form

What is the value of 3 in 2308? *300*

Write 32 084 in expanded form. *30 000 + 2000 + 80 + 4*

What is the value of 6 in these numbers?

26		162	
12 612		6130	
13 036		9764	

36 904	
567 902	
17 632	

What is the value of 4 in these numbers?

14 300		942	
10 408		1043	
6045		804 001	

8764	
45 987	
694	

Circle the numbers that have a 7 with the value of seventy thousand.

457 682	67 924	870 234	372 987
171 345	767 707	79 835	16 757

Write the numbers in expanded form.

34 897

508 061

50 810

8945

60 098

Cubes of small numbers

What is 2^3?

$2 \times 2 \times 2 = 8$

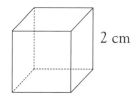

2 cm

What is the volume of this cube?

$2 \text{ cm} \times 2 \text{ cm} \times 2 \text{ cm} = 8 \text{ cm}^3$

You find the volume of a cube in the same way you work out the cube of a number.

Use extra paper here if you need to. What is...

3^3

4^3

6^3

5^3

1^3

2^3

What are the volumes of these cubes?

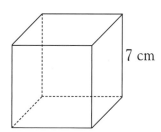

7 cm

cm³

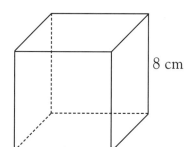

8 cm

cm³

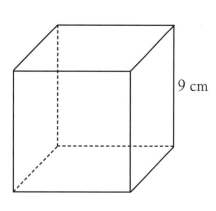

9 cm

cm³

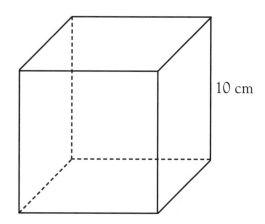

10 cm

cm³

Multiplying fractions

Write the product.

$$\frac{3}{\underset{2}{8}} \times \frac{\overset{1}{4}}{7} = \boxed{\frac{3}{14}} \qquad\qquad \overset{1}{5} \times \frac{3}{\underset{2}{10}} = \boxed{\frac{3}{2} = 1\frac{1}{2}}$$

Write the product.

$$\frac{1}{4} \times \frac{1}{4} = \boxed{} \qquad \frac{3}{10} \times \frac{2}{6} = \boxed{} \qquad 6 \times \frac{3}{4} = \boxed{} = \boxed{}$$

$$8 \times \frac{1}{4} = \boxed{} \qquad \frac{2}{5} \times \frac{5}{7} = \boxed{} \qquad \frac{2}{5} \times \frac{5}{6} = \boxed{}$$

$$\frac{2}{5} \times \frac{2}{3} = \boxed{} \qquad 4 \times \frac{3}{16} = \boxed{} \qquad \frac{3}{8} \times 10 = \boxed{} = \boxed{}$$

$$\frac{1}{3} \times 15 = \boxed{} \qquad \frac{5}{9} \times \frac{1}{5} = \boxed{} \qquad \frac{3}{4} \times \frac{4}{9} = \boxed{}$$

$$\frac{1}{4} \times \frac{2}{7} = \boxed{} \qquad \frac{2}{9} \times \frac{3}{4} = \boxed{} \qquad 12 \times \frac{3}{10} = \boxed{} = \boxed{}$$

$$\frac{2}{3} \times \frac{1}{3} = \boxed{} \qquad \frac{1}{12} \times 2 = \boxed{} \qquad \frac{3}{4} \times \frac{1}{4} = \boxed{}$$

$$\frac{5}{6} \times 8 = \boxed{} = \boxed{} \qquad 7 \times \frac{1}{8} = \boxed{} \qquad \frac{1}{6} \times \frac{5}{6} = \boxed{}$$

$$\frac{1}{2} \times 25 = \boxed{} = \boxed{} \qquad \frac{7}{10} \times \frac{5}{7} = \boxed{} \qquad 4 \times \frac{3}{4} = \boxed{}$$

More complex fraction problems

Find $\frac{3}{5}$ of $30.00.

Find $\frac{1}{5}$: $30 ÷ 5 = $6

$6 x 3 = $18

So, $\frac{3}{5}$ of $30 is $18

Find $\frac{7}{10}$ of 60 cm

Find $\frac{1}{10}$: 60 cm ÷ 10 = 6 cm

6 cm x 7 = 42 cm

So, $\frac{7}{10}$ of 60 cm is 42 cm

Find $\frac{3}{5}$ of these amounts.

40 cm

$50

$10.50

80 m

75 ml

45 kg

Find $\frac{7}{10}$ of these amounts.

48 m

$98.00

75 km

Find $\frac{2}{3}$ of these amounts.

48 cm

120 kg

$24.00

Finding percentages

Find 30% of 140.

$$\frac{140}{100} \times 30 = 42$$

(Divide by 100 to find 1% and then multiply by 30 to find 30%.)

Find 12% of 75.

$$\frac{75^{3}}{100_{4_1}} \times 12^{3} = 9$$

(Divide by 100 to find 1% and then multiply by 12 to find 12%.)

Find 30% of these numbers.

620

240

80

160

Find 60% of these numbers.

60

100

160

580

Find 45% of these numbers.

80 g

40 cm

240 ml

600 km

Find 12% of these numbers.

$150

$600

125 m

775 m

Addition

Work out the answer to each problem.

```
  1 1
  634
 4812
+1428
─────
 6874
```

```
  1 3 1
 1 472
    96
 8 391
+  564
──────
10 523
```

Remember to regroup if you need to.

Find each sum.

```
  5831
  8375
+  219
──────
```

```
  3724
  9942
+  623
──────
```

```
  9994
  7358
+  471
──────
```

```
   524
  7034
+   95
──────
```

```
  7341
   299
+ 5143
──────
```

```
  9328
   347
+ 8222
──────
```

```
  7159
    39
+  748
──────
```

```
   208
  4943
+   55
──────
```

Find each sum.

```
  8594
   629
  9878
+   96
──────
```

```
  7362
   843
  4732
+   53
──────
```

```
  3041
   571
  5210
+   71
──────
```

```
  7641
    93
  8521
+  843
──────
```

```
  8795
   659
  3212
+  961
──────
```

```
  6043
     4
   147
+ 8948
──────
```

```
    27
   153
  8612
+  127
──────
```

```
   146
  3714
    26
+ 5003
──────
```

More addition

Work out the answer to each problem.

```
  11  1            12 1
  23 714           11 541
   9 024              861
 +   348           29 652
 ─────────         +     5
  33 086           ─────────
                    42 059
```

Remember to regroup if you need to.

Find each sum.

```
   17 203          29 521          65 214          25 046
      112           6 211             973              15
 +  5 608        +      58       +  1 291        +     263
 ─────────       ─────────       ─────────       ─────────
```

```
    6 958          73 009          11 536          87 019
       71               3              48             127
 + 16 911        +     581       +  2 435        +  5 652
 ─────────       ─────────       ─────────       ─────────
```

Find each sum.

```
   79 622          64 599           6 940          72 148
    8 011             122             936             999
   47 391           6 375          58 274           7 481
 +      7        +      91       +      36        + 21 685
 ─────────       ─────────       ─────────        ─────────
```

```
   58 975          36 403               8              23
      858              73          22 849          99 951
    8 423             712             502             358
 +     27        +  6 229        +  4 034        +  6 231
 ─────────       ─────────       ─────────       ─────────
```

Dividing by ones

$477 \div 2$ can be written in two ways:

$$238\frac{1}{2}$$ $$238 \, r \, 1$$

or

$$2\overline{)477}$$ $$2\overline{)477}$$

Work out the answers to these problems. Use fraction remainders.

$$2\overline{)479}$$ $$4\overline{)863}$$ $$5\overline{)579}$$ $$7\overline{)860}$$

$$2\overline{)175}$$ $$3\overline{)167}$$ $$9\overline{)457}$$ $$3\overline{)293}$$

Work out the answers to these problems. Use unit remainders.

$$2\overline{)705}$$ $$5\overline{)637}$$ $$4\overline{)330}$$ $$7\overline{)921}$$

Dividing by ones

361 ÷ 2 can be written in two ways:

$$180\frac{1}{2}$$

or

180 r 1

2) 361   2) 361

Work out the answers to these problems. Use fraction remainders.

4) 320   7) 490   8) 349   9) 547

2) 807   2) 437   2) 943   3) 361

Work out the answers to these problems. Use unit remainders.

5) 417   9) 810   3) 303   4) 366

Dividing

$589 \div 5$ can be written in two ways:

$117\frac{4}{5}$ or   117 r 4

$5\overline{)589}$ $5\overline{)589}$

Work out the answers to these problems. Use fractions remainders.

$8\overline{)435}$ $9\overline{)359}$ $7\overline{)452}$ $7\overline{)792}$

$8\overline{)937}$ $7\overline{)799}$ $9\overline{)289}$ $6\overline{)854}$

Work out the answers to these problems. Use unit remainders.

$9\overline{)653}$ $4\overline{)545}$ $8\overline{)952}$ $6\overline{)411}$

Everyday problems

A plumber has 6 m of copper tubing. If he uses 2.36 m, how much will he have left?

3.64 m

```
        9
      5 1010
      6.00
    - 2.36
      3.64
```

If he buys another 4.5 m of copper tubing, how much will he now have?

8.14 m

```
      1
      3.64
    + 4.50
      8.14
```

A man spends $35.65, $102.43, $68.99 and $36.50 in 4 different stores. How much money did he spend altogether?

A gas station has 10 400 litres of gasoline delivered on Monday, 13 350 litres on Tuesday, 14 755 litres on Wednesday, 9656 litres on Thursday, and 15 975 litres on Friday. How much did they have delivered from Monday through Friday?

If they sold 59 248 litres that week, how much gasoline did they have left?

Daniel runs 22.56 km in a charity fun run. Sandra runs 8420 m less. How far does Sandra run?

What is the combined distance run by Daniel and Sandra?

Dianne is 1 m 30 cm tall. Tania is 1 m 54 cm tall. How much taller is Tania?

Real-life problems

A man walks 18.34 km on Saturday and 16.57 km on Sunday. How far did he walk that weekend?

34.91 km

How much farther did he walk on Saturday?

1.77 km

$$\begin{array}{r} \overset{1}{1}\overset{1}{8}.34 \\ +\ 16.57 \\ \hline 34.91 \end{array}$$

$$\begin{array}{r} \overset{7}{1}\overset{12}{\cancel{8}}.\overset{2\,14}{\cancel{3}\cancel{4}} \\ -\ 16.57 \\ \hline 1.77 \end{array}$$

A rectangular field measures 103.7 m by 96.5 m. What is the perimeter of the field?

When Joe and Kerry stand on a scale it reads 91 kg.
When Joe steps off, it reads 31.5 kg.
How much does Joe weigh?

A rectangular room has an area of 32.58 m². When a carpet is put down there is still 7.99 m² of floor showing. What is the area of the carpet?

A brother's and sister's combined height is 270 cm. If the sister is $120\frac{1}{2}$ cm tall, how tall is the brother?

A province has 4 highways: Rte 1, which is 1246 km long; Rte 2 which is 339 km long; Rte 3 which is 1573 km long; and Rte 4 which is 48 km long. How much highway does the province have in total?

Jenny's aquarium holds $25\frac{1}{2}$ litres of water. She buys a new one that holds 32 litres. How much extra water do her fish have?

Real-life problems

Deborah's school bag has a mass of $6\frac{1}{2}$ kg.
Asha's has a mass of $4\frac{1}{2}$ kg. How much heavier is
Deborah's bag than Asha's?

2 kg

What is the total mass of the two bags?

11 kg

$$6\frac{1}{2}$$
$$-4\frac{1}{2}$$
$$\overline{2}$$

$$6\frac{1}{2}$$
$$+4\frac{1}{2}$$
$$\overline{10\frac{2}{2}} = 11$$

Mr Shaw needs to put weather stripping around four
sides of his front door. The door is 200 cm high and
90 cm wide. How many centimetres of weather
stripping does he need?

Bert earns \$24 632 a year, Ernie earns
\$34 321 a year, and Oscar earns \$22 971 a
year. How much do they earn altogether?

How much more than Bert does
Ernie earn?

How much more than Oscar does
Bert earn?

How much more than Oscar does
Ernie earn?

An elevator says, "Maximum weight 636 kg."
If four people get in, weighing 90 kg, 60 kg, 115 kg, and
78 kg, how much more mass will the elevator hold?

Multiplication by 2-digit numbers

Work out the answer to each problem.

```
    27              34
  x 76            x 58
  ----            ----
   162             272
  1890            1700
  ----            ----
  2052            1972
```

Work out the answer to each problem.

```
    26              95              32              78
  x 84            x 65            x 39            x 49
  ----            ----            ----            ----
```

```
    97              94              32              47
  x 46            x 37            x 64            x 75
  ----            ----            ----            ----
```

```
    28              47              36              45
  x 95            x 62            x 87            x 33
  ----            ----            ----            ----
```

```
    46              29              85              63
  x 85            x 72            x 29            x 84
  ----            ----            ----            ----
```

Division by ones

47 ÷ 2 can be written in two ways:

$$23\frac{1}{2}$$

2)47
 4
 7
 6
 1

or

$$23\text{ r }1$$

2)47
 4
 7
 6
 1

Write the quotients for these problems with fraction remainders.

2)1768   4)1972   3)1637   4)3761

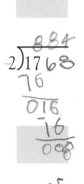

3)2986   2)4598   5)8735   5)4960

Write the quotients for these problems with unit remainders.

2)73   2)85   2)39   4)59

4)71   4)83   5)29   5)47

107

Dividing

$646 \div 3$ can be written in two ways:

$$215\frac{1}{3}$$

or

$$215 \text{ r } 1$$

$$3\overline{)646}$$

$$3\overline{)646}$$

Work out the answer to each problem. Use fraction remainders.

$4\overline{)377}$ $2\overline{)169}$ $7\overline{)158}$ $4\overline{)368}$

$5\overline{)197}$ $9\overline{)636}$ $2\overline{)325}$ $4\overline{)787}$

Work out the answer to each problem. Use unit remainders.

$5\overline{)947}$ $3\overline{)731}$ $7\overline{)878}$ $9\overline{)875}$

Division of 3-digit decimal numbers

Work out these division sums.

$$\begin{array}{r} 0.89 \\ 3\overline{)2.67} \\ 24 \\ \hline 27 \\ 27 \\ \hline 0 \end{array}$$

0.89

$$\begin{array}{r} 0.74 \\ 4\overline{)2.96} \\ 28 \\ \hline 16 \\ 16 \\ \hline 0 \end{array}$$

0.74

Work out these division problems.

$2\overline{)2.94}$ $4\overline{)7.32}$ $4\overline{)6.12}$ $2\overline{)3.24}$

$2\overline{)9.98}$ $3\overline{)9.72}$ $4\overline{)6.24}$ $4\overline{)7.48}$

$4\overline{)2.24}$ $3\overline{)2.22}$ $3\overline{)2.25}$ $3\overline{)2.61}$

Division of 3-digit decimal numbers

Work out these division problems.

```
      1.99
  5)9.95
     5
     49
     45
     45
     45
      0
```
1.99

```
      1.61
  6)9.66
     6
     36
     36
      6
      6
      0
```
1.61

Work out these division problems.

```
  5)8.15        5)9.25        5)6.35        6)9.12
```

```
  6)2.16        7)8.82        7)4.83        8)5.92
```

```
  8)8.72        9)8.19        9)5.67        6)6.36
```

Real-life problems

A builder uses 1600 kg of sand a day.
How much will he use in 5 days?

8000 kg

$$\begin{array}{r} \scriptstyle 3 \\ 1600 \\ \times\ \ 5 \\ \hline 8000 \end{array}$$

If he uses 9500 kg the next week,
how much more has he used than
the week before?

1500 kg

$$\begin{array}{r} 9500 \\ -\ 8000 \\ \hline 1500 \end{array}$$

An electrician uses 184 m of cable while
working on four houses. If he uses the same
amount on each house, how much does
he use on one house?

A family looks at vacations in two different resorts.
The first one costs $846.95. The second costs $932.
How much will the family save if they choose
the cheaper resort?

Doris has 5 sections of fence, each 96 cm
wide. If she puts them together, how much
of her yard can she fence off?

Shula goes on a sponsored walk and collects
$15.95 from her mother, $8.36 from her uncle,
$4.65 from her brother, and $2.75 from her aunt.
How much does she
collect altogether?

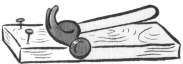

A taxi company has 9 cars.
If each car holds 40.4 litres of gasoline,
how many litres will it take to fill all
of the cars?

Rounding money

Round to the nearest dollar.

$3.95 rounds to $4

$2.25 rounds to $2

Round to the nearest ten dollars.

$15.50 rounds to $20

$14.40 rounds to $10

Round to the nearest dollar.

$2.60 rounds to $8.49 rounds to $3.39 rounds to

$9.55 rounds to $1.75 rounds to $4.30 rounds to

$7.15 rounds to $6.95 rounds to $2.53 rounds to

Round to the nearest ten dollars.

$37.34 rounds to $21.75 rounds to $85.03 rounds to

$71.99 rounds to $66.89 rounds to $52.99 rounds to

$55.31 rounds to $12.79 rounds to $15.00 rounds to

Round to the nearest hundred dollars.

$307.12 rounds to $175.50 rounds to $115.99 rounds to

$860.55 rounds to $417.13 rounds to $650.15 rounds to

$739.10 rounds to $249.66 rounds to $367.50 rounds to

Estimating sums of money

Round to the leading digit. Estimate the sum.

$3.26 → $3
+ $4.82 → + $5
is about $8

$68.53 → $70
+ $34.60 → + $30
is about $100

Round to the leading digit. Estimate the sum.

$52.61 →
+ $27.95 →
is about

$19.20 →
+ $22.13 →
is about

$70.75 →
+ $12.49 →
is about

$701.34 →
+ $100.80 →
is about

$339.50 →
+ $422.13 →
is about

$160.07 →
+ $230.89 →
is about

$25.61 →
+ $72.51 →
is about

$61.39 →
+ $19.50 →
is about

$18.32 →
+ $13.90 →
is about

$587.35 →
+ $251.89 →
is about

$109.98 →
+ $210.09 →
is about

$470.02 →
+ $203.17 →
is about

Round to the leading digit. Estimate the sum.

$75.95 + $17.95 →

$41.67 + $20.35 →

$49.19 + $38.70 →

$784.65 + $101.05 →

$516.50 + $290.69 →

$58.78 + $33.25 →

$82.90 + $11.79 →

$90.09 + $14.50 →

Estimating differences of money

Round the numbers to the leading digit. Estimate the differences.

$$\begin{array}{r} \$8.75 \rightarrow \$9 \\ - \$5.10 \rightarrow - \$5 \\ \hline \text{is about} \quad \$4 \end{array} \qquad \begin{array}{r} \$61.47 \rightarrow \$60 \\ - \$35.64 \rightarrow - \$40 \\ \hline \text{is about} \quad \$20 \end{array}$$

Round the numbers to the leading digit. Estimate the differences.

$$\begin{array}{r} \$17.90 \rightarrow \\ - \$12.30 \rightarrow \\ \hline \text{is about} \end{array} \qquad \begin{array}{r} \$6.40 \rightarrow \\ - \$3.75 \rightarrow \\ \hline \text{is about} \end{array} \qquad \begin{array}{r} \$87.45 \rightarrow \\ - \$54.99 \rightarrow \\ \hline \text{is about} \end{array}$$

$$\begin{array}{r} \$34.90 \rightarrow \\ - \$12.60 \rightarrow \\ \hline \text{is about} \end{array} \qquad \begin{array}{r} \$8.68 \rightarrow \\ - \$4.39 \rightarrow \\ \hline \text{is about} \end{array} \qquad \begin{array}{r} \$363.24 \rightarrow \\ - \$127.66 \rightarrow \\ \hline \text{is about} \end{array}$$

$$\begin{array}{r} \$78.75 \rightarrow \\ - \$24.99 \rightarrow \\ \hline \text{is about} \end{array} \qquad \begin{array}{r} \$64.21 \rightarrow \\ - \$28.56 \rightarrow \\ \hline \text{is about} \end{array} \qquad \begin{array}{r} \$723.34 \rightarrow \\ - \$487.12 \rightarrow \\ \hline \text{is about} \end{array}$$

Round the numbers to the leading digit. Estimate the differences.

$8.12 – $1.35 $49.63 – $27.85
→   =   →   =

$7.50 – $3.15 $85.15 – $42.99
→   =   →   =

$5.85 – $4.75 $634.60 – $267.25
→   =   →   =

$37.35 – $16.99 $842.17 – $169.54
→   =   →   =

$56.95 – $20.58 $628.37 – $252.11
→   =   →   =

Estimating sums and differences

Round the numbers to the leading digit. Estimate the sum or difference.

685 →	21 481 →	7834 →
+ 489 → _____	− 12 500 → _____	+ 3106 → _____
is about	is about	is about

682 778 →	58 499 →	902 276 →
+ 130 001 → _____	− 22 135 → _____	− 615 999 → _____
is about	is about	is about

46 801 →	9734 →	65 606 →
+ 34 700 → _____	− 8306 → _____	+ 85 943 → _____
is about	is about	is about

5218 →	745 →	337 297 →
− 3673 → _____	+ 451 → _____	− 168 931 → _____
is about	is about	is about

Write < or > for each problem.

329 + 495 ▢ 800   11 569 − 6146 ▢ 6000

563 − 317 ▢ 300   8193 − 6668 ▢ 1000

41 924 − 12 445 ▢ 50 000   634 577 + 192 556 ▢ 800 000

18 885 + 12 691 ▢ 30 000   713 096 − 321 667 ▢ 400 000

Estimating products

Round to the leading digit. Estimate the product.

3456 x 6
3000 x 6 = 18 000

73 x 46
70 x 50 = 3500

Round to the leading digit. Estimate the sum.

1908 x 8
_____ x 8 = _____

5 x 6099
5 x _____ = _____

7 x 1108
7 x _____ = _____

5239 x 9
_____ x 9 = _____

81 x 32
_____ x _____ = _____

19 x 62
_____ x _____ = _____

39 x 44
_____ x _____ = _____

94 x 12
_____ x _____ = _____

Estimate the product.

6 x 7243		4785 x 4		3 x 8924	
2785 x 5		6298 x 4		7 x 7105	
8 x 2870		4176 x 7		5 x 4803	
6777 x 9		6 x 8022		3785 x 4	
42 x 51		54 x 28		23 x 75	
16 x 32		47 x 54		59 x 52	
17 x 74		33 x 22		81 x 18	
31 x 91		38 x 87		46 x 77	

Estimating quotients

Round to compatible numbers. Estimate the quotient.

$3156 \div 6$
$3000 \div 6 =$ 500

$2159 \div 5$
$2500 \div 5 =$ 500

Round to compatible numbers. Estimate the quotient.

$1934 \div 8$
$\div 8 =$

$4066 \div 5$
$\div 5 =$

$1108 \div 4$
$\div 4 =$

$5657 \div 9$
$\div 9 =$

$3998 \div 6$
$\div 6 =$

$5525 \div 7$
$\div 7 =$

$1701 \div 3$
$\div 3 =$

$1304 \div 2$
$\div 2 =$

Estimate the quotient.

$4798 \div 7$

$8205 \div 9$

$5022 \div 5$

$3785 \div 4$

$5528 \div 6$

$2375 \div 8$

$1632 \div 3$

$4251 \div 4$

$4754 \div 9$

$7352 \div 8$

$1774 \div 2$

$3322 \div 7$

$3591 \div 6$

$2887 \div 5$

$5746 \div 2$

$3703 \div 3$

$2392 \div 6$

$6621 \div 8$

Rounding mixed numbers

Round to the closest whole number.

$2\frac{5}{6}$

$\frac{5}{6}$ is more than $\frac{1}{2}$,

so, $2\frac{5}{6}$ rounds up to 3.

$3\frac{2}{5}$

$\frac{2}{5}$ is less than $\frac{1}{2}$,

so, $3\frac{2}{5}$ rounds down to 3.

Circle the fractions that are more than $\frac{1}{2}$.

$\frac{3}{7}$ $\qquad$ $\frac{2}{9}$ $\qquad$ $\frac{6}{7}$ $\qquad$ $\frac{5}{9}$ $\qquad$ $\frac{3}{8}$ $\qquad$ $\frac{1}{7}$ $\qquad$ $\frac{2}{3}$ $\qquad$ $\frac{4}{7}$

$\frac{7}{10}$ $\qquad$ $\frac{2}{5}$ $\qquad$ $\frac{1}{3}$ $\qquad$ $\frac{5}{6}$ $\qquad$ $\frac{3}{4}$ $\qquad$ $\frac{2}{9}$ $\qquad$ $\frac{5}{8}$ $\qquad$ $\frac{3}{5}$

Circle the fractions that are less than $\frac{1}{2}$.

$\frac{1}{8}$ $\qquad$ $\frac{3}{9}$ $\qquad$ $\frac{4}{5}$ $\qquad$ $\frac{2}{7}$ $\qquad$ $\frac{3}{5}$ $\qquad$ $\frac{2}{5}$ $\qquad$ $\frac{7}{10}$ $\qquad$ $\frac{2}{9}$

$\frac{3}{4}$ $\qquad$ $\frac{1}{3}$ $\qquad$ $\frac{4}{9}$ $\qquad$ $\frac{3}{10}$ $\qquad$ $\frac{5}{6}$ $\qquad$ $\frac{1}{4}$ $\qquad$ $\frac{3}{7}$ $\qquad$ $\frac{5}{9}$

Round to the closest whole number.

$4\frac{3}{8}$ $\qquad$ $2\frac{6}{7}$ $\qquad$ $5\frac{3}{4}$ $\qquad$ $3\frac{2}{9}$

$2\frac{5}{6}$ $\qquad$ $1\frac{7}{8}$ $\qquad$ $2\frac{2}{5}$ $\qquad$ $5\frac{1}{7}$

$3\frac{1}{6}$ $\qquad$ $5\frac{3}{8}$ $\qquad$ $3\frac{3}{5}$ $\qquad$ $7\frac{8}{13}$

$6\frac{3}{5}$ $\qquad$ $1\frac{1}{4}$ $\qquad$ $4\frac{5}{6}$ $\qquad$ $9\frac{3}{4}$

$5\frac{2}{3}$ $\qquad$ $3\frac{3}{7}$ $\qquad$ $1\frac{6}{7}$ $\qquad$ $6\frac{3}{4}$

Calculate the mean

What is the mean of 6 and 10? $(6+10) \div 2 = 8$

David is 9, Asha is 10, and
Daniel is 5. What is their mean age? $(9 + 10 + 5) \div 3 = 8$ years

Calculate the mean of these amounts.

9 and 5   6 and 8

5 and 7   11 and 7

8 and 12   13 and 15

19 and 21   40 and 60

Calculate the mean of these amounts.

5, 7, and 3   11, 9, and 7

14, 10, and 6   12, 8, and 4

7, 3, 5, and 9 $1, $1.50, $2.50, and $3

16¢, 9¢, 12¢, and 3¢   5 g, 7 g, 8 g, and 8 g

Calculate these answers.

The mean of two numbers is 7. If one of the numbers
is 6, what is the other number?

The mean of three numbers is 4. If two of the numbers
are 4 and 5, what is the third number?

The mean of four numbers is 12. If three of the numbers
are 9, 15, and 8, what is the fourth number?

Two children record their
last five spelling-test scores.

| Gayle | 17 | 18 | 16 | 14 | 15 |
| Sally | 19 | 20 | 12 | 13 | 11 |

Which child has the best mean score?

Mean, median, and mode

Sian throws a dice 7 times. Here are her results:
4, 2, 1, 2, 4, 2, 6

What is the mean? $(4 + 2 + 1 + 2 + 4 + 2 + 6) \div 7 = 3$

What is the median? Put the numbers in order of size and find the middle number, example, 1, 2, 2, 2, 4, 4, 6.

The median is 2.

What is the mode?   The most common result, which is 2.

A school scoccer team scores the following number of goals in their first 9 matches:
2, 2, 1, 3, 2, 1, 2, 4, 1

What is the mean score?

What is the median score?

Write down the mode for their results.

The ages of the local hockey players are:
17, 15, 16, 19, 17, 19, 22, 17, 18, 21, 17

What is the mean of their ages?

What is their median age?

Write down the mode for their ages.

The results of Susan's last 11 spelling tests were:
15, 12, 15, 17, 11, 16, 19, 11, 3, 11, 13

What is the mean of her scores?

What is her median score?

Write down the mode for her scores.

Line graphs

Look at this graph.

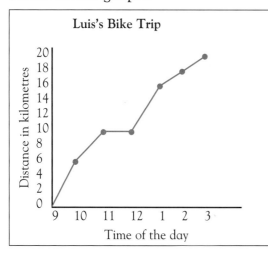

Luis's Bike Trip

Distance in kilometres
20 18 16 14 12 10 8 6 4 2 0

9 10 11 12 1 2 3

Time of the day

How many kilometres did Luis ride during the first hour of his trip?

6 kilometres

How many hours did Luis's trip take?

6 hours

How far did he travel in all?

20 kilometres

Luis stopped for lunch for one hour. What time did he stop?

Did Luis cover more distance between 12 and 1 or between 1 and 2?

Between which two hours did Luis travel 4 kilometres?

During which hours did Luis ride the fastest?

Did Luis travel farther before or after his lunch break?

How much longer did it take Luis to ride 10 kilometres after lunch?

Coordinates

Write the coordinates of:

A   (2, 4)

B   (3, 1)

C   (1, 1)

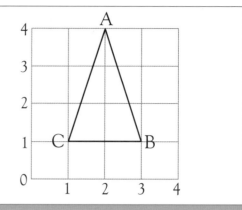

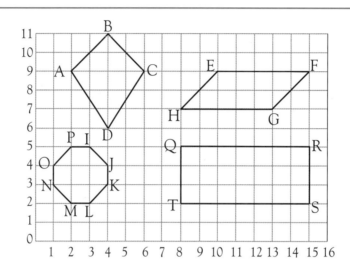

Write the coordinates of:

A		B		C		D		E	
F		G		H		I		J	
K		L		M		N		O	
P		Q		R		S		T	

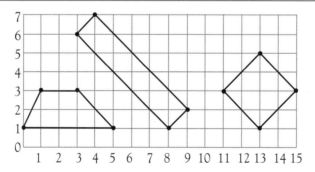

Plot these points on the grid, and connect them up in the right order.

(0, 1) (1, 3) (3, 3) (5, 1) (0, 1). What shape does this make?

(3, 6) (4, 7) (9, 2) (8, 1) (3, 6). What shape does this make?

(11, 3) (13, 5) (15, 3) (13, 1) (11, 3). What shape does this make?

Drawing angles

Acute angles are between 0° and 90°.   Obtuse angles are between 90° and 180°.

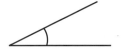

When you get to 180° you have a straight line.

Use a protractor to draw these angles. Remember to mark the angle you have drawn.

150°	135°
45°	110°
10°	20°

Reading and writing numbers

264 346 in words is Two hundred sixty-four thousand three hundred forty-six

One million three hundred twelve thousand five hundred two is 1 312 502

Write each of these numbers in words.

326 208

704 543

240 701

278 520

Write each of these in numbers.

Five hundred seventeen thousand forty-two

Six hundred ninety-four thousand seven hundred eleven

Eight hundred nine thousand two hundred three

Nine hundred thousand four hundred four

Write each of these numbers in words.

9 307 012

5 042 390

9 908 434

8 400 642

Write each of these in numbers.

Eight million two hundred fifty-one

Two million forty thousand four hundred four

Seven million three hundred two thousand one hundred one

Two million five hundred forty-one thousand five

Multiplying and dividing by 10

Write the answer in the box.

26 x 10 = 260

40 ÷ 10 = 4

Write the answer in the box.

76 x 10 =

43 x 10 =

93 x 10 =

66 x 10 =

13 x 10 =

47 x 10 =

147 x 10 =

936 x 10 =

284 x 10 =

364 x 10 =

821 x 10 =

473 x 10 =

Write the answer in the box.

30 ÷ 10 =

20 ÷ 10 =

70 ÷ 10 =

60 ÷ 10 =

50 ÷ 10 =

580 ÷ 10 =

310 ÷ 10 =

270 ÷ 10 =

100 ÷ 10 =

540 ÷ 10 =

890 ÷ 10 =

710 ÷ 10 =

Write the number that has been multiplied by 10.

x 10 = 370

x 10 = 640

x 10 = 740

x 10 = 810

x 10 = 100

x 10 = 830

x 10 = 7140

x 10 = 3070

x 10 = 5290

x 10 = 2640

x 10 = 8290

x 10 = 6480

Write the number that has been divided by 10.

÷ 10 = 3

÷ 10 = 2

÷ 10 = 9

÷ 10 = 42

÷ 10 = 93

÷ 10 = 74

÷ 10 = 57

÷ 10 = 38

÷ 10 = 86

Identifying patterns

Continue each pattern.

Steps of 9:   5   14   23   *32*   *41*   *50*

Steps of 14:   20   34   48   *62*   *76*   *90*

Continue each pattern.

21	38	55	72	89	106	123	140
13	37	61	85	109	133	157	181
7	25	43	61	79	97	115	133
32	48	64	80	96	112	128	144
12	31	50	69	88	107	126	145
32	54	76	98	120	142	164	186
24	64	104	144	184	224	264	304
4	34	64	94	124	154	184	214
36	126	216	306	396	486	576	666
12	72	132	192	252	312	372	432
25	45	65	85	105	125	145	165
22	72	122	172	222	272	322	372
25	100	175	250	325	400	475	550
60	165	270	375	480	585	690	795
8	107	206	305	404	503	602	701
10	61	112	163	214	265	316	367
26	127	228	329	430	531	632	733
48	100	152	204	256	308	360	412

Recognizing multiples of 6, 7, and 8

Circle the multiples of 6.

8   (12)   15   (18)   20   (24)

Circle the multiples of 6.

8	22	14	18	36	40
16	38	44	25	30	60
6	21	19	54	56	24
12	48	10	20	35	26
42	39	23	28	36	32

Circle the multiples of 7.

7	17	24	59	42	55
15	20	21	46	12	70
14	27	69	36	47	49
65	19	57	28	38	63
33	34	35	37	60	56

Circle the multiples of 8.

40	26	15	25	38	56
26	8	73	41	64	12
75	58	62	24	31	72
12	80	32	46	38	78
16	42	66	28	48	68

Circle the number that is a multiple of 6 *and* 7.

| 18 | 54 | 42 | 21 | 28 | 63 |

Circle the numbers that are multiples of 6 *and* 8.

| 16 | 24 | 36 | 48 | 54 | 42 |

Circle the number that is a multiple of 7 *and* 8.

| 24 | 32 | 40 | 28 | 42 | 56 |

Factors of numbers from 1 to 30

The factors of 10 are   1   2   5   10

Circle the factors of 4.   (1)   (2)   3   (4)

Write all the factors of each number.

The factors of 26 are

The factors of 30 are

The factors of 9 are

The factors of 12 are

The factors of 15 are

The factors of 22 are

The factors of 20 are

The factors of 21 are

The factors of 24 are

Circle all the factors of each number.

Which numbers are factors of 14?   1   2   3   5   7   9   12   14

Which numbers are factors of 13?   1   2   3   4   5   6   7   8   9   10   11   13

Which numbers are factors of 7?   1   2   3   4   5   6   7

Which numbers are factors of 11?   1   2   3   4   5   6   7   8   9   10   11

Which numbers are factors of 6?   1   2   3   4   5   6

Which numbers are factors of 8?   1   2   3   4   5   6   7   8

Which numbers are factors of 17?   1   2   5   7   12   14   16   17

Which numbers are factors of 18?   1   2   3   4   5   6   8   9   10   12   18

Some numbers only have factors of 1 and themselves. They are called prime numbers. Write down all the prime numbers that are less than 30 in the box.

Recognizing equivalent fractions

Make each pair of fractions equal by writing a number in the box.

$$\frac{1}{2} = \frac{2}{4} \qquad\qquad \frac{1}{3} = \frac{2}{6}$$

Make each pair of fractions equal by writing a number in the box.

$$\frac{1}{2} = \frac{}{10} \qquad \frac{3}{4} = \frac{}{8} \qquad \frac{1}{3} = \frac{}{9}$$

$$\frac{2}{3} = \frac{}{12} \qquad \frac{6}{12} = \frac{}{6} \qquad \frac{4}{8} = \frac{}{2}$$

$$\frac{1}{5} = \frac{}{10} \qquad \frac{4}{12} = \frac{}{6} \qquad \frac{3}{5} = \frac{}{10}$$

$$\frac{1}{4} = \frac{}{8} \qquad \frac{6}{18} = \frac{}{3} \qquad \frac{3}{12} = \frac{}{4}$$

$$\frac{3}{9} = \frac{1}{} \qquad \frac{4}{10} = \frac{2}{} \qquad \frac{3}{4} = \frac{9}{}$$

$$\frac{4}{16} = \frac{1}{} \qquad \frac{15}{20} = \frac{3}{} \qquad \frac{6}{12} = \frac{1}{}$$

$$\frac{3}{5} = \frac{6}{} \qquad \frac{3}{6} = \frac{1}{} \qquad \frac{9}{12} = \frac{3}{}$$

Make each row of fractions equal by writing a number in each box.

$$\frac{1}{2} = \frac{}{4} = \frac{3}{} = \frac{}{8} = \frac{}{10} = \frac{6}{}$$

$$\frac{1}{4} = \frac{2}{} = \frac{}{12} = \frac{4}{} = \frac{5}{} = \frac{}{24}$$

$$\frac{3}{4} = \frac{6}{} = \frac{}{12} = \frac{12}{} = \frac{}{20} = \frac{18}{}$$

$$\frac{1}{3} = \frac{}{6} = \frac{3}{} = \frac{4}{} = \frac{}{15} = \frac{12}{}$$

$$\frac{1}{5} = \frac{}{10} = \frac{}{15} = \frac{4}{} = \frac{5}{} = \frac{}{30}$$

$$\frac{2}{3} = \frac{}{6} = \frac{}{9} = \frac{8}{} = \frac{10}{} = \frac{14}{}$$

Rounding decimals

Round each decimal to the nearest whole number.

3.4	3
5.7	6
4.5	5

If the whole number has 5 after it, round it to the whole number above.

Round each decimal to the nearest whole number.

6.2		2.5		1.5		3.8	
5.5		2.8		3.2		8.5	
5.4		7.9		3.7		2.3	
1.1		8.6		8.3		9.2	
4.7		6.3		7.3		8.7	

Round each decimal to the nearest whole number.

14.4		42.3		74.1		59.7	
29.9		32.6		63.5		96.4	
18.2		37.5		39.6		76.3	
40.1		28.7		26.9		12.5	
29.5		38.5		87.2		41.6	

Round each decimal to the nearest whole number.

137.6		423.5		426.2		111.8	
641.6		333.5		805.2		246.8	
119.5		799.6		562.3		410.2	
682.4		759.6		531.5		829.9	
743.4		831.1		276.7		649.3	

Real-life problems

Write the answer in the box.

Yasmin has $4.60 and she is given another $1.20.
How much money does she have?

$5.80

$4.60
+ $1.20
$5.80

David has 120 marbles.
He divides them equally among his 5 friends.
How many marbles
does each get?

24

```
      24
  5)120
    10
    20
    20
     0
```

Write the answer in the box.

Michael buys a ball for $5.50 and a flashlight for $3.65.
How much does he spend?

How much does he have left from $10?

The 32 children of a class bring in $5 each for a school trip.
What is the total of the amount brought in?

A set of 5 shelves can be made from a piece of wood 4 metres
long. What fraction of a metre will each shelf be?

Each of 5 children has $16.
How much do they have altogether?

If the above total were shared among 8 children, how much would
each child have?

Real-life problems

Find the answer to each problem.

A box is 16 cm wide. How wide will 6 boxes side by side be?

96 cm

$$
\begin{array}{r}
3 \\
16 \text{ cm} \\
\times 6 \\
\hline
96 \text{ cm}
\end{array}
$$

Josh is 1.20 m tall. His sister is 1.55 m tall. How much taller than Josh is his sister?

0.35 m

$$
\begin{array}{r}
1.55 \text{ m} \\
- 1.20 \text{ m} \\
\hline
0.35 \text{ m}
\end{array}
$$

Find the answer to each problem.

A can contains 56 g of lemonade mix. If 12 g are used, how much is left?

A large jar of coffee has a mass of 280 g. A smaller jar has a mass of 130 g. How much heavier is the larger jar than the smaller jar?

There are 7 shelves of books. 5 shelves are 1.2 m long. 2 shelves are 1.5 m long. What is the total length of the 7 shelves?

A rock star can sign 36 photographs in a minute. How many can he sign in 30 seconds?

Shana has read 5 pages of a 20-page comic book. If it has taken her 9 minutes, how long is it likely to take her to read the whole comic book?

Problems involving time

Find the answer to this problem.

A train leaves the station at 7:30 A.M. and arrives at the end of the line at 10:45 A.M. How long did the journey take?

3 hours 15 minutes

7:30 → 10:30 = 3 h
10:30 → 10:45 = 15 min
Total = 3 h 15 min

Find the answer to each problem.

A film starts at 7:00 P.M. and finishes at 8:45 P.M. How long is the film?

A cake takes 2 hours 25 minutes to bake. If it begins baking at 1:35 P.M., at what time will the cake be done?

Sanjay needs to clean his bedroom and wash the car. It takes him 1 hour 10 minutes to clean his room and 45 minutes to clean the car. If he starts at 10:00 A.M., at what time will he finish?

A car is taken in for repair at 7:00 A.M. It is finished at 1:50 P.M. How long did the repairs take?

Claire has to be at school by 8:50 A.M. If she takes 1 hour 30 minutes to get ready, and the trip takes 35 minutes, at what time does she need to get up?

A bus leaves the bus station at 8:45 A.M. and arrives back at 10:15 A.M. How long has its trip taken?

Elapsed time

Write the answer in the box.

10:40   11:40   12:40   1:20

1 hour→   1 hour→   40 minutes→

Carmen's gymnastics class starts at 10:40 A.M. and ends at 1:20 P.M. How long does it last?

2 hours and 40 minutes

Write the answer in the box.

The ferry leaves the mainland at 11:00 A.M. and docks on the island at 3 P.M. How long is the ride?

The movie starts at 6:05 P.M. and ends at 9:17 P.M. How long is it?

Pat works an 8-hour shift at the fairgrounds. If he starts work at 9 A.M., at what time is he finished?

Keesha wants to videotape a program that starts at 11:30 P.M. It lasts 1 hour and 45 minutes. What time will it end?

Mai finished painting her porch at 4:25 P.M. The instructions said she should wait at least 15 hours to paint the trim. What is the earliest time when she could start painting the trim?

Recognizing multiples

Circle the multiples of 10.

| 14 | (20) | 25 | (30) | 47 | (60) |

Circle the multiples of 6.

20	48	56	72	25	35
1	3	6	16	26	36

Circle the multiples of 7.

14	24	35	27	47	49
63	42	52	37	64	71

Circle the multiples of 8.

25	31	48	84	32	8
18	54	64	35	72	28

Circle the multiples of 9.

17	81	27	35	92	106
45	53	108	90	33	95
64	9	28	18	36	98

Circle the multiples of 10.

15	35	20	46	90	100
44	37	30	29	50	45

Circle the multiples of 11.

24	110	123	54	66	90
45	33	87	98	99	121
43	44	65	55	21	22

Circle the multiples of 12.

136	134	144	109	108	132
24	34	58	68	48	60
35	29	72	74	84	94

Bar graphs

Use this bar graph to answer each question.

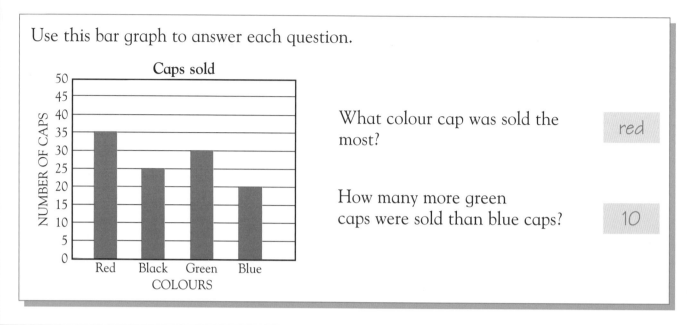

What colour cap was sold the most?   red

How many more green caps were sold than blue caps?   10

Use this bar graph to answer each question.

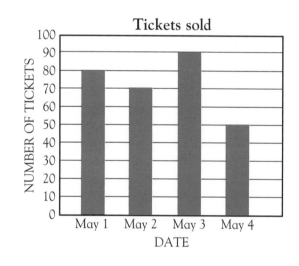

How many tickets were sold on May 1?

How many more tickets were sold on May 2 than on May 4?

On which date were 90 tickets sold?

Use this bar graph to answer each question.

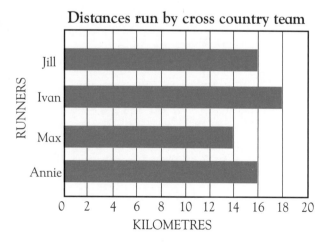

Which runner ran 14 kilometres?

Which runner ran the same distance as Annie?

How much farther did Ivan run than Max?

Triangles

Look at these different triangles.

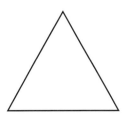  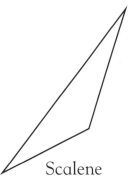 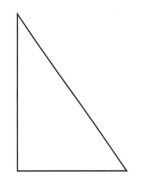

Equilateral
(all sides equal;
is also isosceles)

Isosceles
(two sides equal)

Scalene
(all sides different)

Right angle
(may be isosceles or
scalene, but one angle
must be a right angle)

1 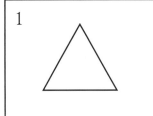 2 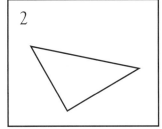 3 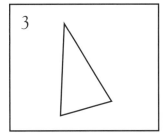 4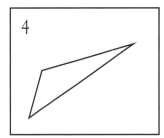

5 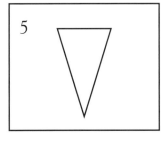 6 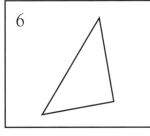 7 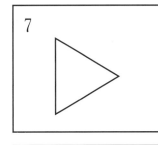 8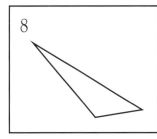

9 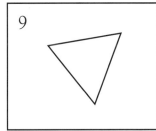 10 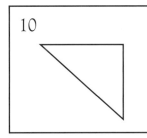 11 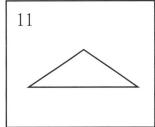 12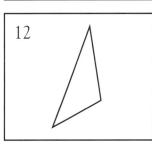

List the triangles that are:

Equilateral _____

Isosceles _____

Scalene _____

Right angle _____

Place value to 10 000 000

| How many hundreds are there in 7000? | 70 | hundreds (70 x 100 = 7000) |
| What is the value of the 9 in 694? | 90 | (because the 9 is in the tens column) |

Write how many tens there are in:

400	tens	600	tens	900	tens
200	tens	1300	tens	4700	tens
4800	tens	1240	tens	1320	tens
2630	tens	5920	tens	4350	tens

What is the value of the 7 in these numbers?

| 76 | | 720 | | 137 | |
| 7122 | | 74 301 | | 724 | |

What is the value of the 3 in these numbers?

| 324 126 | | 3 927 141 | | 214 623 | |
| 8 254 320 | | 3 711 999 | | 124 372 | |

Write how many hundreds there are in:

6400	hundreds	8500	hundreds
19 900	hundreds	36 200	hundreds
524 600	hundreds	712 400	hundreds

What is the value of the 8 in these numbers?

| 8 214 631 | | 2 398 147 | | 463 846 | |
| 287 034 | | 8 110 927 | | 105 428 | |

Multiplying and dividing by 10

Write the answer in the box.

37 x 10 = | 370 | 58 ÷ 10 = | 5.8 |

Write the product in the box.

94 x 10 = [ ]   13 x 10 = [ ]   37 x 10 = [ ]

36 x 10 = [ ]   47 x 10 = [ ]   54 x 10 = [ ]

236 x 10 = [ ]   419 x 10 = [ ]   262 x 10 = [ ]

531 x 10 = [ ]   674 x 10 = [ ]   801 x 10 = [ ]

Write the quotient in the box.

92 ÷ 10 = [ ]   48 ÷ 10 = [ ]   37 ÷ 10 = [ ]

18 ÷ 10 = [ ]   29 ÷ 10 = [ ]   54 ÷ 10 = [ ]

345 ÷ 10 = [ ]   354 ÷ 10 = [ ]   723 ÷ 10 = [ ]

531 ÷ 10 = [ ]   262 ÷ 10 = [ ]   419 ÷ 10 = [ ]

Find the missing factor.

[ ] x 10 = 230   [ ] x 10 = 750   [ ] x 10 = 990

[ ] x 10 = 480   [ ] x 10 = 130   [ ] x 10 = 250

[ ] x 10 = 520   [ ] x 10 = 390   [ ] x 10 = 270

[ ] x 10 = 620   [ ] x 10 = 860   [ ] x 10 = 170

Find the dividend.

[ ] ÷ 10 = 4.7   [ ] ÷ 10 = 6.8   [ ] ÷ 10 = 12.4

[ ] ÷ 10 = 25.7   [ ] ÷ 10 = 36.2   [ ] ÷ 10 = 31.4

[ ] ÷ 10 = 40.8   [ ] ÷ 10 = 67.2   [ ] ÷ 10 = 80.9

[ ] ÷ 10 = 92.4   [ ] ÷ 10 = 32.7   [ ] ÷ 10 = 56.3

Appropriate units of measure

Choose the best units to measure the length of each item.

millimetres	centimetres	metres

desk	tooth	swimming pool
centimetres	millimetres	metres

Choose the best units to measure the length of each item.

centimetres	metres	kilometres

bed	bicycle	toothbrush	football field

shoe	driveway	sailboat	highway

The height of a door is about 2 ⬚ .

The length of a pencil is about 17 ⬚ .

The height of a flagpole is about 7 ⬚ .

Choose the best units to measure the mass of each item.

grams	kilograms	tonnes

train	kitten	watermelon	tennis ball

shoe	bag of potatoes	elephant	washing machine

The mass of a hamburger is about 26 ⬚ .

The mass of a bag of apples is about 2 ⬚ .

The mass of a truck is about 4 ⬚ .

Identifying patterns

Continue each pattern.

Intervals of 6:   1   7   13   19 | 25 | 31 | 37 |

Intervals of 3:   27 24 21 18 | 15 | 12 | 9 |

Continue each pattern.

0	10	20				
15	20	25				
5	7	9				
2	9	16				
4	7	10			19	
2	10	18		34		

Continue each pattern.

44	38	32				
33	29	25				
27	23	19				
56	48	40			16	
49	42	35				
28	25	22				10

Continue each pattern.

36	30	24		12		
5	14	23				
3	8	13				
47	40	33			12	
1	4	7				

The factors of 40 are   1   2   4   5   8   10   20   40

Circle the factors of 56.

(1)   (2)   3   (4)   5   6   (7)   (8)   (14)   (28)   32   (56)

Find all the factors of each number.

The factors of 31 are

The factors of 47 are

The factors of 60 are

The factors of 50 are

The factors of 42 are

The factors of 32 are

The factors of 48 are

The factors of 35 are

The factors of 52 are

Circle all the factors of each number.

Which numbers are factors of 39?

| 1 | 2 | 3 | 4 | 5 | 8 | 9 | 10 | 13 | 14 | 15 | 20 | 25 | 39 |

Which numbers are factors of 45?

| 1 | 3 | 4 | 5 | 8 | 9 | 12 | 15 | 16 | 21 | 24 | 36 | 40 | 44 | 45 |

Which numbers are factors of 61?

| 1 | 3 | 4 | 5 | 6 | 10 | 15 | 16 | 18 | 20 | 26 | 31 | 40 | 61 |

Which numbers are factors of 65?

| 1 | 2 | 4 | 5 | 6 | 8 | 9 | 10 | 12 | 13 | 14 | 15 | 30 | 60 | 65 |

Some numbers have only factors of 1 and themselves. They are called prime numbers.
Write all the prime numbers between 31 and 65 in the box.

Greatest common factor

Circle the common factors.
Write the greatest common factor (GCF).

24: ①, ②, ③, 4, ⑥, 8, 12, 24
60: ①, ②, ③, 4, 5, ⑥, 8, 10, 12, 60   The GCF is 6
42: ①, ②, ③, ⑥, 7, 14

Find the factors. Circle the common factors.

45:                          36:

28:                          54:

Find the factors. Write the GCF.

35:                          80:

The GCF is

32:                          64:

The GCF is

12:              24:   15:

The GCF is

54:              72:   18:

The GCF is

143

Writing equivalent fractions

Make these fractions equal by writing a number in the box.

$$\frac{10}{100} = \frac{\boxed{}}{10} \qquad \frac{8}{100} = \frac{\boxed{}}{25} \qquad \frac{4}{100} = \frac{\boxed{}}{25}$$

$$\frac{2}{20} = \frac{\boxed{}}{10} \qquad \frac{5}{100} = \frac{\boxed{}}{20} \qquad \frac{6}{20} = \frac{\boxed{}}{10}$$

$$\frac{3}{5} = \frac{\boxed{}}{20} \qquad \frac{5}{6} = \frac{\boxed{}}{12} \qquad \frac{2}{8} = \frac{\boxed{}}{24}$$

$$\frac{2}{3} = \frac{\boxed{}}{24} \qquad \frac{2}{18} = \frac{\boxed{}}{9} \qquad \frac{4}{50} = \frac{\boxed{}}{25}$$

$$\frac{11}{12} = \frac{\boxed{}}{36} \qquad \frac{12}{15} = \frac{\boxed{}}{5} \qquad \frac{8}{20} = \frac{\boxed{}}{5}$$

$$\frac{2}{12} = \frac{1}{\boxed{}} \qquad \frac{5}{20} = \frac{1}{\boxed{}} \qquad \frac{5}{8} = \frac{10}{\boxed{}}$$

$$\frac{7}{8} = \frac{21}{\boxed{}} \qquad \frac{15}{100} = \frac{3}{\boxed{}} \qquad \frac{6}{24} = \frac{1}{\boxed{}}$$

$$\frac{5}{25} = \frac{1}{\boxed{}} \qquad \frac{8}{20} = \frac{2}{\boxed{}} \qquad \frac{15}{20} = \frac{3}{\boxed{}}$$

$$\frac{5}{30} = \frac{1}{\boxed{}} \qquad \frac{12}{14} = \frac{6}{\boxed{}} \qquad \frac{1}{5} = \frac{4}{\boxed{}}$$

$$\frac{9}{18} = \frac{1}{\boxed{}} \qquad \frac{24}{30} = \frac{4}{\boxed{}} \qquad \frac{25}{30} = \frac{5}{\boxed{}}$$

$$\frac{1}{8} = \frac{\boxed{}}{16} = \frac{3}{\boxed{}} = \frac{\boxed{}}{32} = \frac{\boxed{}}{40} = \frac{6}{\boxed{}}$$

$$\frac{20}{100} = \frac{\boxed{}}{25} = \frac{2}{\boxed{}} = \frac{1}{\boxed{}} = \frac{\boxed{}}{50} = \frac{\boxed{}}{200}$$

$$\frac{2}{5} = \frac{6}{\boxed{}} = \frac{\boxed{}}{20} = \frac{10}{\boxed{}} = \frac{\boxed{}}{50} = \frac{40}{\boxed{}}$$

$$\frac{1}{6} = \frac{\boxed{}}{12} = \frac{3}{\boxed{}} = \frac{4}{\boxed{}} = \frac{5}{\boxed{}} = \frac{6}{\boxed{}}$$

$$\frac{2}{3} = \frac{\boxed{}}{24} = \frac{\boxed{}}{36} = \frac{\boxed{}}{21} = \frac{6}{\boxed{}} = \frac{\boxed{}}{300}$$

Fraction models

Write the missing numbers to show what part is shaded.

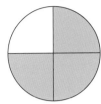

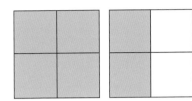

$$\frac{3 \text{ shaded parts}}{4 \text{ parts}} = \frac{3}{4}$$

$\frac{4}{4} = 1$ and $\frac{2}{4} = \frac{1}{2}$

So, shaded part $= 1\frac{1}{2}$

Write the missing numbers to show what part is shaded.

   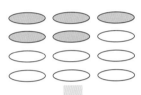

 $\frac{}{9}$ $\frac{1}{}$ $\frac{}{}$ $\frac{}{}$

Write the fraction for the part that is shaded.

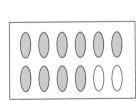

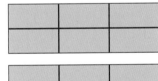
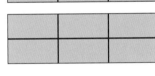

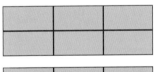
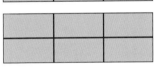

 $\frac{}{}$ or $\frac{}{}$ 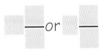 $\frac{}{}$ or $\frac{}{}$ 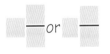 $\frac{}{}$ or $\frac{}{}$

Write the fraction for the part that is shaded.

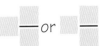 $\frac{}{}$ or $\frac{}{}$ $\frac{}{}$ or $\frac{}{}$ $\frac{}{}$

Multiplying by one-digit numbers

Find each product. Remember to regroup.

$$
\begin{array}{r}
^{1\ 1}465 \\
\times\quad 3 \\
\hline
1395
\end{array}
\qquad
\begin{array}{r}
^{3}391 \\
\times\quad 4 \\
\hline
1564
\end{array}
\qquad
\begin{array}{r}
^{3\ 4}278 \\
\times\quad 5 \\
\hline
1390
\end{array}
$$

Find each product.

$$
\begin{array}{r}
563 \\
\times\quad 3 \\
\hline
\end{array}
\qquad
\begin{array}{r}
910 \\
\times\quad 2 \\
\hline
\end{array}
\qquad
\begin{array}{r}
437 \\
\times\quad 3 \\
\hline
\end{array}
\qquad
\begin{array}{r}
812 \\
\times\quad 2 \\
\hline
\end{array}
$$

$$
\begin{array}{r}
572 \\
\times\quad 4 \\
\hline
\end{array}
\qquad
\begin{array}{r}
831 \\
\times\quad 3 \\
\hline
\end{array}
\qquad
\begin{array}{r}
406 \\
\times\quad 5 \\
\hline
\end{array}
\qquad
\begin{array}{r}
394 \\
\times\quad 6 \\
\hline
\end{array}
$$

Find each product.

$$
\begin{array}{r}
318 \\
\times\quad 3 \\
\hline
\end{array}
\qquad
\begin{array}{r}
223 \\
\times\quad 4 \\
\hline
\end{array}
\qquad
\begin{array}{r}
542 \\
\times\quad 4 \\
\hline
\end{array}
\qquad
\begin{array}{r}
217 \\
\times\quad 3 \\
\hline
\end{array}
$$

$$
\begin{array}{r}
127 \\
\times\quad 4 \\
\hline
\end{array}
\qquad
\begin{array}{r}
275 \\
\times\quad 5 \\
\hline
\end{array}
\qquad
\begin{array}{r}
798 \\
\times\quad 6 \\
\hline
\end{array}
\qquad
\begin{array}{r}
365 \\
\times\quad 6 \\
\hline
\end{array}
$$

$$
\begin{array}{r}
100 \\
\times\quad 5 \\
\hline
\end{array}
\qquad
\begin{array}{r}
372 \\
\times\quad 4 \\
\hline
\end{array}
\qquad
\begin{array}{r}
881 \\
\times\quad 4 \\
\hline
\end{array}
\qquad
\begin{array}{r}
953 \\
\times\quad 3 \\
\hline
\end{array}
$$

Solve each problem.

A middle school has 255 students. A high school has 6 times as many students. How many children are there at the high school?

A train can carry 365 passengers. How many could it carry on

four trips?

six trips?

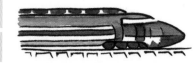

Multiplying by one-digit numbers

Find each product. Remember to regroup.

33	12	4 4
456	823	755
x 6	x 8	x 9
2736	6584	6795

Find each product.

394	736	827	943
x 7	x 7	x 8	x 9

643	199	821	547
x 6	x 6	x 7	x 8

501	377	843	222
x 7	x 8	x 8	x 9

471	223	606	513
x 9	x 8	x 6	x 7

500	800	900	200
x 9	x 9	x 8	x 9

Solve each problem.

A crate holds 550 apples. How many apples are there in 8 crates?

Keyshawn swims 760 laps each week. How many laps does he swim in 5 weeks?

147

Real-life problems

Find the answer to each problem.

Jacob spent $4.68 at the store and had $4.77 left.
How much did he have to start with?

$9.45

```
        1  1
     4.77
   + 4.68
   _____
     9.45
```

Tracy receives a weekly allowance of $3.00 a week.
How much will she have if she saves all of it for 8 weeks?

$24.00

```
     3.00
   ×    8
   _____
    24.00
```

Find the answer to each problem.

A theater charges $4 for each matinee
ticket. If it sells 360 tickets for a matinee
performance, how much does it take in?

David has saved $9.59. His sister
has $3.24 less. How much does
she have?

The cost for 9 children to go to a
theme park is $72. How much does
each child pay? If only 6 children
go, what will the cost be?

Paul has $3.69. His sister gives him
another $5.25, and he goes out and
buys a CD single for $3.99. How
much does he have left?

Ian has $20 in savings. He
decides to spend $\frac{1}{4}$ of it. How
much will he have left?

Real-life problems

Find the answer to each problem.

Nina has an hour to do her homework. She plans to spend $\frac{1}{3}$ of her time on math. How many minutes will she spend doing math?

20 minutes

1 hour is 60 minutes

$$3\overline{)60}$$ ... 20

In gym class, David makes 2 long jumps of 1.78 m and 2.19 m. How far does he jump altogether?

3.97 m

$$\begin{array}{r} 1 \\ 1.78\,m \\ +\ 2.19\,m \\ \hline 3.97\,m \end{array}$$

Find the answer to each problem.

Moishe has a can of lemonade containing 400 ml. He drinks $\frac{1}{4}$ of it. How much is left?

David ran 40 m in 8 seconds. At that speed, how far did he run in 1 second?

A large jar of coffee contains 1.75 kg. If 1.48 kg is left in the jar, how much has been used?

A worker can fill 145 boxes of tea in 15 minutes. How many boxes can he fill in 1 hour?

Jennifer's computer is 41.63 cm wide and her printer is 48.37 cm wide. How much space does she have for books if her desk is 1.5 m wide?

Problems involving time

Find the answer to each problem.

Caitlin spends 35 minutes on her homework each day. How many minutes does she spend on her homework in one week from Monday through Friday?

175 minutes

$$\begin{array}{r} \overset{2}{35} \\ \times\ 5 \\ \hline 175 \end{array}$$

Jenny spends 175 minutes on her homework from Monday through Friday. How much time does she spend on homework each day?

35 minutes

$$5\overline{)175}\ ^{35}$$

Find the answer to each problem.

Amy works from 9 A.M. until 5 P.M. She has a lunch break from noon until 1 P.M. How many hours does she work in a 5-day week?

School children have a 15-minute break in the morning and a 10-minute break in the afternoon. How many minutes of break do they have in a week?

It takes 2 hours for one person to do a job. If John shares the work with 3 of his friends, how long will it take?

Mr. Tambo spent 7 days building a patio. If he worked a total of 56 hours and he divided the work evenly among the seven days, how long did he work each day?

It took Ben 45 hours to build a remote-controlled airplane. If he spent 5 hours a day working on it:

How many days did it take?

How many hours per day would he have needed to finish it in 5 days?

Multiplying and dividing

Write the answer in the box.

26 x 10 = 260   26 x 100 = 2600

400 ÷ 10 = 40   400 ÷ 100 = 4

Write the product in the box.

33 x 10 =   21 x 10 =   42 x 10 =

94 x 100 =   36 x 100 =   81 x 100 =

416 x 10 =   204 x 10 =   513 x 10 =

767 x 100 =   821 x 100 =   245 x 100 =

Write the quotient in the box.

120 ÷ 10 =   260 ÷ 10 =   470 ÷ 10 =

300 ÷ 100 =   800 ÷ 100 =   400 ÷ 100 =

20 ÷ 10 =   30 ÷ 10 =   70 ÷ 10 =

500 ÷ 100 =   100 ÷ 100 =   900 ÷ 100 =

Write the number that has been multiplied by 100.

         x 100 =   5900   x 100 = 71 400

         x 100 = 72 100   x 100 = 23 400

         x 100 =   1100   x 100 = 47 000

         x 100 =   8400   x 100 = 44 100

Write the number that has been divided by 100.

         ÷ 100 =   2   ÷ 100 =   8

         ÷ 100 = 21   ÷ 100 = 18

         ÷ 100 = 86   ÷ 100 = 21

         ÷ 100 = 10   ÷ 100 = 59

Identifying patterns

Continue each pattern.

Steps of 2:	$\frac{1}{2}$	$2\frac{1}{2}$	$4\frac{1}{2}$	$6\frac{1}{2}$	$8\frac{1}{2}$	$10\frac{1}{2}$
Steps of 5:	3.5	8.5	13.5	18.5	23.5	28.5

Continue each pattern.

$5\frac{1}{2}$	$10\frac{1}{2}$	$15\frac{1}{2}$			
$1\frac{1}{4}$	$3\frac{1}{4}$	$5\frac{1}{4}$			
$8\frac{1}{3}$	$9\frac{1}{3}$	$10\frac{1}{3}$		$12\frac{1}{3}$	
$55\frac{3}{4}$	$45\frac{3}{4}$	$35\frac{3}{4}$			
$42\frac{1}{2}$	$38\frac{1}{2}$	$34\frac{1}{2}$			$22\frac{1}{2}$
7.5	6.5	5.5			
28.4	25.4	22.4		16.4	
81.6	73.6	65.6			
6.3	10.3	14.3			
12.1	13.1	14.1			17.1
14.6	21.6	28.6			
$11\frac{1}{2}$	$10\frac{1}{2}$	$9\frac{1}{2}$			
8.4	11.4	14.4		20.4	
$7\frac{3}{4}$	$13\frac{3}{4}$	$19\frac{3}{4}$			$37\frac{3}{4}$
57.5	48.5	39.5			

Products with odd and even numbers

Find the products of these numbers.

3 and 4   The product of 3 and 4 is 12.   6 and 8   The product of 6 and 8 is 48.

Find the products of these odd and even numbers.

5 and 6

3 and 2

7 and 4

8 and 3

6 and 3

2 and 9

10 and 3

12 and 5

What do you notice about your answers? _____

Find the products of these odd numbers.

5 and 7

3 and 9

5 and 11

7 and 3

9 and 5

11 and 7

13 and 3

1 and 5

What do you notice about your answers? _____

Find the products of these even numbers.

2 and 4

4 and 6

6 and 2

4 and 8

10 and 2

4 and 10

6 and 10

6 and 8

What do you notice about your answers? _____

Can you write a rule for the products with odd and even numbers?

_____

Factors of numbers from 66 to 100

The factors of 66 are   1   2   3   6   11   22   33   66

Circle the factors of 94.   (1)   (2)   28   32   43   (47)   71   86   (94)

Write the factors of each number in the box.

The factors of 70 are

The factors of 85 are

The factors of 69 are

The factors of 83 are

The factors of 75 are

The factors of 96 are

The factors of 63 are

The factors of 99 are

The factors of 72 are

Circle the factors of 68.

   1   2   3   4   5   6   7   8   9   11   12   17   34   35   62   68

Circle the factors of 95.

   1   2   3   4   5   15   16   17   19   24   37   85   90   95   96

Circle the factors of 88.

   1   2   3   4   5   6   8   10   11   15   22   25   27   44   87   88

Circle the factors of 73.

   1   2   4   5   6   8   9   10   12   13   14   15   30   60   73

A prime number only has two factors, 1 and itself.
Write all the prime numbers between 66 and 100 in the box.

Multiplying by two-digit numbers

Write the product for each problem.

```
    1           2
    1           1
   56          45
 x 32        x 43
 ----        ----
  112         135
 1680        1800
 ----        ----
 1792        1935
```

Write the product for each problem.

```
   56          23          47          84
 x 23        x 24        x 25        x 22
```

```
   73          52          64          51
 x 34        x 35        x 33        x 32
```

Write the product for each problem.

```
   41          65          72          84
 x 62        x 54        x 68        x 71
```

```
   92          57          38          26
 x 63        x 82        x 94        x 75
```

Multiplying by two-digit numbers

Write the product for each problem.

```
    7        7
    6        6
   39       68
 x 87     x 98
  273      544
 3120     6120
 3393     6664
```

Write the product for each problem.

87	76	99	85
x 98	x 78	x 69	x 98

88	67	94	89
x 95	x 76	x 69	x 47

Write the product for each problem.

87	46	58	73
x 79	x 67	x 59	x 98

95	58	78	96
x 67	x 88	x 97	x 79

Extra Practice

This section gives children a chance to further practise what they've learned, helping to reinforce the core skills developed while working through this book.

Contents

In this section, children will review:

- representing, comparing, ordering, and understanding of place value of numbers up to 6 digits
- generating numerical sequences
- solving multi-digit multiplication and division with remainders
- adding, subtracting, and multiplying with decimal notation
- recognizing fraction equivalents to decimals and percentages
- recognizing factors and multiples
- solving money and real-life problems
- calculating perimeters and areas
- representing and interpreting data
- identifying, measuring, and constructing angles
- solving problems with metric units of measurement

The "Keeping skills sharp" pages can act as a test to see how well children are learning the material. Further parents' notes are found in the answer section at the back of the book.

When your child has completed this book, fill out the certificate of achievement and congratulate him or her on a job well done!

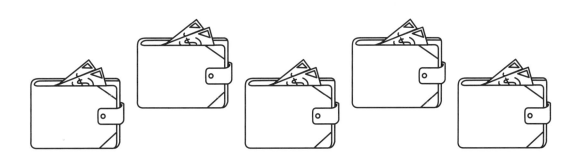

Write each of these using numbers.

Fifteen thousand seven hundred twenty-nine

15 729

Six hundred eighteen thousand two hundred forty-three

Six hundred thousand four

One hundred seven thousand two hundred fifty-six

Three hundred thousand two hundred eighteen

Eight hundred six thousand one hundred seven

Three hundred twenty-one thousand five hundred
fifty-nine

Nine hundred ninety-nine thousand nine hundred
ninety-nine

Two thousand one hundred sixty-nine

Eight hundred five thousand four hundred one

Write each row in order, starting with the smallest number.

21 358	13 560	34 078	100 000

99 000	9999	10 000	9009

Write each number using words.

1502 ....

2416 ....

Write the answers.

269 x 10 = 2690

845 x 10 =

1564 x 10 =

7405 x 10 =

7420 x 10 =

15 645 x 10 =

23 785 x 10 =

54 866 x 10 =

9400 x 10 =

4545 x 10 =

5212 x 10 =

2867 x 100 =

6734 x 100 =

5089 x 100 =

967 x 100 =

3000 x 100 =

7650 ÷ 10 =

52 430 ÷ 10 =

76 400 ÷ 10 =

6000 ÷ 10 =

5290 ÷ 10 =

1350 ÷ 10 =

5500 ÷ 10 =

12 600 ÷ 10 =

1000 ÷ 10 =

6800 ÷ 100 =

6000 ÷ 100 =

5000 ÷ 100 =

5500 ÷ 100 =

60 200 ÷ 100 =

40 000 ÷ 100 =

66 000 ÷ 100 =

Write each row in order, starting with the smallest number.

7 m	690 cm	1.6 km	900 m	1700 m
690 cm				

23 cm	240 mm	180 mm	20 cm	0.21 m

2.8 km	3000 m	2.5 km	2600 m	1.9 km

678 g	0.5 kg	2.3 kg	1400 g	0.95 kg

1200 mL	1.6 L	0.9 L	850 mL	1400 mL

$5.50	280 ¢	$0.75	600 ¢	$3.90

12 L	11 000 mL	8.5 L	110.45 mL	6.85 L

150 seconds	3 minutes	1 hour	130 minutes	600 seconds

$\frac{1}{2}$ L	$\frac{3}{5}$ L	1.2 L	0.25 L	2 L

2 hours	50 minutes	$3\frac{1}{2}$ hours	100 minutes	$1\frac{1}{2}$ hours

Continue each sequence.

1.6	2.2	2.8	3.4	4.0	4.6		
3.7	4.2	4.7	5.2	5.7			
$1\frac{1}{2}$	$4\frac{1}{2}$	$7\frac{1}{2}$	$10\frac{1}{2}$	$13\frac{1}{2}$			
35	28	21	14	7			
5.9	4.9	3.9	2.9	1.9			
$6\frac{1}{4}$	$5\frac{3}{4}$	$5\frac{1}{4}$	$4\frac{3}{4}$	$4\frac{1}{4}$			
−6.5	−5.6	−4.7	−3.8	−2.9			
34	45	56	67	78			
8.6	9.2	9.8	10.4	11.0			
30	45	60	75	90			
−50	−44	−38	−32	−26			
0.6	1.1	1.6	2.1	2.6			
4.6	7.6	10.6	13.6	16.6			
14.4	13.9	13.4	12.9	12.4			
7.3	6.3	5.3	4.3	3.3			

Write each row in order, beginning with the lowest number.

8	4	−3	−7	0	9	−5
−7						

−10	5	10	0	−5	12	14

7	−3	9	−4	−6	6	5

0	5	−5	4	−4	3	−3

0.5	1.5	−0.5	0	−1.5	−0.2	0.2

14	8	0	9	−3	12	−20

−8	−6	−10	0	−4	−1	6

30	0	50	−60	−30	20	−10

−5	12	−20	30	40	−10	50

$\frac{1}{2}$	$\frac{1}{3}$	$\frac{1}{4}$	$\frac{9}{10}$	$-\frac{1}{4}$	−1	−2

Use the thermometer to count the number of degrees from one temperature to another to answer these questions.

What is the difference in temperatures?

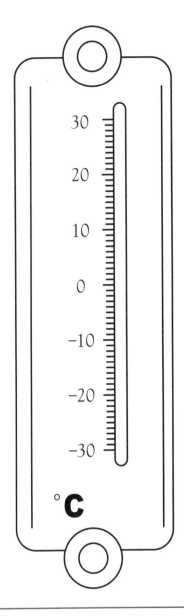

5°C and 12°C	7°C	10°C and 3°C	
1°C and 14°C		4°C and 0°C	
8°C and 20°C		18°C and 30°C	
15°C and 25°C		10°C and 14°C	
19°C and 12°C		5°C and –2°C	
–3°C and 7°C		8°C and –1°C	
–4°C and 4°C		9°C and 0°C	
6°C and –3°C		–8°C and 3°C	
10°C and –3°C		–5°C and 12°C	
–3°C and –4°C		–6°C and –8°C	
0°C and –5°C		0°C and –20°C	
–10°C and –30°C		–4°C and –12°C	

The temperature in Calgary, Alberta is 5°C but the temperature in Moscow, Russia is 8°C colder. What is the temperature in Moscow?

The temperature in Madrid, Spain is 12°C warmer than the temperature in Toronto, Ontario. The temperature in Toronto is –3°C. What is the temperature in Madrid?

The temperature in Paris, France is 7°C and in Montreal, Quebec is –4°C. What is the difference in temperature between Paris and Montreal?

Ordering decimals

Write each row in order, starting with the smallest number.

3.89	9.83	8.93	9.38	3.98
3.89				

0.67	7.06	6.7	7.6	6.07

12.65	16.52	26.51	62.15	26.25

30.06	36.0	6.03	63.0	30.6

3.16	3.61	0.36	36.01	3.06

3.42 cm	4.85 cm	1.65 cm	2.33 cm	3.76 cm

5.23 m	12.08 m	3.76 m	11.82 m	9.65 m

4.56 mm	3.88 mm	1.26 mm	6.07 mm	4.5 mm

10.08 L	9.45 L	3.45 L	6.5 L	5.1 L

7 km	6.8 km	7.03 km	5 km	7.34 km

Round each number to the nearest whole number.

3.65	1.87	4.52	6.3	2.01	5.45
4					

4.88	5.5	7.43	9.09	4.83	6.21

4.86 mm	5.23 m	7.6 km	4.9 mm	8.28 m	7.06 cm

0.69 g	7.26 cm	5.46 g	27.06 mL	9.99 g	46.34 kg

Round each amount to the nearest whole dollar.

$2.58	$1.60	$4.12	$5.85	$16.17	$8.30

$1.56	$9.45	$6.01	$8.51	$21.76	$79.90

Round each number to the nearest tenth.

12.42	11.76	12.38	14.75	17.48	5.69

3.47	4.92	13.31	24.44	18.09	15.63

2.31	2.85	3.65	8.12	19.49	6.10

5.67	14.67	5.55	0.78	0.50	1.46

Write five fractions that are equivalent to $\frac{1}{2}$.

$\frac{1}{2}$ $\frac{2}{4}$

Write five fractions that are equivalent to $\frac{1}{5}$.

$\frac{1}{5}$

Write five fractions that are equivalent to $\frac{3}{5}$.

$\frac{3}{5}$

Write five fractions that are equivalent to $\frac{1}{10}$.

$\frac{1}{10}$

Write five fractions that are equivalent to $\frac{3}{4}$.

$\frac{3}{4}$

Write five fractions that are equivalent to $\frac{3}{10}$.

$\frac{3}{10}$

Write five fractions that are equivalent to $\frac{2}{3}$.

$\frac{2}{3}$

Fractions of amounts

What is one-quarter ($\frac{1}{4}$) of each amount?

| 12 ¢ | 3 ¢ | 40 ¢ | | 60 ¢ | | $1.00 | | $8.00 | |

| 24 cm | | 36 cm | | 4 m | | 16 cm | | 240 cm | |

| 8 kg | | 28 mL | | 44 g | | 52 kg | | 120 mL | |

What is two-thirds ($\frac{2}{3}$) of each amount?

| 21 km | | 27 kg | | 15 ¢ | | $30 | | 18 cm | |

| 12 litres | | 9 cm | | 30 m | | 45 kg | | 60 mm | |

| 24 mL | | 36 m | | 90 km | | 48 cm | | $120 | |

What is three-quarters ($\frac{3}{4}$) of each amount?

| $1.00 | | $1.60 | | $1.12 | | $1.40 | | $10.00 | |

| 96 ¢ | | 84 ¢ | | 72 ¢ | | 56 ¢ | | 104 ¢ | |

| 240 m | | 400 m | | 600 m | | 480 m | | 220 m | |

What is four-fifths ($\frac{4}{5}$) of each amount?

| 350 mL | | 8 m | | $5 | | 15 km | | 20 m | |

| 100 mm | | 80 m | | 60 ¢ | | 90 cm | | 30 ¢ | |

| 500 km | | $2 | | 250 ¢ | | $120 | | 900 m | |

Write each fraction in its decimal form.

$\frac{1}{2}$ [0.5] $\frac{1}{4}$ [ ] $\frac{3}{4}$ [ ] $\frac{1}{5}$ [ ] $\frac{2}{5}$ [ ]

$\frac{3}{5}$ [ ] $\frac{4}{5}$ [ ] $\frac{1}{3}$ [ ] $\frac{2}{3}$ [ ] $\frac{1}{10}$ [ ]

$\frac{2}{10}$ [ ] $\frac{3}{10}$ [ ] $\frac{5}{10}$ [ ] $\frac{6}{10}$ [ ] $\frac{9}{10}$ [ ]

Write each number in its decimal form.

$1\frac{1}{2}$ [1.5] $7\frac{1}{2}$ [ ] $4\frac{1}{5}$ [ ] $7\frac{2}{5}$ [ ] $9\frac{1}{4}$ [ ]

$6\frac{1}{5}$ [ ] $9\frac{3}{10}$ [ ] $2\frac{9}{10}$ [ ] $12\frac{1}{5}$ [ ] $15\frac{2}{5}$ [ ]

$8\frac{4}{5}$ [ ] $5\frac{3}{4}$ [ ] $7\frac{8}{10}$ [ ] $15\frac{3}{5}$ [ ] $2\frac{4}{10}$ [ ]

$14\frac{2}{5}$ [ ] $18\frac{3}{4}$ [ ] $12\frac{3}{4}$ [ ] $2\frac{1}{2}$ [ ] $15\frac{6}{10}$ [ ]

Join the shaded fraction to its decimal form with a line.

$\frac{3}{10}$ 0.4

$\frac{4}{5}$ 0.75

$\frac{9}{10}$ 0.2

$\frac{1}{5}$ 0.3

$\frac{3}{4}$ 0.9

$\frac{2}{5}$ 0.8

Percentages and conversions

Change each fraction to its percentage equivalent.

$\frac{1}{2}$ = 50% $\frac{1}{4}$ = $\frac{3}{4}$ = $\frac{1}{5}$ =

$\frac{2}{5}$ = $\frac{3}{5}$ = $\frac{4}{5}$ = $\frac{1}{10}$ =

$\frac{2}{10}$ = $\frac{3}{10}$ = $\frac{4}{10}$ = $\frac{5}{10}$ =

$\frac{6}{10}$ = $\frac{7}{10}$ = $\frac{8}{10}$ = $\frac{9}{10}$ =

$\frac{50}{100}$ = $\frac{80}{100}$ = $\frac{10}{100}$ = $\frac{20}{100}$ =

$\frac{90}{100}$ = $\frac{40}{100}$ = $\frac{70}{100}$ = $\frac{30}{100}$ =

$\frac{60}{100}$ = $\frac{25}{100}$ = $\frac{75}{100}$ = $\frac{5}{100}$ =

$\frac{17}{100}$ = $\frac{28}{100}$ = $\frac{35}{100}$ = $\frac{46}{100}$ =

$\frac{52}{100}$ = $\frac{63}{100}$ = $\frac{76}{100}$ = $\frac{83}{100}$ =

Write each amount in dollars.

27 ¢   35 ¢   60 ¢   90 ¢

41 ¢   12 ¢   42 ¢   79 ¢

75 ¢   56 ¢   30 ¢   80 ¢

Write each amount in cents.

$2.00 $5.00 $10.00 $40.00

Ten people win a lottery prize of $345 270. The prize is shared equally between them. How much will they each receive?

A scientist has to put some animals on display in order of their length. The smallest animal must go first. Below are the lengths of some animals. Put these lengths in order, starting with the shortest.

27 m	3750 cm	18.25 m	99 mm	0.87 m

A child reduces each of these amounts by 8 units every minute. What will the amounts be after 5 minutes?

	After 1 min	After 2 min	After 3 min	After 4 min	After 5 min
62 g					
79 cm					
102 mL					

The temperature in a freezer drops steadily by 3°C per hour. If the freezer starts at 0°C, what will the temperature be after six hours?

Put each row in order, starting with the smallest number.

7.5	5.7	7.05	5.07	5.55	5.75

12.8	1.28	0.12	0.28	2.18	1.82

34.06	30.46	36.4	36.04	30.64	34.6

Circle the fractions that are equivalent to $\frac{3}{4}$.

$\frac{30}{40}$ $\frac{9}{10}$ $\frac{4}{6}$ $\frac{12}{16}$ $\frac{300}{400}$ $\frac{18}{30}$

Boris has five children. Each child has a certain amount of money.

Annie
$12.00

Billy
$20.00

Carol
$18.00

Doris
$24.00

David
$8.00

Boris tells each child they must give one-fifth of their money to charity.
How much will each child give?

Annie	Billy	Carol	Doris	David

Write the answers.

$\frac{4}{5}$ of $14 = $ $\frac{3}{4}$ of 80 cm = $\frac{3}{10}$ of 2 m =

$\frac{2}{5}$ of 4 m = $\frac{2}{3}$ of 60 km = $\frac{9}{10}$ of 800 g =

Circle the fractions that are equivalent to 0.4.

$\frac{3}{4}$ $\frac{2}{5}$ $\frac{1}{2}$ $\frac{1}{3}$ $\frac{4}{10}$ $\frac{4}{8}$

What is $\frac{2}{3}$ of each amount?

$9   3 m   150 cm

$21   60 mL $210

Find the sum.

265 m	482 km	359 cm
177 m	209 km	423 cm
564 m	788 km	630 cm
+ 443 m	+ 734 km	+ 823 cm
1449 m		

894 g	412 g	4530 g
653 g	745 g	523 g
506 g	211 g	9 g
+ 789 g	+ 295 g	+ 3423 g

7564 m	8675 km	5321 cm
7345 m	4173 km	3123 cm
6445 m	8347 km	5264 cm
+ 9673 m	+ 2331 km	+ 5234 cm

2756 mm	9678 mm	675 g
452 mm	4500 mm	8 g
174 mm	657 mm	56 g
+ 1894 mm	+ 4336 mm	+ 3445 g

Find the difference.

5565 − 4331	6723 − 5694	9786 − 7564
1234		

7407 − 2321	3321 − 1665	8564 − 3423

7008 − 1745	4505 − 1534	3202 − 1332

2000 − 1500	5000 − 1320	7000 − 2312

6500 − 2310	6200 − 5300	7800 − 4305

6578 − 789	4312 − 656	4560 − 206

Circle the multiples of 12.

50   (24)   60   144

38   70   80   100   90

     36   120   56   94

Circle the multiples of 15.

     45   10   130

80   70   75   100   90

     1   150   50   65

Circle the multiples of 20.

     15   20   310   110

60   90   70   100   400

     500   130   200   30

Circle the multiples of 50.

     50   20   350

750   1000   70   400

     300   240   470

Write the factors of these numbers. Always begin with 1.

Remember: If a number is even, 2 will always be a factor.

The factors of 10 are   1, 2, 5, 10

The factors of 12 are

The factors of 18 are

The factors of 51 are

The factors of 61 are

The factors of 71 are

The factors of 81 are

The factors of 60 are

The factors of 70 are

The factors of 75 are

The factors of 85 are

The factors of 29 are

The factors of 53 are

The factors of 24 are

By now you should know up to the 12-times tables very well.

Write the products.

Be quick and accurate!

6 x 12 = 72   5 x 9 =   4 x 10 =   3 x 8 =

2 x 7 =   5 x 12 =   6 x 9 =   7 x 10 =

8 x 8 =   3 x 7 =   4 x 12 =   7 x 9 =

8 x 10 =   7 x 8 =   4 x 7 =   3 x 12 =

9 x 8 =   10 x 10 =   12 x 12 =   11 x 9 =

6 x 8 =   6 x 7 =   4 x 11 =   3 x 9 =

5 x 6 =   7 x 5 =   8 x 4 =   9 x 7 =

1 x 7 =   3 x 6 =   4 x 9 =   7 x 6 =

When a number is multiplied by itself, the answer is a square number or perfect square.

Write the answers.

1 x 1 =   2 x 2 =   3 x 3 =   4 x 4 =

5 x 5 =   6 x 6 =   7 x 7 =   8 x 8 =

9 x 9 =   10 x 10 =   11 x 11 =   12 x 12 =

Work out these multiplication problems, using the method you prefer.

```
        48              67              79              54
    x   11          x   12          x   13          x   14
    _____         _____         _____         _____
        48
  +    480
    _____
       528
```

```
        23              85              35              46
    x   15          x   16          x   17          x   18
    _____         _____         _____         _____
```

```
        59             123              68             154
    x   19          x   21          x   23          x   25
    _____         _____         _____         _____
```

```
       143             135             214             167
    x   27          x   13          x   15          x   16
    _____         _____         _____         _____
```

★ Dividing with remainders

You may have been shown different ways to work out these problems.
Use the method you prefer to find the quotient and remainders.

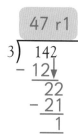

47 r1

$3\overline{)142}$
$-12\downarrow$
  22
-21
   1

$4\overline{)89}$

$5\overline{)130}$

$6\overline{)124}$

$7\overline{)130}$

$8\overline{)78}$

$9\overline{)150}$

$2\overline{)167}$

$3\overline{)76}$

$4\overline{)106}$

$5\overline{)178}$

$6\overline{)126}$

$7\overline{)184}$

$8\overline{)166}$

$9\overline{)190}$

$2\overline{)49}$

$3\overline{)92}$

$4\overline{)101}$

$5\overline{)74}$

$6\overline{)111}$

Find the quotient and remainders.

15 r6

10) 156
 − 10↓
    56
 − 50
     6

10) 189

10) 130

10) 46

10) 232

10) 178

10) 80

10) 110

10) 150

10) 14

10) 186

10) 200

10) 172

10) 100

10) 120

10) 143

10) 155

10) 179

10) 180

10) 201

Write the operation (+, −, x, ÷) that makes each question true.

12 x 8 = 96   50 ☐ 6 = 8 r2   15 ☐ 3 = 18

15 ☐ 3 = 45   6 ☐ 20 = 120   42 ☐ 12 = 30

11 ☐ 8 = 3   100 ☐ 12 = 8 r4   12 ☐ 4 = 8

29 ☐ 8 = 21   50 ☐ 7 = 7 r1   12 ☐ 6 = 6

7 ☐ 9 = 63   14 ☐ 5 = 70   15 ☐ 3 = 5

50 ☐ 20 = 30   21 ☐ 3 = 63   35 ☐ 7 = 5

10 ☐ 9 = 90   100 ☐ 8 = 12 r4   24 ☐ 3 = 8

20 ☐ 9 = 11   40 ☐ 8 = 320   22 ☐ 3 = 66

50 ☐ 2 = 25   62 ☐ 17 = 79   16 ☐ 3 = 5 r1

Use the box to show your work if needed.

A baseball team scores 432 runs. Two players at bat score a total of 278 runs. How many runs do the rest of the players score?

154 runs

```
  432
 -278
 ----
  154
```

125 doughnuts are shared equally between 15 soccer players and the remainder are given to the coach. How many doughnuts does the coach receive?

Jane can cycle at a steady speed of 12 kilometres an hour. How long will it take Jane to travel 66 kilometres?

In a normal year of 365 days, it rains on 187 days. On how many days does it not rain?

In order to go on an amusement park ride, Bobby needs to be 152 centimetres tall. Bobby is 145 centimetres tall. He is short by how much?

Mary's cellphone costs $18 per month. How much will Mary pay each year?

Adding decimals

Write the answers.

3.84 + 1.39 **5.23**	4.29 + 2.66	3.91 + 4.22	5.16 + 3.45
7.43 + 2.66	2.33 + 9.17	8.92 + 3.17	5.26 + 3.75
11.46 + 6.56	19.32 + 3.84	16.67 + 4.21	18.74 + 6.06
15.03 +18.78	14.92 + 2.37	10.45 + 5.93	12.67 +18.06
32.08 + 7.92	46.02 + 19.12	15.01 + 14.99	17.84 + 2.16
423.97 + 67.94	301.75 + 19.12	412.85 + 56.73	213.52 + 68.08

Write the answers.

| 4.78 | 9.52 | 8.74 | 3.97 |
| - 1.44 | - 4.56 | - 3.11 | - 1.84 |

3.34

| 7.82 | 6.13 | 3.27 | 5.24 |
| - 3.49 | - 2.08 | - 1.45 | - 4.01 |

| 9.04 | 6.01 | 8.06 | 4.79 |
| - 2.53 | - 2.67 | - 3.57 | - 1.32 |

| 16.05 | 12.42 | 18.67 | 10.23 |
| - 11.45 | - 8.67 | - 12.37 | - 3.78 |

| 413.65 | 215.07 | 312.56 | 569.72 |
| - 213.65 | - 180.01 | - 121.65 | - 236.09 |

| 500.05 | 150.06 | 200.01 | 420.69 |
| - 1.06 | - 100.09 | - 99.99 | - 89.43 |

★ Money problems

Use the box to show your work if needed.

Dave delivers free magazines to houses and is paid 5 ¢ per magazine. Dave delivers 600 magazines. How much will Dave earn?

Sean wins some money on a game at the fair.
He wins 79 ¢, $1.38, $0.37, and 66 ¢.
How much has Sean won in total?

Harris is a used car dealer and on a good day he sells three cars—a Honda for $7850, a Ford for $5999, and a Toyota for $8499. What was the total value of the cars Harris sold that day?

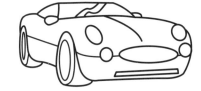

Emmie is given $20 for a birthday present and spends $18.12 on clothes. How much does Emmie have left?

A house on Middle Brook Street costs $285 000.
The house next door is smaller and costs $228 000.
What is the difference in the costs?

A large sack of potatoes costs $12.56.
A smaller sack is half the price of the large sack.
How much does the smaller sack cost?

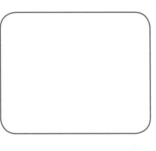

Use the box to show your work if needed.

Gas costs $1.30 per litre. Donny's dad puts
20 litres of gas in the car. How much will
Donny's dad have to pay for the gas?

The highway route between Fredericton and
Moncton is 170 kilometres. A route avoiding
the highway is 196.8 kilometres. How much
shorter is the highway route?

Rashid discovers that one-fifth of the strawberries
in a pack are rotten. The pack contains 75 strawberries.
How many strawberries are not rotten?

Mary measures the growth of a tomato plant.
The plant grows 8 centimetres every week.
How many weeks will it take for the plant to
grow to 104 centimetres?

Nadia measures the distance she has to walk to school.
She walks 950 metres to school. How many metres
will Nadia walk in five days?

A doctor sees one patient every seven minutes.
How long will it take for the doctor to see
25 patients? (Give your answer in hours
and minutes.)

These are the amounts collected at a church in one month.

$213.78 $197.56 $202.67 $184.26

What was the total amount collected in the month?

At the end of the year, each person owes $1250 in taxes to the government. Each person has the following amounts in their savings.

Sean has $12 600   Darius has $9423   Emmie has $10 571

How much will each person have left after paying taxes?

Sean   Darius   Emmie

Write the factors of each number.

32

64

Circle the numbers that are multiples of 12.   21   78

                              50   60

24   90

        110   120   20   132

These are times tables questions given to Jonas in a test. Jonas has written his answers.
Put a smiley face (☺) if Jonas has written the correct answer.
If the answer is wrong, then put a (✗).

6 x 8 = 48   3 x 12 =36   5 x 9 = 54   7 x 8 = 54

6 x 7 = 42   9 x 6 = 45   8 x 9 = 72   12 x 7 = 77

John thinks of a number and then multiplies it by 3.
He adds 6 to the new number and the result is 21.
What number did John start with?

What is the remainder in each division problem?

27 divided by 2

32 divided by 3

60 divided by 8

75 divided by 10

40 divided by 6

49 divided by 9

---

9 walkers each travelled
777 kilometres. What is
the total distance the
9 walkers travelled?

Write the answers.

$$\begin{array}{r} 8.67 \\ + 4.88 \\ \hline \end{array}$$

$$\begin{array}{r} 12.45 \\ + 17.97 \\ \hline \end{array}$$

$$\begin{array}{r} 9.78 \\ + 12.06 \\ \hline \end{array}$$

A storekeeper makes $1312.86 in one day and
then pays his assistant $219.90 for his wages.
How much will the storekeeper have left after
he pays his assistant?

★ Reading schedules

Look at this school schedule.

	Period 1	Period 2	Period 3	Lunch	Period 4	Period 5	Period 6
Monday	Math	Math	Science		English	PE	Social Studies
Tuesday	English	English	Social Studies		Music	Art	Art
Wednesday	Math	Science	Science		PE	English	English
Thursday	Math	English	English		Computer Projects	Computer Projects	Social Studies
Friday	Math	Math	Science		English	Library	Library

Write the answers.

On which days is Science taught?

....

How many periods of Math are taught during the week?

....

How many different subjects are taught during the week?

....

On which day are both Social Studies and Science taught?

....

On which days is PE?

....

Only one subject takes place every day. What subject is that?

....

Which subject is taught for only one period during the week?

....

Which lessons take place during the 6th period?

....

Use the box to show your work if needed.

 A plane journey between London, England and Halifax takes 6 hours 35 minutes. If the plane leaves London at 9:35 a.m., what time will it arrive in Halifax?

Sophie has to go shopping with her mother. They go shopping at 11:15 a.m. and return at 3:45 p.m. How long did the shopping take?

....

 A railway station clock says the time is 3:07 p.m. The clock is 10 minutes fast. What is the actual time?

A bricklayer can lay 180 bricks in one hour. How many bricks will the bricklayer lay in eight hours?

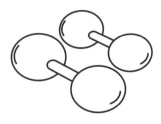 Rashid takes 35 minutes to complete a quarter of his exercises. How long will it take Rashid to complete all his exercises? (Give the answer in hours and minutes.)

....

Lucy and Darius go on a boat trip around Georgian Bay. The trip lasts one and a half hours. If the trip begins at 2:45 p.m., what time will it finish?

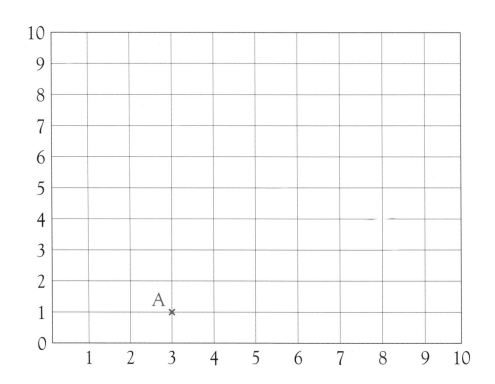

Mark the points A at (3,1) and B at (7,1).
Join A and B with a straight line.
What are the coordinates of the point
halfway between A and B?

Mark the point C at (3,9).
Join A and C with a straight line.
What are the coordinates of the halfway
point between A and C?

Join the points C and B with a straight line.
What kind of triangle have you drawn?

....

Mark the points D at (5,7) and E at (7,7).
Join D and E with a straight line.
What are the coordinates of the halfway
point between D and E?

Mark the point F at (6,3).
Join F to D with a straight line.
Join F to E with a straight line.
What kind of triangle have you drawn?

....

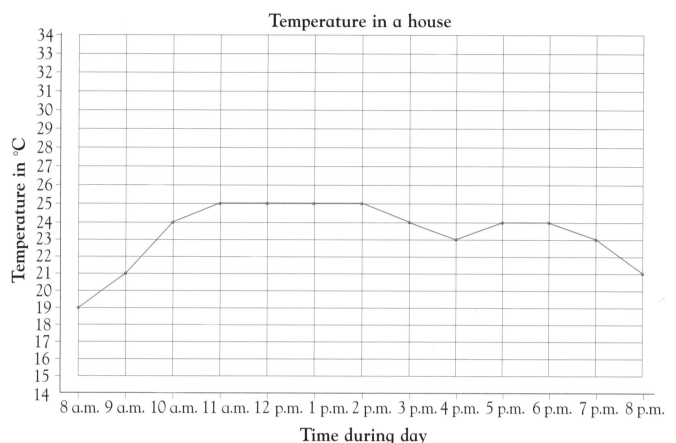

Temperature in a house

Look at the graph and then answer these questions.

What is the coldest temperature in the house?

What is the range of the temperatures?

What is the warmest temperature in the house?

For how long is the temperature at the maximum?

Between which hours does the temperature drop by 2°C?

Between which hours does the temperature rise the quickest?

What is the temperature difference between 8 a.m. and 8 p.m.?

How much does the temperature rise between 10 a.m. and 11 a.m.?

★ | Using data

Children from three grades were asked to vote for their favourite breakfast cereal.

Breakfast cereals	Frequency	Total
Maple Loops	𝍷𝍷𝍷𝍷 𝍷𝍷𝍷𝍷 𝍷𝍷𝍷𝍷 𝍷𝍷	17
Weetynuts	𝍷𝍷𝍷𝍷 𝍷𝍷𝍷𝍷 𝍷𝍷𝍷𝍷 𝍷𝍷𝍷𝍷 𝍷𝍷𝍷𝍷 𝍷	
Corndunks	𝍷𝍷𝍷𝍷 𝍷𝍷𝍷𝍷 𝍷𝍷𝍷𝍷 𝍷𝍷𝍷𝍷 𝍷𝍷𝍷𝍷	
Grainygrit	𝍷𝍷𝍷𝍷 𝍷𝍷𝍷	
Coconutty	𝍷𝍷𝍷𝍷 𝍷𝍷𝍷𝍷 𝍷𝍷𝍷𝍷	

The frequency table shows the results. Look at the frequency table and then answer the questions. Complete the total column.

Which was the most popular breakfast cereal?   ....

What was the mean number of votes?
(**Hint**: Mean means the average.)

What is the median amount of votes?
(**Hint**: Median means the middle number.)

How many more votes did Weetynuts have than Maple Loops?

What was the range of the votes?
(**Hint**: Range means the difference between the most and the least.)

What is the mode of each row?
(**Hint**: Mode means the number used most.)

7	28	14	35	7	28	28	35

$\frac{1}{2}$	$\frac{1}{3}$	$\frac{1}{2}$	$\frac{1}{3}$	$\frac{1}{4}$	$\frac{1}{3}$	$\frac{1}{3}$	$\frac{1}{4}$

Calculate the perimeter of each shape.

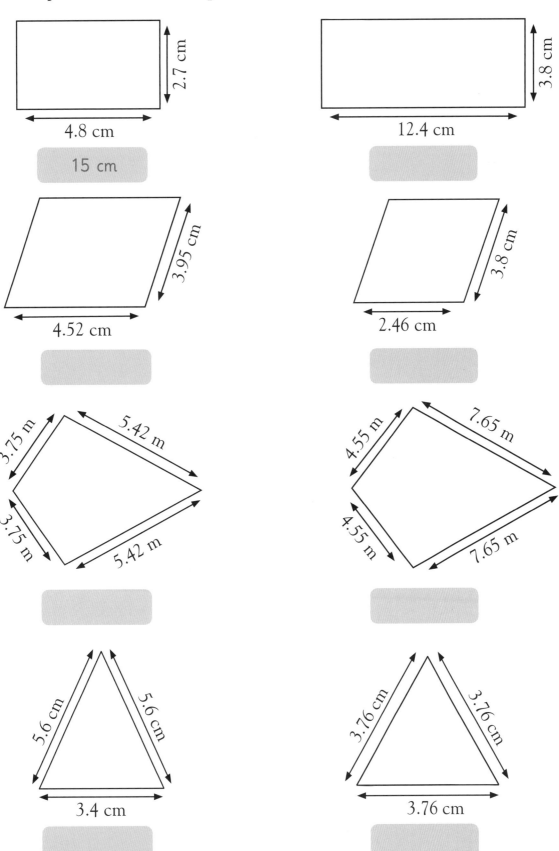

2.7 cm

4.8 cm

15 cm

3.8 cm

12.4 cm

3.95 cm

4.52 cm

3.8 cm

2.46 cm

3.75 m   5.42 m

3.75 m   5.42 m

4.55 m   7.65 m

4.55 m   7.65 m

5.6 cm   5.6 cm

3.4 cm

3.76 cm   3.76 cm

3.76 cm

★ Square numbers

Calculate the area of each square. You may use a calculator.
Round your answers to the nearest hundredth place.

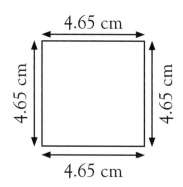

21.62 cm²

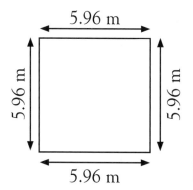

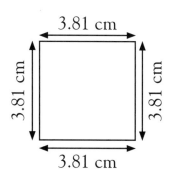

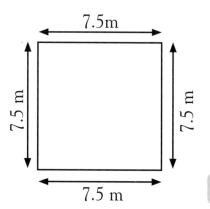

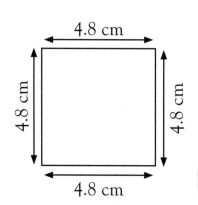

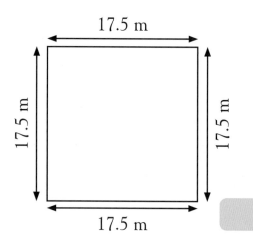

Work out each of these.

15 x 15 =

13 x 13 =

14 x 14 =

16 x 16 =

20 x 20 =

25 x 25 =

Find the area of each shape.

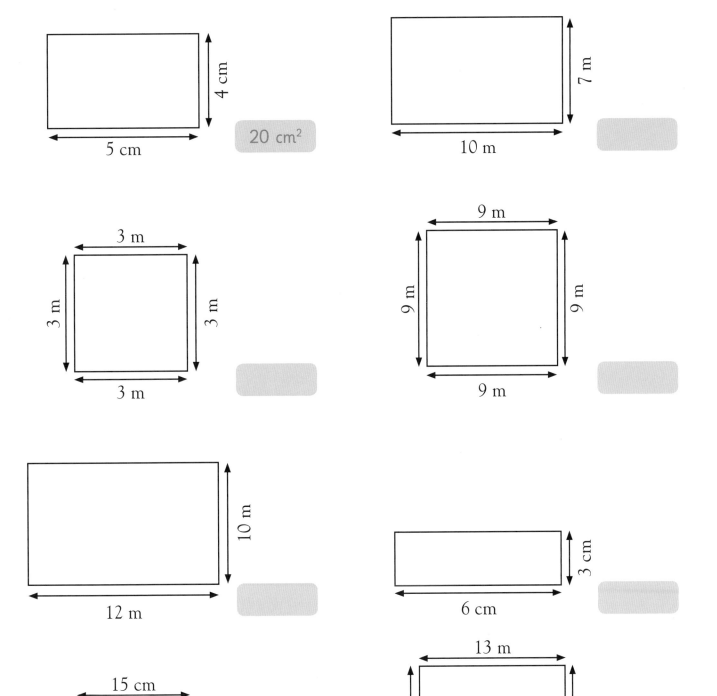

4 cm

5 cm

20 cm²

7 m

10 m

3 m

3 m

3 m

3 m

9 m

9 m

9 m

9 m

10 m

12 m

3 cm

6 cm

15 cm

15 cm

15 cm

15 cm

13 m

13 m

13 m

13 m

Recognizing angles

Write whether these angles are acute, right, obtuse, or reflex.
(**Hint**: Reflex angles are larger than 180° but less than 360°).

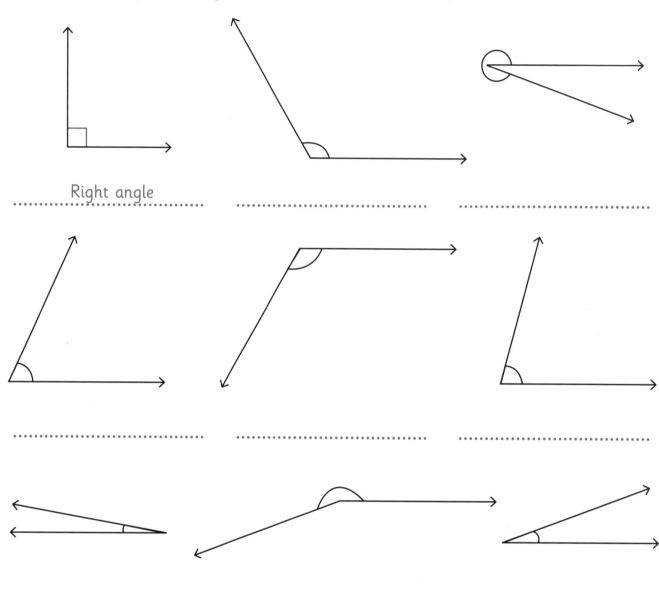

Right angle

....

....

....

Draw an acute angle.

Draw an obtuse angle.

Use a protractor to measure each angle.

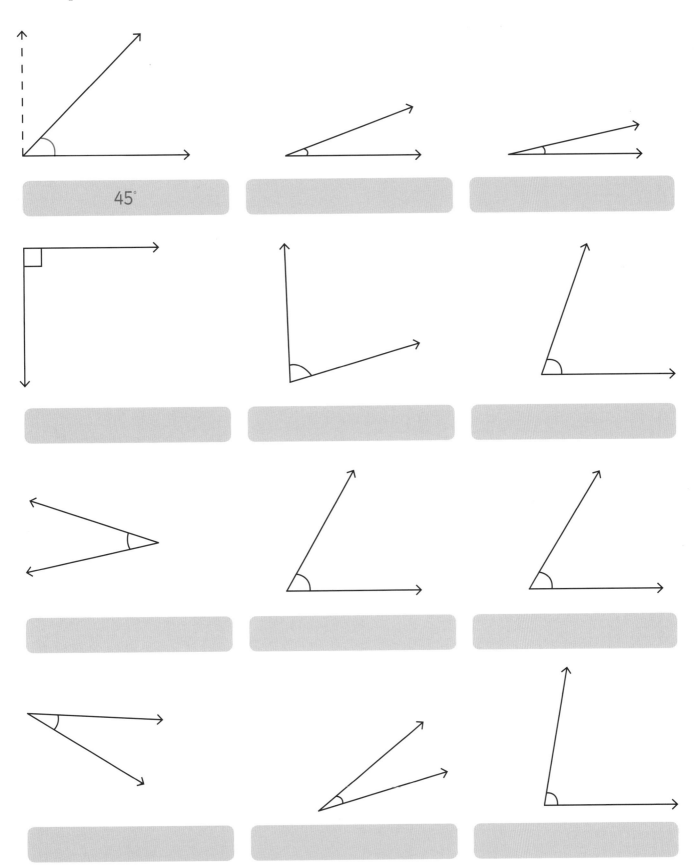

45°

★ 3-D shapes

Name each shape and give the information.

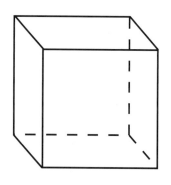

Name ....Cube....

Number
of faces ...6...

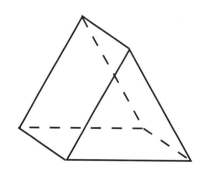

Name ....

Number
of faces ....

Name ....

Number
of bases ....

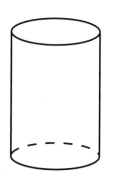

Name ....

Number
of bases ....

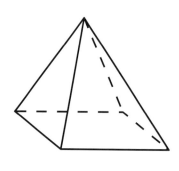

Name ....

Number
of faces ....

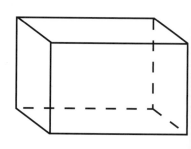

Name ....

Number
of faces ....

Draw a cube of your own choice.

Draw a cylinder of your own choice.

Draw the 3-D shape in the box.

I am made from four triangles. All my triangles are the same size. What is my name?

...............Triangle-based pyramid...............

I am made from four triangles and one square. I might be Egyptian! What is my name?

....

I am made from two circles the same size as each other and a curved middle piece. What is my name?

....

I have six faces which are all squares. What is my name?

....

I just have one curved surface. What is my name?

....

Keeping skills sharp

These two clocks show times in the morning. What is the difference between them?

....

Look at the lengths of these pieces of wood.

   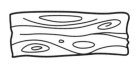 

7 cm   9 cm   20 cm   15 cm   9 cm

What is the mean length?

What is the median length?

What is the mode length?

What is the perimeter of this school playground?

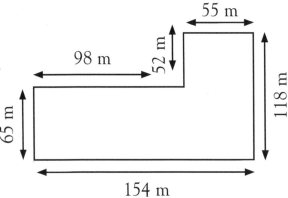

Circle the numbers that are not perfect squares.

16   20   40   60   36   49   100   88   4

Keeping skills sharp

Draw one of each type of angle. You do not need to use a protractor but make sure you mark the angle correctly.

Right angle | Acute angle | Obtuse angle | Reflex angle

Use a protractor to carefully measure each angle.

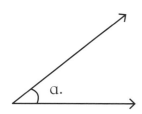

a.

b.

Use a protractor to carefully draw these angles.

67°   45°

Mark the points on this grid.

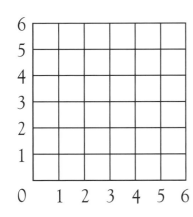

A = (3,5)   B = (5,0)

C = (4, $1\frac{1}{2}$)   D = (0, $5\frac{1}{2}$)

Certificate

Congratulations to

....

for successfully finishing this book.

WELL DONE!

You're a star.

☆ ☆ ☆ ☆ ☆

Date

....

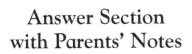

Answer Section with Parents' Notes

Grade 5
ages 10–11
Workbook

This section provides answers to all the activities in the book. These pages will enable you to mark your children's work, or they can be used by your children if they prefer to do their own marking.

The notes for each page help to explain common errors and problems and, where appropriate, indicate the kind of practice needed to ensure that your children understand where and how they have made errors.

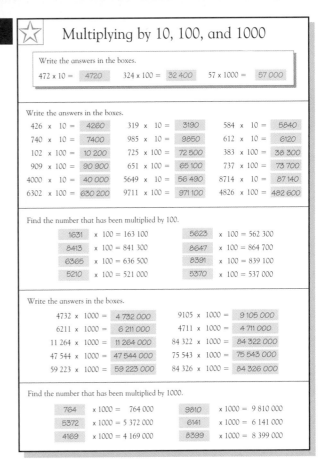

2 ⭐ Multiplying by 10, 100, and 1000

Write the answers in the boxes.

472 x 10 = 4720   324 x 100 = 32 400   57 x 1000 = 57 000

Write the answers in the boxes.

426 x 10 = 4260	319 x 10 = 3190	584 x 10 = 5840
740 x 10 = 7400	985 x 10 = 9850	612 x 10 = 6120
102 x 100 = 10 200	725 x 100 = 72 500	383 x 100 = 38 300
909 x 100 = 90 900	651 x 100 = 65 100	737 x 100 = 73 700
4000 x 10 = 40 000	5649 x 10 = 56 490	8714 x 10 = 87 140
6302 x 100 = 630 200	9711 x 100 = 971 100	4826 x 100 = 482 600

Find the number that has been multiplied by 100.

1631 x 100 = 163 100   5623 x 100 = 562 300
8413 x 100 = 841 300   8647 x 100 = 864 700
6365 x 100 = 636 500   8391 x 100 = 839 100
5210 x 100 = 521 000   5370 x 100 = 537 000

Write the answers in the boxes.

4732 x 1000 = 4 732 000   9105 x 1000 = 9 105 000
6211 x 1000 = 6 211 000   4711 x 1000 = 4 711 000
11 264 x 1000 = 11 264 000   84 322 x 1000 = 84 322 000
47 544 x 1000 = 47 544 000   75 543 x 1000 = 75 543 000
59 223 x 1000 = 59 223 000   84 326 x 1000 = 84 326 000

Find the number that has been multiplied by 1000.

764 x 1000 = 764 000   9810 x 1000 = 9 810 000
5372 x 1000 = 5 372 000   6141 x 1000 = 6 141 000
4169 x 1000 = 4 169 000   8399 x 1000 = 8 399 000

Children should realize that multiplying by 10, 100, or 1000 is the same as adding one, two, or three zeros. In the second and last sections, the child will need to divide the answer to find the number that has been multiplied.

---

3 The simplest form of fractions ⭐

Make these fractions equivalent by putting a number in the box.

$\frac{70}{100} = \frac{7}{10}$ $\frac{4}{12} = \frac{1}{3}$

Make these fractions equivalent by putting a number in each box.

$\frac{30}{100} = \frac{3}{10}$	$\frac{8}{100} = \frac{2}{25}$	$\frac{40}{100} = \frac{4}{10}$	$\frac{15}{100} = \frac{3}{20}$
$\frac{5}{20} = \frac{1}{4}$	$\frac{25}{100} = \frac{1}{4}$	$\frac{12}{60} = \frac{1}{5}$	$\frac{8}{20} = \frac{2}{5}$
$\frac{16}{40} = \frac{2}{5}$	$\frac{2}{6} = \frac{1}{3}$	$\frac{10}{60} = \frac{1}{6}$	$\frac{2}{12} = \frac{1}{6}$
$\frac{9}{18} = \frac{1}{2}$	$\frac{10}{18} = \frac{5}{9}$	$\frac{4}{24} = \frac{1}{6}$	$\frac{7}{28} = \frac{1}{4}$
$\frac{4}{6} = \frac{2}{3}$	$\frac{6}{10} = \frac{3}{5}$	$\frac{9}{15} = \frac{3}{5}$	$\frac{8}{12} = \frac{2}{3}$
$\frac{18}{20} = \frac{9}{10}$	$\frac{21}{28} = \frac{3}{4}$	$\frac{6}{8} = \frac{3}{4}$	$\frac{5}{50} = \frac{1}{10}$
$\frac{15}{25} = \frac{3}{5}$	$\frac{4}{16} = \frac{1}{4}$	$\frac{12}{20} = \frac{3}{5}$	$\frac{12}{18} = \frac{2}{3}$
$\frac{3}{15} = \frac{1}{5}$	$\frac{9}{36} = \frac{1}{4}$	$\frac{9}{27} = \frac{1}{3}$	$\frac{30}{50} = \frac{3}{5}$

Make these rows of fractions equivalent by putting a number in each box.

$\frac{1}{9} = \frac{2}{18} = \frac{3}{27} = \frac{4}{36} = \frac{5}{45} = \frac{6}{54}$

$\frac{1}{10} = \frac{2}{20} = \frac{3}{30} = \frac{4}{40} = \frac{5}{50} = \frac{6}{60}$

$\frac{3}{5} = \frac{12}{20} = \frac{15}{25} = \frac{18}{30} = \frac{21}{35} = \frac{24}{40}$

$\frac{5}{6} = \frac{10}{12} = \frac{15}{18} = \frac{20}{24} = \frac{25}{30} = \frac{30}{36}$

$\frac{1}{7} = \frac{2}{14} = \frac{3}{21} = \frac{4}{28} = \frac{5}{35} = \frac{6}{42}$

$\frac{3}{11} = \frac{12}{44} = \frac{21}{77} = \frac{27}{99} = \frac{30}{110} = \frac{33}{121}$

If children have problems with this page, explain to them that fractions remain the same as long as you multiply or divide the numerator and denominator by the same number.

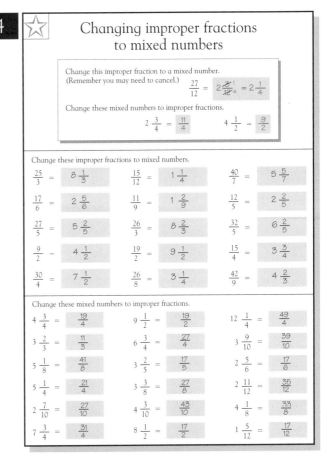

4 ⭐ Changing improper fractions to mixed numbers

Change this improper fraction to a mixed number. (Remember you may need to cancel.) $\frac{27}{12} = 2\frac{3}{12}^{1}_{4} = 2\frac{1}{4}$

Change these mixed numbers to improper fractions.

$2\frac{3}{4} = \frac{11}{4}$ $4\frac{1}{2} = \frac{9}{2}$

Change these improper fractions to mixed numbers.

$\frac{25}{3} = 8\frac{1}{3}$	$\frac{15}{12} = 1\frac{1}{4}$	$\frac{40}{7} = 5\frac{5}{7}$
$\frac{17}{6} = 2\frac{5}{6}$	$\frac{11}{9} = 1\frac{2}{9}$	$\frac{12}{5} = 2\frac{2}{5}$
$\frac{27}{5} = 5\frac{2}{5}$	$\frac{26}{3} = 8\frac{2}{3}$	$\frac{32}{5} = 6\frac{2}{5}$
$\frac{9}{2} = 4\frac{1}{2}$	$\frac{19}{2} = 9\frac{1}{2}$	$\frac{15}{4} = 3\frac{3}{4}$
$\frac{30}{4} = 7\frac{1}{2}$	$\frac{26}{8} = 3\frac{1}{4}$	$\frac{42}{9} = 4\frac{2}{3}$

Change these mixed numbers to improper fractions.

$4\frac{3}{4} = \frac{19}{4}$	$9\frac{1}{2} = \frac{19}{2}$	$12\frac{1}{4} = \frac{49}{4}$
$3\frac{2}{3} = \frac{11}{3}$	$6\frac{3}{4} = \frac{27}{4}$	$3\frac{9}{10} = \frac{39}{10}$
$5\frac{1}{8} = \frac{41}{8}$	$3\frac{2}{5} = \frac{17}{5}$	$2\frac{5}{6} = \frac{17}{6}$
$5\frac{1}{4} = \frac{21}{4}$	$3\frac{3}{8} = \frac{27}{8}$	$2\frac{11}{12} = \frac{35}{12}$
$2\frac{7}{10} = \frac{27}{10}$	$4\frac{3}{10} = \frac{43}{10}$	$4\frac{1}{8} = \frac{33}{8}$
$7\frac{3}{4} = \frac{31}{4}$	$8\frac{1}{2} = \frac{17}{2}$	$1\frac{5}{12} = \frac{17}{12}$

In the first part, children should see that you can divide the denominator by the numerator and place the remainder over the denominator. Use card circles cut into equal parts to reinforce the idea, e.g. how many whole circles can you make from 17 quarter circles?

Rounding decimals ☆

Write these decimals to the nearest tenth.

6.23 is 6.2   6.27 is 6.3

If the second decimal place is a 5, we round up the first decimal place to the next larger number.

6.25 is 6.3

Write these decimals to the nearest tenth.

9.21 is 9.2	4.38 is 4.4	2.47 is 2.5
3.48 is 3.5	8.17 is 8.2	6.28 is 6.3
7.14 is 7.1	3.91 is 3.9	2.56 is 2.6
8.41 is 8.4	2.36 is 2.4	1.53 is 1.5

Write these decimals to the nearest tenth.

9.35 is 9.4	8.71 is 8.7	6.05 is 6.1
1.19 is 1.2	3.65 is 3.7	4.21 is 4.2
8.55 is 8.6	7.35 is 7.4	9.14 is 9.1
6.83 is 6.8	2.15 is 2.2	6.34 is 6.3

Write these decimals to the nearest tenth.

25.61 is 25.6	14.35 is 14.4	11.24 is 11.2
16.85 is 16.9	24.34 is 24.3	71.36 is 71.4
26.85 is 26.9	11.54 is 11.5	37.25 is 37.3
92.42 is 92.4	95.65 is 95.7	27.36 is 27.4
45.17 is 45.2	36.75 is 36.8	22.05 is 22.1

If children experience difficulties, point out that the significant digit to look at is in the second decimal place. The use of a number line may be helpful where the child is still unsure. In the second section, the concept of .05 is introduced. This must be rounded up.

6

☆ Adding with different numbers of digits

Find the total for each problem.

```
   432        11
  + 43       176
  ----      + 97
   475       ----
             273
```

Remember to regroup if you need to.

Find the total for each problem.

```
  148      271      371      938
 + 31     + 17     + 24     + 31
 ----     ----     ----     ----
  179      288      395      969

  942      747      633      101
 + 26     + 34     + 43     + 75
 ----     ----     ----     ----
  968      781      676      176
```

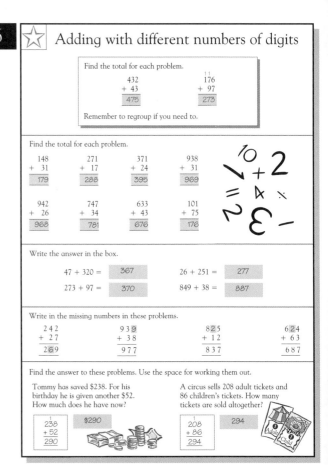

Write the answer in the box.

47 + 320 = 367   26 + 251 = 277

273 + 97 = 370   849 + 38 = 887

Write in the missing numbers in these problems.

```
  242      939      825      624
 + 27     + 38     + 12     + 63
 ----     ----     ----     ----
  269      977      837      687
```

Find the answer to these problems. Use the space for working them out.

Tommy has saved $238. For his birthday he is given another $52. How much does he have now?

```
  238
 + 52       $290
 ----
  290
```

A circus sells 208 adult tickets and 86 children's tickets. How many tickets are sold altogether?

```
  1
  208       294
 + 86
 ----
  294
```

This page and the next should be straightforward. Any errors will probably be due to a failure to carry, or particularly in the second section, may occur where children have added digits with different place values.

7

Adding with different numbers of digits ☆

Work out the answer to each problem.

```
   1 11              1 11
     987            2 767
 + 423 123        + 12 844
 ---------        --------
   424 110          15 611
```

Remember to regroup if you need to.

Work out the answer to each problem.

```
  3 587      8 537 227         27
+ 17 628    +  86 518      + 9964
--------    ---------      ------
  21 215     8 623 745       9 991

    436       387 177       6 770
+ 12 844    +   8 381    + 772 142
--------    ---------    --------
  13 280       395 558     778 912
```

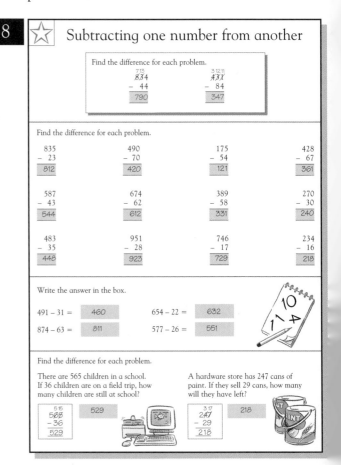

Write the answer in the box.

6 437 501 + 913 548 = 7 351 049

101 876 + 62 725 = 164 601

Write in the missing numbers in these sums.

```
  5 387         3 2 1        6752
 +  849       + 8 1 8 9     + 909
 ------        -------      -----
  6 236          8 5 1 0     7661
```

Work out the answer to the problem. Use the space for working it out.

Jennifer has 1342 stamps in her collection. Dennis has 742. How many do they have altogether?

```
  1342
 + 742       2084
 -----
  2084
```

For problems in which the two numbers are not aligned vertically, ensure that children line up the digits in the ones place on the right side of the numbers. The most common error is not aligning the correct places.

☆ Subtracting one number from another

Find the difference for each problem.

```
   7 13          3 12 11
   834           431
 -  44          - 84
 ----           ----
   790           347
```

Find the difference for each problem.

```
  835      490      175      428
 - 23     - 70     - 54     - 67
 ----     ----     ----     ----
  812      420      121      361

  587      674      389      270
 - 43     - 62     - 58     - 30
 ----     ----     ----     ----
  544      612      331      240

  483      951      746      234
 - 35     - 28     - 17     - 16
 ----     ----     ----     ----
  448      923      729      218
```

Write the answer in the box.

491 – 31 = 460   654 – 22 = 632

874 – 63 = 811   577 – 26 = 551

Find the difference for each problem.

There are 565 children in a school. If 36 children are on a field trip, how many children are still at school?

```
  5 15
  565       529
 - 36
 ----
  529
```

A hardware store has 247 cans of paint. If they sell 29 cans, how many will they have left?

```
  3 17
  247       218
 - 29
 ----
  218
```

The most likely errors to occur in the first section will involve subtractions where a larger digit has to taken away from a smaller digit. Children often take the smaller digit that is on the top away from the larger digit on the bottom.

Subtracting one number from another ⭐

Work out the answer to each problem.

```
  1 16 16 7 15          3 12
  27 6̸8̸5̸          47 4̸2̸3
-  8 726          -  5 351
  18 959            42 072
```

Work out the answer to each problem.

```
  68 231        62 411        11 684        37 481
-  3 846      - 47 566      -  2 845      - 19 804
  64 385        14 845         8 839        17 677

   7965        92 112        67 444         8818
-  3976      - 46 489      - 29 545      -  7465
   3989        45 623        37 899         1353

  52 812         2522          8529          6387
- 37 341       - 1176        - 5892        - 2798
  15 471         1346          2637          3589
```

Write the answer in the box.

55 562 – 24 871 = 30 691

9118 – 8467 = 651

Work out the answer to the problem. Use the space for working it out.

2826 people went to see a rock concert. 135 had to leave early to catch their train. How many were left at the end?

```
  7 12
  2̸8̸2̸6      2691
-  135
  2691
```

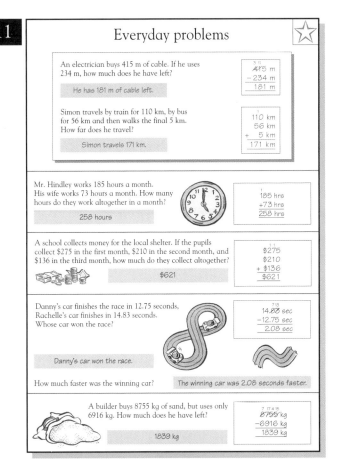

See the notes for page 7.

10

Real-life problems

Toby has $525.95 in the bank and he spends $146.37 on his vacation. How much does he have left?

Toby has $379.58 left.

```
  4 11 5 8 15
  $5̸2̸5̸.9̸5̸
- $146.37
  $379.58
```

A rally driver drives 183 km on the first day of a race and 147 km on the second day. How many kilometres does he travel in the two days?

He drives 330 kilometres.

```
    183 km
  + 147 km
    330 km
```

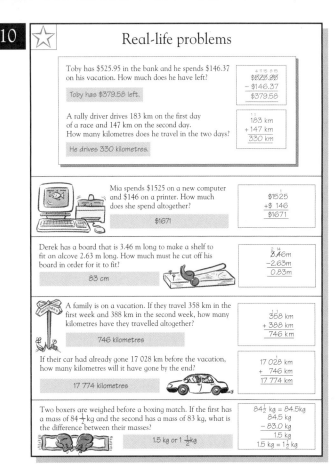

Mia spends $1525 on a new computer and $146 on a printer. How much does she spend altogether?

$1671

```
    1
   $1525
+ $  146
   $1671
```

Derek has a board that is 3.46 m long to make a shelf to fit an alcove 2.63 m long. How much must he cut off his board in order for it to fit?

83 cm

```
  2 14
  3̸.4̸6 m
- 2.63 m
  0.83 m
```

A family is on a vacation. If they travel 358 km in the first week and 388 km in the second week, how many kilometres have they travelled altogether?

746 kilometres

```
  1 1
   358 km
+  388 km
   746 km
```

If their car had already gone 17 028 km before the vacation, how many kilometres will it have gone by the end?

17 774 kilometres

```
  17 028 km
+    746 km
  17 774 km
```

Two boxers are weighed before a boxing match. If the first has a mass of 84½ kg and the second has a mass of 83 kg, what is the difference between their masses?

1.5 kg or 1½ kg

```
  84½ kg = 84.5 kg
           84.5 kg
         - 83.0 kg
            1.5 kg
   1.5 kg = 1½ kg
```

In this page and the following two pages children can apply the skills of addition and subtraction to real-life problems, using various units of measurement. If the child is unsure which operation to use, discuss whether the answer will be larger or smaller.

11

Everyday problems ⭐

An electrician buys 415 m of cable. If he uses 234 m, how much does he have left?

He has 181 m of cable left.

```
  3 11
  4̸1̸5 m
- 234 m
  181 m
```

Simon travels by train for 110 km, by bus for 56 km and then walks the final 5 km. How far does he travel?

Simon travels 171 km.

```
  110 km
   56 km
+   5 km
  171 km
```

Mr. Hindley works 185 hours a month. His wife works 73 hours a month. How many hours do they work altogether in a month?

258 hours

```
  1
  185 hrs
+ 73 hrs
  258 hrs
```

A school collects money for the local shelter. If the pupils collect $275 in the first month, $210 in the second month, and $136 in the third month, how much do they collect altogether?

$621

```
  1 1
  $275
  $210
+ $136
  $621
```

Danny's car finishes the race in 12.75 seconds, Rachelle's car finishes in 14.83 seconds. Whose car won the race?

Danny's car won the race.

```
  7 13
  14.8̸3̸ sec
- 12.75 sec
   2.08 sec
```

How much faster was the winning car?

The winning car was 2.08 seconds faster.

A builder buys 8755 kg of sand, but uses only 6916 kg. How much does he have left?

1839 kg

```
  7 17 4 15
  8̸7̸5̸5̸ kg
- 6916 kg
  1839 kg
```

See the notes for page 10. Point out that an answer that will be larger will require addition, while one that will be smaller will require subtraction.

Everyday problems

Rudy, Andrew, and Rachelle want to put their money together to buy a present for their brother. If Rudy gives $12.50, Andrew gives $14.75, and Rachelle gives $15.25, how much will they have to spend?

They will have $42.50 to spend.

```
   1 1  1
  $12.50
  $14.75
+ $15.25
  $42.50
```

A store has 130 kg of potatoes and sells 80 kg. How much does it have left?

The store has 50 kg left.

```
   13
  1̸30 kg
-  80 kg
   50 kg
```

A bakery orders 145 kg of sugar, 565 kg of salt, and 926 kg of butter. What is the total mass of the order?

The total weight is 1636 kg.

```
  1 1
  145 kg
  565 kg
+ 926 kg
  1636 kg
```

Mr. Jean-Paul travelled in a limo to the airport. After he paid a fare of $65, he had $125 left. How much money did he start with?

He started with $190.

```
   1
  $125
+ $ 65
  $190
```

A vacation in Florida costs $394. A vacation in Majorca costs $876. How much cheaper is the Florida vacation?

The Florida vacation is $482 cheaper.

```
  7 17
  $8̸7̸6
- $394
  $482
```

Chamique is saving up to buy a guitar that costs $159.99. If she already has $65.37, how much more does she need?

She needs $94.62 more.

```
  $159.99
- $ 65.37
  $ 94.62
```

Mr. Lorenzo's garden is 10 m long and 8 m wide. How much fence does he need to surround all four sides?

He needs 36 m of fence.

```
  10 m
  10 m
   8 m
+  8 m
  36 m
```

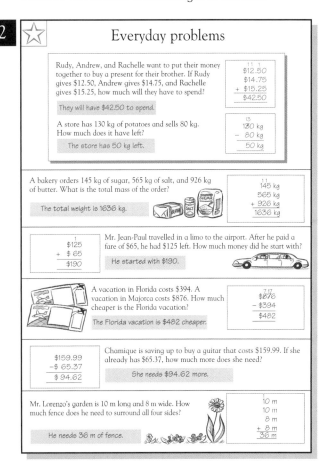

See the notes for pages 10 and 11.

Decimal addition

Write in the answers to these problems.

$$47.15 + 19.36 = 66.51 \qquad 43.99 + 12.76 = 56.75$$

Write the answer to each problem.

53.72 +77.92 = **131.64**	84.17 +68.21 = **152.38**	29.36 +66.84 = **96.20**	23.56 +79.14 = **102.70**	62.49 +18.75 = **81.24**
35.67 +12.99 = **48.66**	29.88 +43.02 = **72.90**	67.39 +81.70 = **149.09**	49.32 +14.95 = **64.27**	27.22 +38.84 = **66.06**

Write the answer to each problem.

76.30 +22.97 = **99.27**	44.29 +11.04 = **55.33**	81.97 +69.14 = **151.11**	29.86 +76.33 = **106.19**	68.25 +84.36 = **152.61**
83.90 +30.24 = **114.14**	45.83 +45.71 = **91.54**	52.17 +90.21 = **142.38**	84.93 +29.37 = **114.30**	72.83 +41.16 = **113.99**

Write the answer to each problem.

$$37.89 + 82.15 = 120.04 \qquad 32.44 + 21.88 = 54.32 \qquad 37.19 + 28.24 = 65.43$$
$$68.67 + 29.82 = 98.49 \qquad 21.99 + 79.32 = 101.31 \qquad 52.45 + 34.58 = 87.03$$
$$84.77 + 39.12 = 123.89 \qquad 63.84 + 29.81 = 93.65 \qquad 34.43 + 25.64 = 60.07$$
$$33.97 + 24.62 = 58.59 \qquad 76.39 + 43.78 = 120.17 \qquad 52.38 + 38.43 = 90.81$$

This page and the next page should follow on from earlier addition work. On these two pages, children are dealing with two decimal places. The most likely mistakes will be errors involving carrying, or in the third section, where they are working horizontally.

14

Decimal addition

Write the sum for each problem.

$$296.48 + 131.70 = 428.18 \qquad 73.00 + 269.23 = 342.23$$

Write the sum for each problem.

91.83 + 37.84 = **129.67**	64.71 + 21.2 = **85.91**	32.045 + 4.99 = **37.035**	306 + 44.24 = **350.24**
71.932 + 55.26 = **127.192**	842.01 + 11.842 = **853.852**	675.82 +105 = **780.82**	37.82 +399.71 = **437.53**
65.24 + 605.27 = **670.51**	178.935 +599.41 = **778.345**	184.70 +372.81 = **557.51**	443.27 + 75 = **518.27**
563 +413.98 = **976.98**	703.95 + 85.11 = **789.06**	825.36 +249.857 = **1075.217**	529.3 +482.56 = **1011.86**

Write the sum for each problem.

$$421 + 136.25 = 557.25 \qquad 92.31 + 241.73 = 334.04$$
$$501.8 + 361.93 = 863.73 \qquad 558.32 + 137.945 = 696.265$$
$$27 + 142.07 = 169.07 \qquad 75.31 + 293.33 = 368.64$$
$$153.3 + 182.02 = 335.32 \qquad 491.445 + 105.37 = 596.815$$
$$253.71 + 62 = 315.71 \qquad 829.2 + 63.74 = 892.94$$

Watch out for misalignment when children work on horizontal subtractions.

Decimal subtraction

Write the difference for each problem.

$$59.76 - 21.47 = 38.29 \qquad 57.18 - 22.09 = 35.09$$

Write the difference for each problem.

64.92 − 26.35 = **38.57**	64.21 − 16.02 = **48.19**	73.71 −19.24 = **54.47**	92.63 − 67.14 = **25.49**
45.76 − 16.18 = **29.58**	73.52 −39.27 = **34.25**	98.98 −39.19 = **59.79**	53.58 − 14.39 = **39.19**
94.87 − 65.28 = **29.59**	21.74 − 12.1 = **9.64**	62.35 −13.16 = **49.19**	81.94 − 28.15 = **53.79**
62.95 − 33.37 = **29.58**	81.42 −25.04 = **56.38**	48.52 − 14.49 = **34.03**	61.55 − 13.26 = **48.29**

Write the difference for each problem.

$$51.52 - 12.13 = 39.39 \qquad 72.41 - 23.18 = 49.23$$
$$91.91 - 22.22 = 69.69 \qquad 53.84 - 19.65 = 34.19$$
$$41.82 - 18.13 = 23.69 \qquad 51.61 - 23.14 = 28.47$$
$$83.91 - 14.73 = 69.18 \qquad 64.65 - 37.26 = 27.39$$
$$53.21 - 35.12 = 18.09 \qquad 77.31 - 28.15 = 49.16$$

On this page and the next two pages, the most likely errors will result from a failure to use decomposition where necessary (see notes for pages 8 and 9). Watch out for misalignment when children work on horizontal subtractions.

Decimal subtraction

Write the difference for each problem.

$$68.17 - 11.40 = 56.77 \qquad 39.20 - 13.15 = 26.05$$

Work out the difference for each problem.

87.23 − 24.4 = **62.83**	95.15 − 31.356 = **63.794**	66.37 −21.9 = **44.47**	85 − 26.32 = **58.68**
72.28 − 1.3 = **70.98**	63.14 −32 = **31.14**	99.235 −33.70 = **65.535**	62.1 −29.34 = **32.76**
77.3 −24.42 = **52.88**	55.492 −27.66 = **27.832**	68 − 31.5 = **36.5**	35.612 −13.207 = **22.405**
82.35 − 23.40 = **58.95**	63.20 −15.36 = **47.84**	53.64 − 23 = **30.64**	35.612 − 26.19 = **9.422**

Write the difference for each problem.

$$63.4 - 24.51 = 38.89 \qquad 92.197 - 63.28 = 28.917$$
$$91.3 - 33 = 58.3 \qquad 41.24 - 14.306 = 26.934$$
$$52.251 - 22.42 = 29.831 \qquad 72.6 - 53.71 = 18.89$$
$$92.84 - 23 = 69.84 \qquad 61.16 - 24.4 = 36.76$$
$$81.815 - 55.90 = 25.915 \qquad 94.31 - 27.406 = 66.904$$

On this page, the most common error will result from not writing the numbers to the same number of decimal places before subtracting.

17

Multiplying larger numbers by ones ☆

Write the product for each problem.

$$\begin{array}{c} \overset{13}{529} \\ \times\ \ 4 \\ \hline 2116 \end{array} \qquad \begin{array}{c} \overset{131}{1273} \\ \times\ \ 5 \\ \hline 6365 \end{array}$$

Write the product for each problem.

724 × 2 = 1448	831 × 3 = 2493	126 × 3 = 378	455 × 4 = 1820
161 × 4 = 644	282 × 5 = 1410	349 × 5 = 1745	253 × 6 = 1518
328 × 6 = 1968	465 × 6 = 2790	105 × 4 = 420	562 × 4 = 2248

Write the product for each problem.

4261 × 3 = 12 783	1582 × 3 = 4746	3612 × 4 = 14 448	4284 × 4 = 17 136
5907 × 5 = 29 535	1263 × 5 = 6315	1303 × 6 = 7818	1467 × 6 = 8802
6521 × 6 = 39 126	8436 × 6 = 50 616	1599 × 6 = 9594	3761 × 6 = 22 566
5837 × 4 = 23 348	6394 × 5 = 31 970	8124 × 6 = 48 744	3914 × 6 = 23 484

Make sure that children understand the convention of multiplication problems, i.e. multiply the ones first, work left, and carry when necessary. This page will generally highlight gaps in knowledge of the 2, 3, 4, 5, and 6 multiplication tables.

18

☆ Multiplying larger numbers by ones

Write the answer to each problem.

$$\begin{array}{c} \overset{14}{417} \\ \times\ \ 7 \\ \hline 2919 \end{array} \qquad \begin{array}{c} \overset{174}{2185} \\ \times\ \ 9 \\ \hline 19\,665 \end{array}$$

Write the answer to each problem.

419 × 7 = 2933	604 × 7 = 4228	715 × 8 = 5720	327 × 7 = 2289
425 × 8 = 3400	171 × 9 = 1539	682 × 8 = 5456	246 × 8 = 1968
436 × 8 = 3488	999 × 9 = 8991	319 × 9 = 2871	581 × 9 = 5229

Work out the answer to each problem.

4331 × 7 = 30 317	2816 × 7 = 19 712	1439 × 8 = 11 512	2617 × 8 = 20 936
3104 × 8 = 24 832	4022 × 8 = 32 176	3212 × 9 = 28 908	2591 × 9 = 23 319
1710 × 9 = 15 390	3002 × 8 = 24 016	2468 × 7 = 17 276	1514 × 8 = 12 112
4624 × 7 = 32 368	2993 × 8 = 23 944	3894 × 8 = 31 152	4361 × 9 = 39 249

Any problems encountered on this page will be similar to those of the previous page. Gaps in the child's knowledge of multiplication tables 7, 8, and 9 will be highlighted here.

19

Real-life multiplication problems ☆

There are 157 apples in a box. How many will there be in three boxes?
$$\overset{12}{157} \times 3 = 471$$ 471 apples

A stamp album can hold 550 stamps. How many stamps will 5 albums hold?
$$\overset{2}{550} \times 5 = 2750$$ 2750 stamps

A train can take 425 passengers. How many can it take in four trips?
$$\overset{12}{425} \times 4 = 1700$$ 1700 passengers

Mr Jenkins puts $256 a month into the bank. How much will he have put in after six months?
$$\overset{33}{256} \times 6 = 1536$$ $1536

A theatre can seat 5524 people. If a play runs for 7 days, what is the maximum number of people who will be able to see it?
$$\overset{312}{5524} \times 7 = 38\,668$$ 38 668 people

A car costs $19 956. How much will it cost a company to buy nine cars for its salespeople?
$$\overset{8855}{19\,956} \times 9 = 179\,604$$ $179 604

Installing a new window for a house costs $435. How much will it cost to install 8 windows of the same size?
$$\overset{24}{435} \times 8 = 3480$$ $3480

An airplane flies at a steady speed of 550 km/h. How far will it travel in 7 hours?
$$\overset{3}{550} \times 7 = 3850$$ 3850 kilometres

This page provides an opportunity for children to apply their skills of multiplication to real-life problems. As with previous multiplication work, gaps in the child's knowledge of multiplication facts will be highlighted here.

☆ Comparing and ordering decimals

Compare the decimals. Which decimal is greater?

2.2 and 3.1   0.45 and 0.6
Line them up vertically.
2.2   0.45
3.1   0.60
3>2, so 3.1>2.2   6>4, so 0.6>0.45

Compare the decimals. Which decimal is greater?

7.9 and 8.1	0.5 and 0.62	3.6 and 0.94	0.4 and 0.67
8.1	0.62	3.6	0.67
1.6 and 1.9	0.31 and 3.10	8.5 and 6.9	6.75 and 6.71
1.9	3.10	8.5	6.75

Find the greatest decimal.

2.9 and 2.75 and 2.6	0.97 and 1.09 and 1.3	4.9 and 3.87 and 4.75
2.9	1.3	4.9

Write the decimals in order from greatest to least.

0.33 3.1 0.3	24.95 23.9 24.5	7.5 6.95 7.58
3.1, 0.33, 0.3	24.95, 24.5, 23.9	7.58, 7.5, 6.95

Find the answer to each problem.

The Weather Bureau reported 5.18 centimetres of rain in March, 6.74 centimetres in April, and 5.23 centimetres in May. Which month had the least rainfall?   5.18<5.23<6.74   March

A postal worker walked 4.5 kilometres on Wednesday, 3.75 kilometres on Thursday, and 4.25 kilometres on Friday. Which day did she walk the farthest?   4.5>4.25>3.75   Wednesday

Before making any comparisons, children should write out each of the numbers with the same number of decimal places, lining up the decimal points vertically.

Converting units of measure

Convert 25 centimetres to millimetres.   Convert 200¢ to dollars.

$25 \times 10 =$ **250 mm** $200 \div 100 =$ **$2**

Convert these centimetres to millimetres.

40 cm	400 mm	15 cm	150 mm	9 cm	90 mm
12 cm	120 mm	34 cm	340 mm	62 cm	620 mm
43 cm	430 mm	96 cm	960 mm	105 cm	1050 mm
92 cm	920 mm	20 cm	200 mm	426 cm	4260 mm

Convert these millimetres to centimetres.

30 mm	3 cm	100 mm	10 cm	120 mm	12 cm
60 mm	6 cm	90 mm	9 cm	200 mm	20 cm
130 mm	13 cm	10 mm	1 cm	400 mm	40 cm

Convert these dollars to cents.

$35	3500¢	$600	60 000¢	$15	1500¢
$12	1200¢	$36	3600¢	$95	9500¢
$72	7200¢	$4	400¢	$250	25 000¢

Convert these cents to dollars.

450¢	$4.50	900¢	$9.00	6000¢	$60.00
250¢	$2.50	400¢	$4.00	150¢	$1.50
100¢	$1.00	300¢	$3.00	750¢	$7.50

This page highlights problems with the relationship between millimetres and centimetres, and dollars and pennies. Use a ruler or money to explain. Look out for answers such as $7.5. Remind children that, with money, we use zero in the hundredths column.

22

Converting units of measure

Convert 300 centimetres to metres.   Convert 4 kilometres to metres.

$300 \div 100 =$ **3 m** $4 \times 1000 =$ **4000 m**

Convert these centimetres to metres.

500 cm	5 m	900 cm	9 m	400 cm	4 m
8000 cm	80 m	3000 cm	30 m	4000 cm	40 m
9800 cm	98 m	8300 cm	83 m	6200 cm	62 m
36 800 cm	368 m	94 200 cm	942 m	73 500 cm	735 m

Convert these metres to centimetres.

47 m	4700 cm	29 m	2900 cm	84 m	8400 cm
69 m	6900 cm	24 m	2400 cm	38 m	3800 cm
146 m	14 600 cm	237 m	23 700 cm	921 m	92 100 cm

Convert these metres to kilometres.

5000 m	5 km	6000 m	6 km	9000 m	9 km
15 000 m	15 km	27 000 m	27 km	71 000 m	71 km
19 000 m	19 km	86 000 m	86 km	42 000 m	42 km

Convert these kilometres to metres.

7 km	7000 m	9 km	9000 m	4 km	4000 m
23 km	23 000 m	46 km	46 000 m	87 km	87 000 m
12 km	12 000 m	96 km	96 000 m	39 km	39 000 m

As with page 21, check that children understand the relationship between centimetres and millimetres, and metres and kilometres. If they are secure in this understanding, this should be a straightforward page of multiplying and dividing by 100 and 1000.

Area of rectangles and squares

Find the area of this rectangle.

To find the area of a rectangle or square, we multiply length (l) by width (w).

Area = **800 cm²**

$$\begin{array}{r} \overset{1}{3}2 \\ \times 25 \\ \hline 160 \\ +640 \\ \hline 800 \end{array} \text{ cm}^2$$

25 cm, (l), (w), 32 cm

Find the area of these rectangles and squares. You may need to do your work on a separate sheet.

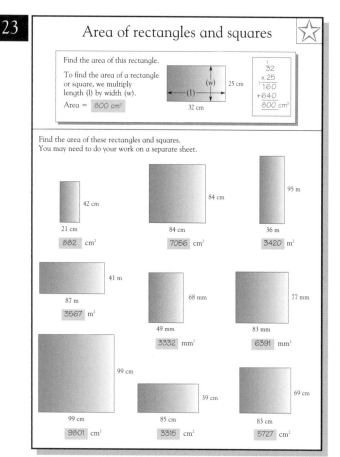

42 cm / 21 cm → **882** cm²	84 cm / 84 cm → **7056** cm²	95 m / 36 m → **3420** m²
41 m / 87 m → **3567** m²	68 mm / 49 mm → **3332** mm²	77 mm / 83 mm → **6391** mm²
99 cm / 99 cm → **9801** cm²	39 cm / 85 cm → **3315** cm²	69 cm / 83 cm → **5727** cm²

For the exercises on this page, children need to multiply the two sides together to arrive at the area. If any answers are wrong, check the long multiplication, and if necessary, revise the method. Children may confuse area and perimeter, and add the sides together.

Perimeter of shapes

Find the perimeter of this rectangle.

To find the perimeter of a rectangle or square, we add the two lengths and the two widths together.

12.4 cm, 27.3 cm

$$\begin{array}{r} \overset{1}{2}\overset{1}{7}.3 \text{ cm} \\ 27.3 \text{ cm} \\ 12.4 \text{ cm} \\ + 12.4 \text{ cm} \\ \hline 79.4 \text{ cm} \end{array}$$

79.4 cm

Find the perimeter of these rectangles and squares. You may need to do your work on a separate sheet.

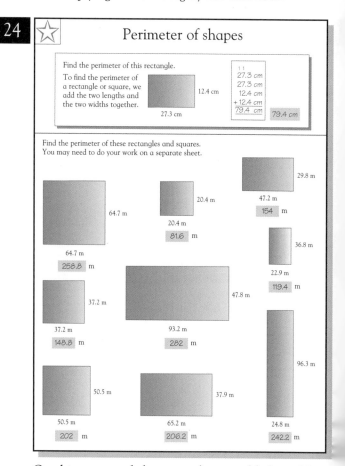

64.7 m / 64.7 m → **258.8** m	20.4 m / 20.4 m → **81.6** m	29.8 m / 47.2 m → **154** m
37.2 m / 37.2 m → **148.8** m	47.8 m / 93.2 m → **282** m	36.8 m / 22.9 m → **119.4** m
50.5 m / 50.5 m → **202** m	37.9 m / 65.2 m → **206.2** m	96.3 m / 24.8 m → **242.2** m

On this page and the next, the most likely problem will be confusion with the area work done previousl Remind children to add the four sides together to get the perimeter.

Decimal place value

☆

Work out the answer to the problem.

2.385
What is the value of the digit 8?

| | 2. Ones | 3 Tenths | 8 Hundredths | 5 Thousandths | 0 Ten-thousandths |

2.3850
8 is in the hundredths place,
so, its value is 8 hundredths.

Name the place of the digit 8 in each of the problems.

0.387	3.87	4.82	8.11
hundredths	tenths	tenths	ones

Name the value of the highlighted digit.

6.5937	5.371	7.403	0.42
9 hundredths	3 tenths	7 ones	2 tenths

6.24	3.611	1.062

Which number has a digit with the value 6 tenths?   3.611

Which number has a digit with the value 6 hundredths?   1.062

Which number has a digit with the value 6 ones?   6.24

How much greater is the second decimal than the first?

7.46 7.56	3.27 3.67	0.82 0.85
one tenth more	four tenths more	three hundredths more

Be sure that children understand that the place value of a digit is the place that it is in, while the value of the digit is the amount that it is worth in that place.

☆

26

Speed problems

How long will it take a bike rider to travel 36 km at a constant speed of 9 kilometres per hour?

4 hours
9)36
Time = Distance ÷ Speed

If a car travelled 150 km at a constant speed in 5 hours, at what speed was it travelling?

30 km/h
5)150
Speed = Distance ÷ Time

If a bus travels for 5 hours at 40 km/h, how far does it travel?

5 × 40 = 200 km
Distance = Speed x Time

A car travels along a road at a steady speed of 60 km/h. How far will it travel in 6 hours?

60 × 6 = 360   360 km

A train covers a distance of 480 km in 8 hours. If it travels at a constant speed, how fast is it travelling?

$\frac{60}{8)480}$ 60 km/h

John walks at a steady speed of 3 km/h. How long will it take him to travel 24 kilometres?

$\frac{8}{3)24}$ 8 hours

A car travels at a constant speed of 65 km/h. How far will it have travelled in 4 hours?

65 × 4 = 260   260 km

Melanie completes a long distance run at an average speed of 6 km/h. If it takes her 3 hours, how far did she run?

6 × 3 = 18   18 km

Sarah cycles 30 km to her grandmother's house at a steady speed of 10 km/h. If she leaves home at 2:00 P.M., what time will she arrive?

$\frac{3}{10)30}$
2 + 3 = 5   5:00 P.M.

If children experience difficulties on this page, ask them what they need to find, i.e. speed, distance, or time, and refer to the formula necessary to do this. Encourage children to develop simple examples that will help them to remember the formulas.

27

Conversion table

☆

This is part of a conversion table that shows how to change dollars to pesos when 10 Mexican pesos (10MN) equal $1.

How many pesos would you get for $2?   20MN

How much is 25MN worth in dollars? $2.50

Canadian Dollars	Mexican Pesos
1	10
2	20
3	30

How many dollars would you get for 40MN? $4.00

How many dollars would you get for 85MN? $8.50

How much is 1MN worth?   10¢

Change $65 into pesos.   650MN

What is $3.50 in pesos?   35MN

Change 250MN into dollars. $25.00

How many pesos could you get for $0.40?   4MN

Canadian Dollars	Mexican Pesos
1	10
2	20
3	30
4	40
5	50
6	60
7	70
8	80
9	90
10	100

The rate then changes to 8MN to the dollar. The conversion chart now looks like the one shown here.

How many pesos are worth $4?   32MN

How many dollars can you get for 56MN? $7.00

How many pesos are worth $9.50?   76MN

How many pesos can you get for $20?   160MN

How many dollars would you get for 120MN? $15.00

What is the value of 4MN?   50¢

Canadian Dollars	Mexican Pesos
1	8
2	16
3	24
4	32
5	40
6	48
7	56
8	64
9	72
10	80

Most of the questions require reading off from a conversion chart. Errors may occur if the chart is not read across accurately. Children may need extra help for questions that involve amounts not on the chart. Check that the right chart is used for the second part.

☆

Interpreting circle graphs

32 children voted for their favourite ice-cream flavours. How many children voted for chocolate?

$\frac{3}{8}$ of 32 is 12   12 children
12 children voted for chocolate.

How many children voted for fudge?

$\frac{1}{8}$ of 32 is 4   4 children
4 children voted for fudge.

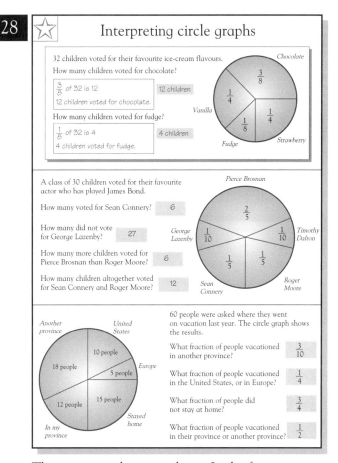

A class of 30 children voted for their favourite actor who has played James Bond.

How many voted for Sean Connery?   6

How many did not vote for George Lazenby?   27

How many more children voted for Pierce Brosnan than Roger Moore?   6

How many children altogether voted for Sean Connery and Roger Moore?   12

---

60 people were asked where they went on vacation last year. The circle graph shows the results.

What fraction of people vacationed in another province? $\frac{3}{10}$

What fraction of people vacationed in the United States, or in Europe? $\frac{1}{4}$

What fraction of people did not stay at home? $\frac{3}{4}$

What fraction of people vacationed in their province or another province? $\frac{1}{2}$

This page introduces pie charts. In the first section children are required to find fractions of an amount. If unsure, remind the child to divide the total by the denominator and multiply by the numerator. The most likely errors will come from misreading the question.

Probability scale 0 to 1

Look at this probability line.

Impossible = 0
Poor chance = 0.25
Fair = 0.5
Good chance = 0.75
Certain = 1

Write each letter in the correct place on the probability line.

a. It will be daylight in New Orleans at midnight.
b. The sun will come up tomorrow.
c. If I toss a coin it will come down heads.

a		c		b
0	0.25	0.5	0.75	1

e	b		a	c	d
0	0.25		0.5	0.75	1

Write each letter in the correct place on the probability line.

a. If I cut a pack of cards I will get a red card.

b. If I cut a pack of cards I will get a diamond.

c. If I cut a pack of cards I will get a diamond, a spade, or a club.

d. If I cut a pack of cards I will get a diamond, a spade, a club, or a heart.

e. If I cut a pack of cards it will be a 15.

b		c		e	d		a
0		0.25		0.5	0.75		1

Write each letter in the correct place on the probability line.

a. Next week, Wednesday will be the day after Tuesday.

b. There will be 33 days in February next year.

c. It will snow in Vancouver in May.

d. It will snow in Newfoundland in January.

e. The next person to knock on the door will be a woman.

The first section assumes a knowledge of the suits of a pack of cards. If children are unfamiliar with cards, some discussion will be necessary. In the second section, the examples have been chosen to fall into the categories listed on the probability line.

30

Likely outcomes

Throw one coin 20 times. Keep a tally.

H	ⅢⅢ ⅢⅠ
T	ⅢⅢ ⅢⅢ Ⅰ

Put your results on a bar graph.

What do you notice?

Heads and tails come up roughly the same number of times because there are only two possible outcomes and they are equally likely.

Predict what you think the outcome will be if you tossed two coins 48 times.

2 heads varies times   2 tails varies times   1 of each varies times

Now actually throw two coins 48 times and record your results on this tally chart.

2 Heads	ⅢⅢ ⅢⅢ ⅢⅢ
2 Tails	ⅢⅢ ⅢⅢ ⅠⅠ
1 of each	ⅢⅢ ⅢⅢ ⅢⅢ ⅢⅢ Ⅰ

Draw a bar graph to show your results.

Which result comes up the most often?   one of each

Can you explain why some results are more probable than others?

The child's answer should explain that there are four possible outcomes and that "one of each" has a two-in-four chance of coming up.

Childrens' predictions in the first question may be considerably different from the result. Once the work is done, check that children use the experience to improve their understanding of likely outcomes. The tally chart may differ from the one shown here.

31

Naming quadrilaterals

Name this shape.

Rhombus

Name these shapes.

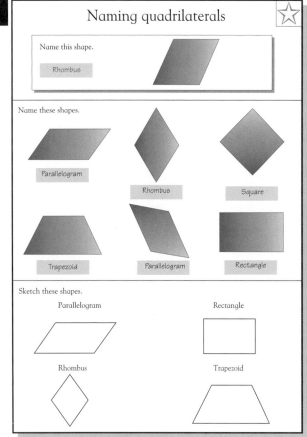

Parallelogram

Rhombus   Square

Trapezoid   Parallelogram   Rectangle

Sketch these shapes.

Parallelogram   Rectangle

Rhombus   Trapezoid

If children have problems identifying these shapes, it may be necessary to provide some more examples for identification practice.

Speed trials

Write the answers as fast as you can, but get them right!

4 x 10 = 40   8 x 2 = 16   6 x 5 = 30

Write the answers as fast as you can, but get them right!

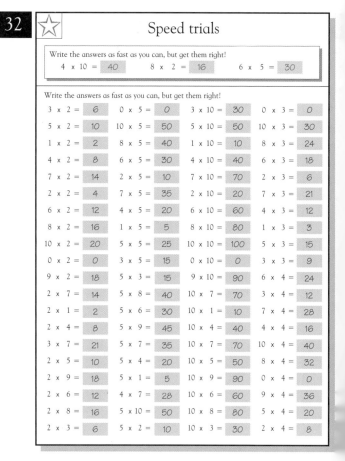

3 x 2 = 6	0 x 5 = 0	3 x 10 = 30	0 x 3 = 0
5 x 2 = 10	10 x 5 = 50	5 x 10 = 50	10 x 3 = 30
1 x 2 = 2	8 x 5 = 40	1 x 10 = 10	8 x 3 = 24
4 x 2 = 8	6 x 5 = 30	4 x 10 = 40	6 x 3 = 18
7 x 2 = 14	2 x 5 = 10	7 x 10 = 70	2 x 3 = 6
2 x 2 = 4	7 x 5 = 35	2 x 10 = 20	7 x 3 = 21
6 x 2 = 12	4 x 5 = 20	6 x 10 = 60	4 x 3 = 12
8 x 2 = 16	1 x 5 = 5	8 x 10 = 80	1 x 3 = 3
10 x 2 = 20	5 x 5 = 25	10 x 10 = 100	5 x 3 = 15
0 x 2 = 0	3 x 5 = 15	0 x 10 = 0	3 x 3 = 9
9 x 2 = 18	5 x 3 = 15	9 x 10 = 90	6 x 4 = 24
2 x 7 = 14	5 x 8 = 40	10 x 7 = 70	3 x 4 = 12
2 x 1 = 2	5 x 6 = 30	10 x 1 = 10	7 x 4 = 28
2 x 4 = 8	5 x 9 = 45	10 x 4 = 40	4 x 4 = 16
3 x 7 = 21	5 x 7 = 35	10 x 7 = 70	10 x 4 = 40
2 x 5 = 10	5 x 4 = 20	10 x 5 = 50	8 x 4 = 32
2 x 9 = 18	5 x 1 = 5	10 x 9 = 90	0 x 4 = 0
2 x 6 = 12	4 x 7 = 28	10 x 6 = 60	9 x 4 = 36
2 x 8 = 16	5 x 10 = 50	10 x 8 = 80	5 x 4 = 20
2 x 3 = 6	5 x 2 = 10	10 x 3 = 30	2 x 4 = 8

All the 3s

You will need to know these:

1 x 3 = 3   2 x 3 = 6   3 x 3 = 9   4 x 3 = 12   5 x 3 = 15   10 x 3 = 30

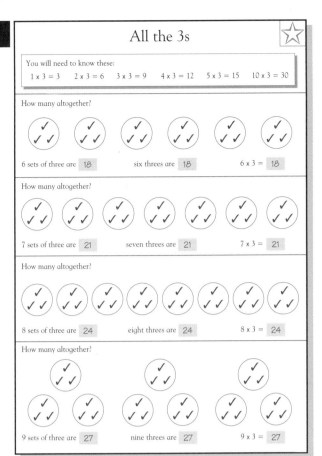

How many altogether?

6 sets of three are 18   six threes are 18   6 x 3 = 18

How many altogether?

7 sets of three are 21   seven threes are 21   7 x 3 = 21

How many altogether?

8 sets of three are 24   eight threes are 24   8 x 3 = 24

How many altogether?

9 sets of three are 27   nine threes are 27   9 x 3 = 27

34

All the 3s again

You should know all of the three times table by now.

1 x 3 = 3   3 x 3 = 9   4 x 3 = 12   5 x 3 = 15
6 x 3 = 18   7 x 3 = 21   8 x 3 = 24   9 x 3 = 27   10 x 3 = 30

Say these to yourself a few times.

Cover the three times table with a sheet of paper so you can't see the numbers.
Write the answers. Be as fast as you can, but get them right!

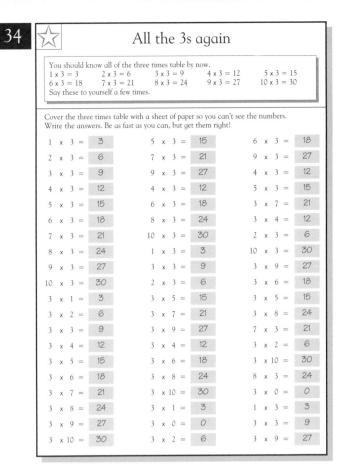

1 x 3 = 3	5 x 3 = 15	6 x 3 = 18
2 x 3 = 6	7 x 3 = 21	9 x 3 = 27
3 x 3 = 9	9 x 3 = 27	4 x 3 = 12
4 x 3 = 12	4 x 3 = 12	5 x 3 = 15
5 x 3 = 15	6 x 3 = 18	3 x 7 = 21
6 x 3 = 18	8 x 3 = 24	3 x 4 = 12
7 x 3 = 21	10 x 3 = 30	2 x 3 = 6
8 x 3 = 24	1 x 3 = 3	10 x 3 = 30
9 x 3 = 27	3 x 3 = 9	3 x 9 = 27
10 x 3 = 30	2 x 3 = 6	3 x 6 = 18
3 x 1 = 3	3 x 5 = 15	3 x 5 = 15
3 x 2 = 6	3 x 7 = 21	3 x 8 = 24
3 x 3 = 9	3 x 9 = 27	7 x 3 = 21
3 x 4 = 12	3 x 4 = 12	3 x 2 = 6
3 x 5 = 15	3 x 6 = 18	3 x 10 = 30
3 x 6 = 18	3 x 8 = 24	8 x 3 = 24
3 x 7 = 21	3 x 10 = 30	3 x 0 = 0
3 x 8 = 24	3 x 1 = 3	1 x 3 = 3
3 x 9 = 27	3 x 0 = 0	3 x 3 = 9
3 x 10 = 30	3 x 2 = 6	3 x 9 = 27

35

All the 4s

You should know these:

1 x 4 = 4   2 x 4 = 8   3 x 4 = 12   4 x 4 = 16   5 x 4 = 20   10 x 4 = 40

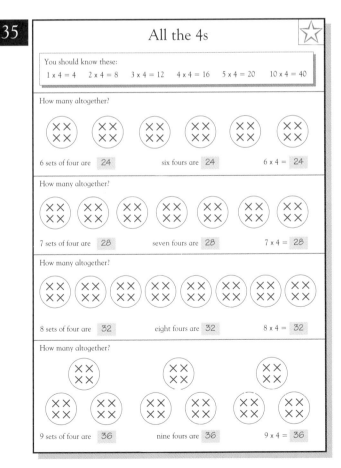

How many altogether?

6 sets of four are 24   six fours are 24   6 x 4 = 24

How many altogether?

7 sets of four are 28   seven fours are 28   7 x 4 = 28

How many altogether?

8 sets of four are 32   eight fours are 32   8 x 4 = 32

How many altogether?

9 sets of four are 36   nine fours are 36   9 x 4 = 36

All the 4s again

You should know all of the four times table by now.

1 x 4 = 4   3 x 4 = 12   4 x 4 = 16   5 x 4 = 20
6 x 4 = 24   7 x 4 = 28   8 x 4 = 32   9 x 4 = 36   10 x 4 = 40

Say these to yourself a few times.

Cover the four times table with a sheet of paper so you can't see the numbers.
Write the answers. Be as fast as you can, but get them right!

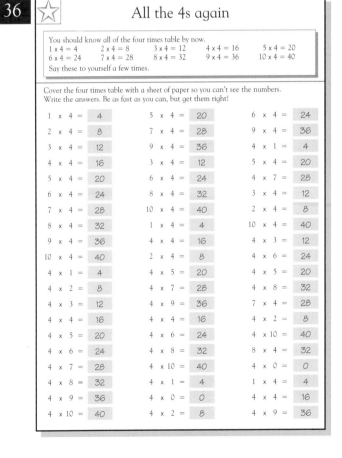

1 x 4 = 4	5 x 4 = 20	6 x 4 = 24
2 x 4 = 8	7 x 4 = 28	9 x 4 = 36
3 x 4 = 12	9 x 4 = 36	4 x 1 = 4
4 x 4 = 16	3 x 4 = 12	5 x 4 = 20
5 x 4 = 20	6 x 4 = 24	4 x 7 = 28
6 x 4 = 24	8 x 4 = 32	3 x 4 = 12
7 x 4 = 28	10 x 4 = 40	2 x 4 = 8
8 x 4 = 32	1 x 4 = 4	10 x 4 = 40
9 x 4 = 36	4 x 4 = 16	4 x 3 = 12
10 x 4 = 40	2 x 4 = 8	4 x 6 = 24
4 x 1 = 4	4 x 5 = 20	4 x 5 = 20
4 x 2 = 8	4 x 7 = 28	4 x 8 = 32
4 x 3 = 12	4 x 9 = 36	7 x 4 = 28
4 x 4 = 16	4 x 4 = 16	4 x 2 = 8
4 x 5 = 20	4 x 6 = 24	4 x 10 = 40
4 x 6 = 24	4 x 8 = 32	8 x 4 = 32
4 x 7 = 28	4 x 10 = 40	4 x 0 = 0
4 x 8 = 32	4 x 1 = 4	1 x 4 = 4
4 x 9 = 36	4 x 0 = 0	4 x 4 = 16
4 x 10 = 40	4 x 2 = 8	4 x 9 = 36

Speed trials

You should know all of the 1, 2, 3, 4, 5, and 10 times tables by now, but how quickly can you do them?
Ask someone to time you as you do this page.
Remember, you must be fast but also correct.

4 x 2 = 8	6 x 3 = 18	9 x 5 = 45
8 x 3 = 24	3 x 4 = 12	8 x 10 = 80
7 x 4 = 28	7 x 5 = 35	7 x 2 = 14
6 x 5 = 30	3 x 10 = 30	6 x 3 = 18
8 x 10 = 80	1 x 2 = 2	5 x 4 = 20
8 x 2 = 16	7 x 3 = 21	4 x 5 = 20
5 x 3 = 15	4 x 4 = 16	3 x 10 = 30
9 x 4 = 36	6 x 5 = 30	2 x 2 = 4
5 x 5 = 25	4 x 10 = 40	1 x 3 = 3
7 x 10 = 70	6 x 2 = 12	0 x 4 = 0
0 x 2 = 0	5 x 3 = 15	10 x 5 = 50
4 x 3 = 12	8 x 4 = 32	9 x 2 = 18
6 x 4 = 24	0 x 5 = 0	8 x 3 = 24
3 x 5 = 15	2 x 10 = 20	7 x 4 = 28
4 x 10 = 40	7 x 2 = 14	6 x 5 = 30
7 x 2 = 14	8 x 3 = 24	5 x 10 = 50
3 x 3 = 9	9 x 4 = 36	4 x 0 = 0
2 x 4 = 8	5 x 5 = 25	3 x 2 = 6
7 x 5 = 35	7 x 10 = 70	2 x 8 = 16
9 x 10 = 90	5 x 2 = 10	1 x 9 = 9

38

Some of the 6s

You should already know parts of the 6 times table because they are parts of the 1, 2, 3, 4, 5, and 10 times tables.
1 x 6 = 6   2 x 6 = 12   3 x 6 = 18
4 x 6 = 24   5 x 6 = 30   10 x 6 = 60
Find out if you can remember them quickly and correctly.

Cover the six times table with paper so you can't see the numbers.
Write the answers as quickly as you can.

What is three sixes? 18		What is ten sixes? 60
What is two sixes? 12		What is four sixes? 24
What is one six? 6		What is five sixes? 30

Write the answers as quickly as you can.

How many sixes make 12? 2	How many sixes make 6? 1
How many sixes make 30? 5	How many sixes make 18? 3
How many sixes make 24? 4	How many sixes make 60? 10

Write the answers as quickly as you can.

Multiply six by three. 18	Multiply six by ten. 60
Multiply six by two. 12	Multiply six by five. 30
Multiply six by one. 6	Multiply six by four. 24

Write the answers as quickly as you can.

4 x 6 = 24	2 x 6 = 12	10 x 6 = 60
5 x 6 = 30	1 x 6 = 6	3 x 6 = 18

Write the answers as quickly as you can.
A box contains six eggs. A man buys five boxes. How many eggs does he have? 30

A pack contains six sticks of gum.
How many sticks will there be in 10 packs? 60

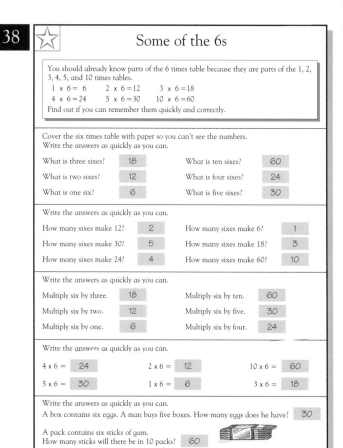

The rest of the 6s

You need to learn these:
6 x 6 = 36   7 x 6 = 42   8 x 6 = 48   9 x 6 = 54

This work will help you remember the 6 times table.

Complete these sequences.

6   12   18   24   30   36   42   48   54   60

5 x 6 = 30   so   6 x 6 = 30 plus another 6 = 36

18   24   30   36   42   48   54   60

6 x 6 = 36   so   7 x 6 = 36 plus another 6 = 42

6   12   18   24   30   36   42   48   54   60

7 x 6 = 42   so   8 x 6 = 42 plus another 6 = 48

6   12   18   24   30   36   42   48   54   60

8 x 6 = 48   so   9 x 6 = 48 plus another 6 = 54

6   12   18   24   30   36   42   48   54   60

Test yourself on the rest of the 6 times table.
Cover the above part of the page with a sheet of paper.

What is six sixes? 36	What is seven sixes? 42
What is eight sixes? 48	What is nine sixes? 54

8 x 6 = 48   7 x 6 = 42   6 x 6 = 36   9 x 6 = 54

Practise the 6s

You should know all of the 6 times table now, but how quickly can you remember it?
Ask someone to time you as you do this page.
Remember, you must be fast but also correct.

1 x 6 = 6	2 x 6 = 12	7 x 6 = 42
2 x 6 = 12	4 x 6 = 24	3 x 6 = 18
3 x 6 = 18	6 x 6 = 36	9 x 6 = 54
4 x 6 = 24	8 x 6 = 48	6 x 4 = 24
5 x 6 = 30	10 x 6 = 60	1 x 6 = 6
6 x 6 = 36	1 x 6 = 6	6 x 2 = 12
7 x 6 = 42	3 x 6 = 18	6 x 8 = 48
8 x 6 = 48	5 x 6 = 30	0 x 6 = 0
9 x 6 = 54	7 x 6 = 42	6 x 3 = 18
10 x 6 = 60	9 x 6 = 54	5 x 6 = 30
6 x 1 = 6	6 x 3 = 18	6 x 7 = 42
6 x 2 = 12	6 x 5 = 30	2 x 6 = 12
6 x 3 = 18	6 x 7 = 42	6 x 9 = 54
6 x 4 = 24	6 x 9 = 54	4 x 6 = 24
6 x 5 = 30	6 x 2 = 12	8 x 6 = 48
6 x 6 = 36	6 x 4 = 24	10 x 6 = 60
6 x 7 = 42	6 x 6 = 36	6 x 5 = 30
6 x 8 = 48	6 x 8 = 48	6 x 0 = 0
6 x 9 = 54	6 x 10 = 60	6 x 1 = 6
6 x 10 = 60	6 x 0 = 0	6 x 6 = 36

Speed trials

You should know all of the 1, 2, 3, 4, 5, 6, and 10 times tables by now, but how quickly can you remember them?
Ask someone to time you as you do this page.
Remember, you must be fast but also correct.

4 x 6 = 24	6 x 3 = 18	9 x 6 = 54
5 x 3 = 15	8 x 6 = 48	8 x 6 = 48
7 x 3 = 21	6 x 6 = 36	7 x 3 = 21
6 x 5 = 30	3 x 10 = 30	6 x 6 = 36
6 x 10 = 60	6 x 2 = 12	5 x 4 = 20
8 x 2 = 16	7 x 3 = 21	4 x 6 = 24
5 x 3 = 15	4 x 6 = 24	3 x 6 = 18
9 x 6 = 54	6 x 5 = 30	2 x 6 = 12
5 x 5 = 25	6 x 10 = 60	6 x 3 = 18
7 x 6 = 42	6 x 2 = 12	0 x 6 = 0
0 x 2 = 0	5 x 3 = 15	10 x 5 = 50
6 x 3 = 18	8 x 4 = 32	6 x 2 = 12
6 x 6 = 36	0 x 6 = 0	8 x 3 = 24
3 x 5 = 15	5 x 10 = 50	7 x 6 = 42
4 x 10 = 40	7 x 6 = 42	6 x 5 = 30
7 x 10 = 70	8 x 3 = 24	5 x 10 = 50
3 x 6 = 18	9 x 6 = 54	6 x 0 = 0
2 x 4 = 8	5 x 5 = 25	3 x 10 = 30
6 x 9 = 54	7 x 10 = 70	2 x 8 = 16
9 x 10 = 90	5 x 6 = 30	1 x 8 = 8

42

Some of the 7s

You should already know parts of the 7 times table because they are parts of the 1, 2, 3, 4, 5, 6 and 10 times tables.
1 x 7 = 7   2 x 7 = 14   3 x 7 = 21   4 x 7 = 28
5 x 7 = 35   6 x 7 = 42   10 x 7 = 70
Find out if you can remember them quickly and correctly.

Cover the seven times table with paper and write the answers to these questions as quickly as you can.

What is three sevens?	21	What is ten sevens?	70
What is two sevens?	14	What is four sevens?	28
What is six sevens?	42	What is five sevens?	35

Write the answers as quickly as you can.

How many sevens make 14?	2	How many sevens make 42?	6
How many sevens make 35?	5	How many sevens make 21?	3
How many sevens make 28?	4	How many sevens make 70?	10

Write the answers as quickly as you can.

Multiply seven by three.	21	Multiply seven by ten.	70
Multiply seven by two.	14	Multiply seven by five.	35
Multiply seven by six.	42	Multiply seven by four.	28

Write the answers as quickly as you can.

4 x 7 = 28	2 x 7 = 14	10 x 7 = 70
5 x 7 = 35	1 x 7 = 7	3 x 7 = 21

Write the answers as quickly as you can.
A bag has seven candies. Ann buys five bags. How many candies does she have? 35

How many days are there in six weeks? 42

The rest of the 7s

You should now know all of the 1, 2, 3, 4, 5, 6, and 10 times tables.
You need to learn only these parts of the seven times table.
7 x 7 = 49   8 x 7 = 56   9 x 7 = 63

This work will help you remember the 7 times table.

Complete these sequences.

7   14   21   28   35   42   49   56   63   70

6 x 7 = 42   so   7 x 7 = 42 plus another 7 = 49

21   28   35   42   49   56   63   70

7 x 7 = 49   so   8 x 7 = 49 plus another 7 = 56

7   14   21   28   35   42   49   56   63   70

8 x 7 = 56   so   9 x 7 = 56 plus another 7 = 63

7   14   21   28   35   42   49   56   63   70

Test yourself on the rest of the 7 times table.
Cover the section above with a sheet of paper.

What is seven sevens?	49	What is eight sevens?	56
What is nine sevens?	63	What is ten sevens?	70

8 x 7 = 56   7 x 7 = 49   9 x 7 = 63   10 x 7 = 70

How many days are there in eight weeks? 56

A package contains seven pens.
How many pens will there be in nine packets? 63

How many sevens make 56? 8

Practise the 7s

You should know all of the 7 times table now, but how quickly can you remember it?
Ask someone to time you as you do this page.
Remember, you must be fast but also correct.

1 x 7 = 7	2 x 7 = 14	7 x 6 = 42
2 x 7 = 14	4 x 7 = 28	3 x 7 = 21
3 x 7 = 21	6 x 7 = 42	9 x 7 = 63
4 x 7 = 28	8 x 7 = 56	7 x 4 = 28
5 x 7 = 35	10 x 7 = 70	1 x 7 = 7
6 x 7 = 42	1 x 7 = 7	7 x 2 = 14
7 x 7 = 49	3 x 7 = 21	7 x 8 = 56
8 x 7 = 56	5 x 7 = 35	0 x 7 = 0
9 x 7 = 63	7 x 7 = 49	7 x 3 = 21
10 x 7 = 70	9 x 7 = 63	5 x 7 = 35
7 x 1 = 7	7 x 3 = 21	7 x 7 = 49
7 x 2 = 14	7 x 5 = 35	2 x 7 = 14
7 x 3 = 21	7 x 7 = 49	7 x 9 = 63
7 x 4 = 28	7 x 9 = 63	4 x 7 = 28
7 x 5 = 35	7 x 2 = 14	8 x 7 = 56
7 x 6 = 42	7 x 4 = 28	10 x 7 = 70
7 x 7 = 49	7 x 6 = 42	7 x 5 = 35
7 x 8 = 56	7 x 8 = 56	7 x 0 = 0
7 x 9 = 63	7 x 10 = 70	7 x 1 = 7
7 x 10 = 70	7 x 0 = 0	6 x 7 = 42

Speed trials

You should know all of the 1, 2, 3, 4, 5, 6, 7, and 10 times tables by now,
but how quickly can you remember them?
Ask someone to time you as you do this page.
Remember, you must be fast but also correct.

4 x 7 =	28	7 x 3 =	21	9 x 7 =	63
5 x 10 =	50	8 x 7 =	56	7 x 6 =	42
7 x 5 =	35	6 x 6 =	36	8 x 3 =	24
6 x 5 =	30	5 x 10 =	50	6 x 6 =	36
6 x 10 =	60	6 x 3 =	18	7 x 4 =	28
8 x 7 =	56	7 x 5 =	35	4 x 6 =	24
5 x 8 =	40	4 x 6 =	24	3 x 7 =	21
9 x 6 =	54	6 x 5 =	30	2 x 8 =	16
5 x 7 =	35	7 x 10 =	70	7 x 3 =	21
7 x 6 =	42	6 x 7 =	42	0 x 6 =	0
0 x 5 =	0	5 x 7 =	35	10 x 7 =	70
6 x 3 =	18	8 x 4 =	32	6 x 2 =	12
6 x 7 =	42	0 x 7 =	0	8 x 7 =	56
3 x 5 =	15	5 x 8 =	40	7 x 7 =	49
4 x 7 =	28	7 x 6 =	42	6 x 5 =	30
7 x 10 =	70	8 x 3 =	24	5 x 10 =	50
7 x 8 =	56	9 x 6 =	54	7 x 0 =	0
2 x 7 =	14	7 x 7 =	49	3 x 10 =	30
4 x 9 =	36	9 x 10 =	90	2 x 7 =	14
9 x 10 =	90	5 x 6 =	30	7 x 8 =	56

46

Some of the 8s

You should already know some of the 8 times table because it is part of the
1, 2, 3, 4, 5, 6, 7, and 10 times tables.
1 x 8 = 8   2 x 8 = 16   3 x 8 = 24   4 x 8 = 32
5 x 8 = 40   6 x 8 = 48   7 x 8 = 56   10 x 8 = 80
Find out if you can remember them quickly and correctly.

Cover the 8 times table with paper so you can't see the numbers.
Write the answers as quickly as you can.

What is three eights?	24	What is ten eights?	80
What is two eights?	16	What is four eights?	32
What is six eights?	48	What is five eights?	40

Write the answers as quickly as you can.

How many eights equal 16?	2	How many eights equal 40?	5
How many eights equal 32?	4	How many eights equal 24?	3
How many eights equal 56?	7	How many eights equal 48?	6

Write the answers as quickly as you can.

Multiply eight by three.	24	Multiply eight by ten.	80
Multiply eight by two.	16	Multiply eight by five.	40
Multiply eight by six.	48	Multiply eight by four.	32

Write the answers as quickly as you can.

6 x 8 =	48	2 x 8 =	16	10 x 8 =	80
5 x 8 =	40	7 x 8 =	56	3 x 8 =	24

Write the answers as quickly as you can.
A pizza has eight slices. John buys six pizzas.
How many slices does he have? 48

Which number multiplied by 8 gives the answer 56? 7

The rest of the 8s

You need to learn only these parts of the eight times table.
8 x 8 = 64   9 x 8 = 72

This work will help you remember the 8 times table.

Complete these sequences.

8   16   24   32   40   48   56   64   72   80

7 x 8 = 56   so   8 x 8 = 56 plus another 8 = 64

24   32   40   48   56   64   72   80

8 x 8 = 64   so   9 x 8 = 64 plus another 8 = 72

8   16   24   32   40   48   56   64   72   80

8   16   24   32   40   48   56   64   72   80

Test yourself on the rest of the 8 times table.
Cover the section above with a sheet of paper.

What is seven eights?	56	What is eight eights?	64
What is nine eights?	72	What is eight nines?	72

8 x 8 = 64   9 x 8 = 72   8 x 9 = 72   10 x 8 = 80

What number multiplied by 8 gives the answer 72? 9

A number multiplied by 8 gives the answer 80. What is the number? 10

David puts out building bricks in piles of 8.
How many bricks will there be in 10 piles? 80

What number multiplied by 5 gives the answer 40? 8

How many 8s make 72? 9

Practise the 8s

You should know all of the 8 times table now, but how quickly can you remember it?
Ask someone to time you as you do this page.
Be fast but also correct.

1 x 8 =	8	2 x 8 =	16	8 x 6 =	48
2 x 8 =	16	4 x 8 =	32	3 x 8 =	24
3 x 8 =	24	6 x 8 =	48	9 x 8 =	72
4 x 8 =	32	8 x 8 =	64	8 x 4 =	32
5 x 8 =	40	10 x 8 =	80	1 x 8 =	8
6 x 8 =	48	1 x 8 =	8	8 x 2 =	16
7 x 8 =	56	3 x 8 =	24	7 x 8 =	56
8 x 8 =	64	5 x 8 =	40	0 x 8 =	0
9 x 8 =	72	7 x 8 =	56	8 x 3 =	24
10 x 8 =	80	9 x 8 =	72	5 x 8 =	40
8 x 1 =	8	8 x 3 =	24	8 x 8 =	64
8 x 2 =	16	8 x 5 =	40	2 x 8 =	16
8 x 3 =	24	8 x 8 =	64	8 x 9 =	72
8 x 4 =	32	8 x 9 =	72	4 x 8 =	32
8 x 5 =	40	8 x 2 =	16	8 x 6 =	48
8 x 6 =	48	8 x 4 =	32	10 x 8 =	80
8 x 7 =	56	8 x 6 =	48	8 x 5 =	40
8 x 8 =	64	8 x 8 =	64	8 x 0 =	0
8 x 9 =	72	8 x 10 =	80	8 x 1 =	8
8 x 10 =	80	8 x 0 =	0	6 x 8 =	48

Speed trials

You should know all of the 1, 2, 3, 4, 5, 6, 7, 8, and 10 times tables now,
but how quickly can you remember them?
Ask someone to time you as you do this page.
Be fast but also correct.

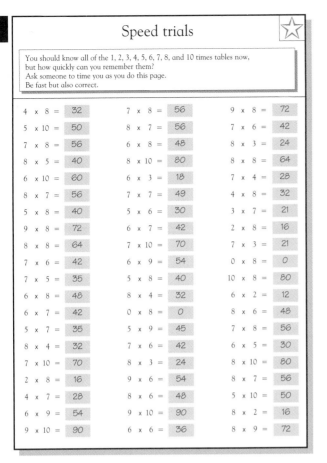

4 x 8 = 32	7 x 8 = 56	9 x 8 = 72
5 x 10 = 50	8 x 7 = 56	7 x 6 = 42
7 x 8 = 56	6 x 8 = 48	8 x 3 = 24
8 x 5 = 40	8 x 10 = 80	8 x 8 = 64
6 x 10 = 60	6 x 3 = 18	7 x 4 = 28
8 x 7 = 56	7 x 7 = 49	4 x 8 = 32
5 x 8 = 40	5 x 6 = 30	3 x 7 = 21
9 x 8 = 72	6 x 7 = 42	2 x 8 = 16
8 x 8 = 64	7 x 10 = 70	7 x 3 = 21
7 x 6 = 42	6 x 9 = 54	0 x 8 = 0
7 x 5 = 35	5 x 8 = 40	10 x 8 = 80
6 x 8 = 48	8 x 4 = 32	6 x 2 = 12
6 x 7 = 42	0 x 8 = 0	8 x 6 = 48
5 x 7 = 35	5 x 9 = 45	7 x 8 = 56
8 x 4 = 32	7 x 6 = 42	6 x 5 = 30
7 x 10 = 70	8 x 3 = 24	8 x 10 = 80
2 x 8 = 16	9 x 6 = 54	8 x 7 = 56
4 x 7 = 28	8 x 6 = 48	5 x 10 = 50
6 x 9 = 54	9 x 10 = 90	8 x 2 = 16
9 x 10 = 90	6 x 6 = 36	8 x 9 = 72

50

Some of the 9s

You should already know nearly all of the 9 times table because it is part of the
1, 2, 3, 4, 5, 6, 7, 8, and 10 times tables.

1 x 9 = 9	2 x 9 = 18	3 x 9 = 27	4 x 9 = 36
6 x 9 = 54	7 x 9 = 63	8 x 9 = 72	10 x 9 = 90

5 x 9 = 45

Find out if you can remember them quickly and correctly.

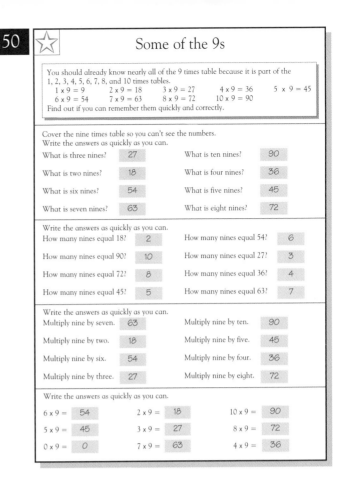

Cover the nine times table so you can't see the numbers.
Write the answers as quickly as you can.

What is three nines?	27	What is ten nines?	90
What is two nines?	18	What is four nines?	36
What is six nines?	54	What is five nines?	45
What is seven nines?	63	What is eight nines?	72

Write the answers as quickly as you can.

How many nines equal 18?	2	How many nines equal 54?	6
How many nines equal 90?	10	How many nines equal 27?	3
How many nines equal 72?	8	How many nines equal 36?	4
How many nines equal 45?	5	How many nines equal 63?	7

Write the answers as quickly as you can.

Multiply nine by seven.	63	Multiply nine by ten.	90
Multiply nine by two.	18	Multiply nine by five.	45
Multiply nine by six.	54	Multiply nine by four.	36
Multiply nine by three.	27	Multiply nine by eight.	72

Write the answers as quickly as you can.

6 x 9 = 54	2 x 9 = 18	10 x 9 = 90
5 x 9 = 45	3 x 9 = 27	8 x 9 = 72
0 x 9 = 0	7 x 9 = 63	4 x 9 = 36

51

The rest of the 9s

You need to learn only this part of the nine times table.
9 x 9 = 81

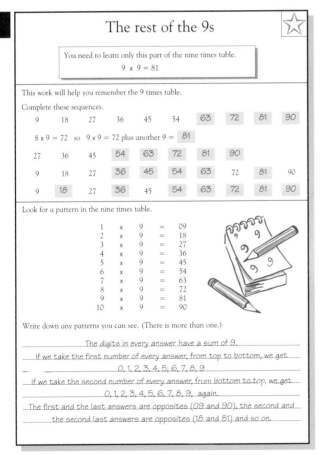

This work will help you remember the 9 times table.

Complete these sequences.

9 18 27 36 45 54 63 72 81 90

8 x 9 = 72 so 9 x 9 = 72 plus another 9 = 81

27 36 45 54 63 72 81 90

9 18 27 36 45 54 63 72 81 90

9 18 27 36 45 54 63 72 81 90

Look for a pattern in the nine times table.

1	x	9	=	09
2	x	9	=	18
3	x	9	=	27
4	x	9	=	36
5	x	9	=	45
6	x	9	=	54
7	x	9	=	63
8	x	9	=	72
9	x	9	=	81
10	x	9	=	90

Write down any patterns you can see. (There is more than one.)

The digits in every answer have a sum of 9.
If we take the first number of every answer, from top to bottom, we get
0, 1, 2, 3, 4, 5, 6, 7, 8, 9
If we take the second number of every answer, from bottom to top, we get
0, 1, 2, 3, 4, 5, 6, 7, 8, 9, again.
The first and the last answers are opposites (09 and 90), the second and
the second last answers are opposites (18 and 81) and so on.

Practise the 9s

You should know all of the 9 times table now, but how quickly can you remember it?
Ask someone to time you as you do this page.
Be fast and correct.

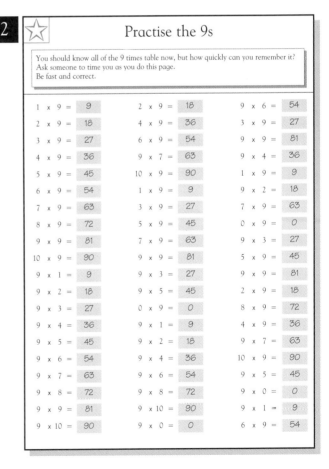

1 x 9 = 9	2 x 9 = 18	9 x 6 = 54
2 x 9 = 18	4 x 9 = 36	3 x 9 = 27
3 x 9 = 27	6 x 9 = 54	9 x 9 = 81
4 x 9 = 36	9 x 7 = 63	9 x 4 = 36
5 x 9 = 45	10 x 9 = 90	1 x 9 = 9
6 x 9 = 54	1 x 9 = 9	9 x 2 = 18
7 x 9 = 63	3 x 9 = 27	7 x 9 = 63
8 x 9 = 72	5 x 9 = 45	0 x 9 = 0
9 x 9 = 81	7 x 9 = 63	9 x 3 = 27
10 x 9 = 90	9 x 9 = 81	5 x 9 = 45
9 x 1 = 9	9 x 3 = 27	9 x 9 = 81
9 x 2 = 18	9 x 5 = 45	2 x 9 = 18
9 x 3 = 27	0 x 9 = 0	8 x 9 = 72
9 x 4 = 36	9 x 1 = 9	4 x 9 = 36
9 x 5 = 45	9 x 2 = 18	9 x 7 = 63
9 x 6 = 54	9 x 4 = 36	10 x 9 = 90
9 x 7 = 63	9 x 6 = 54	9 x 5 = 45
9 x 8 = 72	9 x 8 = 72	9 x 0 = 0
9 x 9 = 81	9 x 10 = 90	9 x 1 = 9
9 x 10 = 90	9 x 0 = 0	6 x 9 = 54

Encourage children to notice patterns. It does not
matter how they express these. One pattern is to
deduct 1 from the number being multiplied. This
gives the first digit of the answer. Then deduct this
first digit from 9 to get the second digit of the answer.

Speed trials

You should know all of the times tables by now, but how quickly can you remember them?
Ask someone to time you as you do this page.
Be fast and correct.

6 x 8 = 48	4 x 8 = 32	8 x 10 = 80
9 x 10 = 90	9 x 8 = 72	7 x 9 = 63
5 x 8 = 40	6 x 6 = 36	8 x 5 = 40
7 x 5 = 35	8 x 9 = 72	8 x 7 = 56
6 x 4 = 24	6 x 4 = 24	7 x 4 = 28
8 x 8 = 64	7 x 3 = 21	4 x 9 = 36
5 x 10 = 50	5 x 9 = 45	6 x 7 = 42
9 x 8 = 72	6 x 8 = 48	4 x 6 = 24
8 x 3 = 24	7 x 7 = 49	7 x 8 = 56
7 x 7 = 49	6 x 9 = 54	6 x 9 = 54
9 x 5 = 45	7 x 8 = 56	10 x 8 = 80
4 x 8 = 32	8 x 4 = 32	6 x 5 = 30
6 x 7 = 42	0 x 9 = 0	8 x 8 = 64
2 x 9 = 18	10 x 10 = 100	7 x 6 = 42
8 x 4 = 32	7 x 6 = 42	6 x 8 = 48
7 x 10 = 70	8 x 7 = 56	9 x 10 = 90
2 x 8 = 16	9 x 6 = 54	8 x 4 = 32
4 x 7 = 28	8 x 6 = 48	7 x 10 = 70
6 x 9 = 54	9 x 9 = 81	5 x 8 = 40
9 x 9 = 81	6 x 7 = 42	8 x 9 = 72

54

Times tables for division

Knowing the times tables can also help with division problems.
Look at these examples.
3 x 6 = 18 which means that 18 ÷ 3 = 6 and that 18 ÷ 6 = 3
4 x 5 = 20 which means that 20 ÷ 4 = 5 and that 20 ÷ 5 = 4
9 x 3 = 27 which means that 27 ÷ 3 = 9 and that 27 ÷ 9 = 3

Use your knowledge of the times tables to work these division problems.

3 x 8 = 24 which means that 24 ÷ 3 = 8 and that 24 ÷ 8 = 3
4 x 7 = 28 which means that 28 ÷ 4 = 7 and that 28 ÷ 7 = 4
3 x 5 = 15 which means that 15 ÷ 3 = 5 and that 15 ÷ 5 = 3
4 x 3 = 12 which means that 12 ÷ 3 = 4 and that 12 ÷ 4 = 3
3 x 10 = 30 which means that 30 ÷ 3 = 10 and that 30 ÷ 10 = 3
4 x 8 = 32 which means that 32 ÷ 4 = 8 and that 32 ÷ 8 = 4
3 x 9 = 27 which means that 27 ÷ 3 = 9 and that 27 ÷ 9 = 3
4 x 10 = 40 which means that 40 ÷ 4 = 10 and that 40 ÷ 10 = 4

These division problems help practise the 3 and 4 times tables.

20 ÷ 4 = 5	15 ÷ 3 = 5	16 ÷ 4 = 4
24 ÷ 4 = 6	27 ÷ 3 = 9	30 ÷ 3 = 10
12 ÷ 3 = 4	18 ÷ 3 = 6	28 ÷ 4 = 7
24 ÷ 3 = 8	32 ÷ 4 = 8	21 ÷ 3 = 7

How many fours in 36? 9	Divide 27 by three. 9
Divide 28 by 4. 7	How many threes in 21? 7
How many fives in 35? 7	Divide 40 by 5. 8
Divide 15 by 3. 5	How many eights in 48? 6

55

Times tables for division

This page will help you remember times tables by dividing by 2, 3, 4, 5, and 10.
20 ÷ 5 = 4   18 ÷ 3 = 6   60 ÷ 10 = 6

Complete the problems.

40 ÷ 10 = 4	14 ÷ 2 = 7	32 ÷ 4 = 8
25 ÷ 5 = 5	21 ÷ 3 = 7	16 ÷ 4 = 4
24 ÷ 4 = 6	28 ÷ 4 = 7	12 ÷ 2 = 6
45 ÷ 5 = 9	35 ÷ 5 = 7	12 ÷ 3 = 4
10 ÷ 2 = 5	40 ÷ 10 = 4	12 ÷ 4 = 3
20 ÷ 10 = 2	20 ÷ 2 = 10	20 ÷ 2 = 10
6 ÷ 2 = 3	18 ÷ 3 = 6	20 ÷ 4 = 5
24 ÷ 3 = 8	32 ÷ 4 = 8	20 ÷ 5 = 4
30 ÷ 5 = 6	40 ÷ 5 = 8	20 ÷ 10 = 2
30 ÷ 10 = 3	80 ÷ 10 = 8	18 ÷ 2 = 9
40 ÷ 5 = 8	6 ÷ 2 = 3	18 ÷ 3 = 6
21 ÷ 3 = 7	15 ÷ 3 = 5	15 ÷ 3 = 5
14 ÷ 2 = 7	24 ÷ 4 = 6	15 ÷ 5 = 3
27 ÷ 3 = 9	15 ÷ 5 = 3	24 ÷ 3 = 8
90 ÷ 10 = 9	10 ÷ 10 = 1	24 ÷ 4 = 6
15 ÷ 5 = 3	4 ÷ 2 = 2	50 ÷ 5 = 10
15 ÷ 3 = 5	9 ÷ 3 = 3	50 ÷ 10 = 5
20 ÷ 5 = 4	4 ÷ 4 = 1	30 ÷ 3 = 10
20 ÷ 4 = 5	10 ÷ 5 = 2	30 ÷ 5 = 6
16 ÷ 2 = 8	100 ÷ 10 = 10	30 ÷ 10 = 3

Times tables for division

This page will help you remember times tables by dividing by 2, 3, 4, 5, 6, and 10.
30 ÷ 6 = 5   12 ÷ 6 = 2   60 ÷ 10 = 6

Complete the problems.

18 ÷ 6 = 3	27 ÷ 3 = 9	48 ÷ 6 = 8
30 ÷ 10 = 3	18 ÷ 6 = 3	35 ÷ 5 = 7
14 ÷ 2 = 7	20 ÷ 2 = 10	36 ÷ 4 = 9
18 ÷ 3 = 6	24 ÷ 6 = 4	24 ÷ 3 = 8
20 ÷ 4 = 5	24 ÷ 3 = 8	20 ÷ 2 = 10
15 ÷ 5 = 3	24 ÷ 4 = 6	30 ÷ 6 = 5
36 ÷ 6 = 6	30 ÷ 10 = 3	25 ÷ 5 = 5
50 ÷ 10 = 5	18 ÷ 2 = 9	32 ÷ 4 = 8
8 ÷ 2 = 4	18 ÷ 3 = 6	27 ÷ 3 = 9
15 ÷ 3 = 5	36 ÷ 4 = 9	16 ÷ 2 = 8
16 ÷ 4 = 4	36 ÷ 6 = 6	42 ÷ 6 = 7
25 ÷ 5 = 5	40 ÷ 5 = 8	5 ÷ 5 = 1
6 ÷ 6 = 1	100 ÷ 10 = 10	4 ÷ 4 = 1
10 ÷ 10 = 1	16 ÷ 4 = 4	28 ÷ 4 = 7
42 ÷ 6 = 7	42 ÷ 6 = 7	14 ÷ 2 = 7
24 ÷ 4 = 6	48 ÷ 6 = 8	24 ÷ 6 = 4
54 ÷ 6 = 9	54 ÷ 6 = 9	18 ÷ 6 = 3
90 ÷ 10 = 9	60 ÷ 6 = 10	54 ÷ 6 = 9
30 ÷ 6 = 5	60 ÷ 10 = 6	60 ÷ 6 = 10
30 ÷ 5 = 6	30 ÷ 6 = 5	40 ÷ 5 = 8

Times tables for division

This page will help you remember times tables by dividing by 2, 3, 4, 5, 6, and 7.

$14 \div 7 = 2$ $28 \div 7 = 4$ $70 \div 7 = 10$

Complete the problems.

$21 \div 7 = 3$	$18 \div 6 = 3$	$49 \div 7 = 7$
$35 \div 5 = 7$	$28 \div 7 = 4$	$35 \div 5 = 7$
$14 \div 2 = 7$	$24 \div 6 = 4$	$35 \div 7 = 5$
$18 \div 6 = 3$	$24 \div 4 = 6$	$24 \div 6 = 4$
$20 \div 5 = 4$	$24 \div 2 = 12$	$21 \div 3 = 7$
$15 \div 3 = 5$	$21 \div 7 = 3$	$70 \div 7 = 10$
$36 \div 4 = 9$	$42 \div 7 = 6$	$42 \div 7 = 6$
$56 \div 7 = 8$	$18 \div 3 = 6$	$32 \div 4 = 8$
$18 \div 2 = 9$	$49 \div 7 = 7$	$27 \div 3 = 9$
$15 \div 5 = 3$	$36 \div 4 = 9$	$16 \div 4 = 4$
$49 \div 7 = 7$	$36 \div 6 = 6$	$42 \div 6 = 7$
$25 \div 5 = 5$	$40 \div 5 = 8$	$45 \div 5 = 9$
$7 \div 7 = 1$	$70 \div 7 = 10$	$40 \div 4 = 10$
$63 \div 7 = 9$	$24 \div 3 = 8$	$24 \div 3 = 8$
$42 \div 7 = 6$	$42 \div 6 = 7$	$14 \div 7 = 2$
$24 \div 6 = 4$	$48 \div 6 = 8$	$24 \div 4 = 6$
$54 \div 6 = 9$	$54 \div 6 = 9$	$18 \div 3 = 6$
$28 \div 7 = 4$	$60 \div 6 = 10$	$56 \div 7 = 8$
$30 \div 6 = 5$	$63 \div 7 = 9$	$63 \div 7 = 9$
$35 \div 7 = 5$	$25 \div 5 = 5$	$48 \div 6 = 8$

Times tables for division

This page will help you remember times tables by dividing by 2, 3, 4, 5, 6, 7, 8, and 9.

$16 \div 8 = 2$ $35 \div 7 = 5$ $27 \div 9 = 3$

Complete the problems.

$42 \div 6 = 7$	$81 \div 9 = 9$	$56 \div 7 = 8$
$32 \div 8 = 4$	$56 \div 7 = 8$	$45 \div 5 = 9$
$14 \div 7 = 2$	$72 \div 9 = 8$	$35 \div 7 = 5$
$18 \div 9 = 2$	$24 \div 8 = 3$	$18 \div 9 = 2$
$63 \div 7 = 9$	$27 \div 9 = 3$	$21 \div 3 = 7$
$72 \div 9 = 8$	$72 \div 9 = 8$	$28 \div 7 = 4$
$72 \div 8 = 9$	$42 \div 6 = 7$	$64 \div 8 = 8$
$56 \div 7 = 8$	$27 \div 3 = 9$	$32 \div 8 = 4$
$18 \div 6 = 3$	$14 \div 7 = 2$	$27 \div 9 = 3$
$81 \div 9 = 9$	$36 \div 4 = 9$	$16 \div 8 = 2$
$63 \div 9 = 7$	$36 \div 6 = 6$	$42 \div 6 = 7$
$45 \div 5 = 9$	$48 \div 8 = 6$	$45 \div 9 = 5$
$54 \div 9 = 6$	$21 \div 7 = 3$	$40 \div 4 = 10$
$70 \div 7 = 10$	$24 \div 3 = 8$	$24 \div 8 = 3$
$42 \div 7 = 6$	$40 \div 8 = 5$	$63 \div 7 = 9$
$30 \div 5 = 6$	$45 \div 9 = 5$	$24 \div 6 = 4$
$54 \div 6 = 9$	$54 \div 6 = 9$	$18 \div 3 = 6$
$56 \div 8 = 7$	$42 \div 7 = 6$	$56 \div 8 = 7$
$30 \div 5 = 6$	$63 \div 9 = 7$	$63 \div 9 = 7$
$35 \div 7 = 5$	$50 \div 5 = 10$	$48 \div 8 = 6$

Times tables practice grids

This is a times tables grid.

X	3	4	5
7	21	28	35
8	24	32	40

Complete each times tables grid.

X	1	3	5	7	9
2	2	6	10	14	18
3	3	9	15	21	27

X	4	6
6	24	36
7	28	42
8	32	48

X	6	7	8	9	10
3	18	21	24	27	30
4	24	28	32	36	40
5	30	35	40	45	50

X	10	7	8	4
3	30	21	24	12
5	50	35	40	20
7	70	49	56	28

X	6	2	4	7
5	30	10	20	35
10	60	20	40	70

X	8	7	9	6
9	72	63	81	54
7	56	49	63	42

Times tables practice grids

Here are more times tables grids.

X	2	4	6
5	10	20	30
7	14	28	42

X	8	3	9	2
5	40	15	45	10
6	48	18	54	12
7	56	21	63	14

X	2	3	4	5
8	16	24	32	40
9	18	27	36	45

X	10	9	8	7
6	60	54	48	42
5	50	45	40	35
4	40	36	32	28

X	3	8
2	6	16
3	9	24
4	12	32
5	15	40
6	18	48
7	21	56

X	2	4	6	8
1	2	4	6	8
3	6	12	18	24
5	10	20	30	40
7	14	28	42	56
9	18	36	54	72
0	0	0	0	0

Times tables practice grids

Here are some other times tables grids.

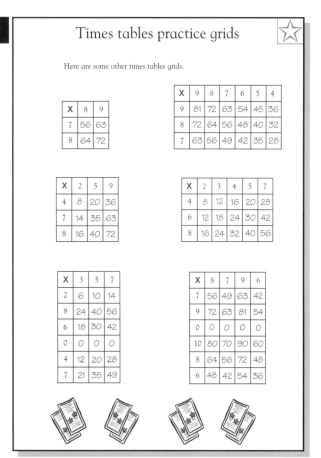

X	8	9
7	56	63
8	64	72

X	9	8	7	6	5	4
9	81	72	63	54	45	36
8	72	64	56	48	40	32
7	63	56	49	42	35	28

X	2	5	9
4	8	20	36
7	14	35	63
8	16	40	72

X	2	3	4	5	7
4	8	12	16	20	28
6	12	18	24	30	42
8	16	24	32	40	56

X	3	5	7
2	6	10	14
8	24	40	56
6	18	30	42
0	0	0	0
4	12	20	28
7	21	35	49

X	8	7	9	6
7	56	49	63	42
9	72	63	81	54
0	0	0	0	0
10	80	70	90	60
8	64	56	72	48
6	48	42	54	36

Speed trials

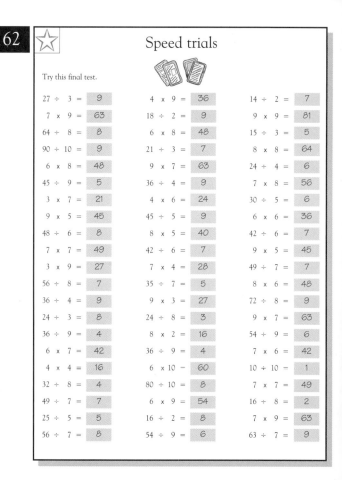

Try this final test.

27 ÷ 3 = 9	4 x 9 = 36	14 ÷ 2 = 7
7 x 9 = 63	18 ÷ 2 = 9	9 x 9 = 81
64 ÷ 8 = 8	6 x 8 = 48	15 ÷ 3 = 5
90 ÷ 10 = 9	21 ÷ 3 = 7	8 x 8 = 64
6 x 8 = 48	9 x 7 = 63	24 ÷ 4 = 6
45 ÷ 9 = 5	36 ÷ 4 = 9	7 x 8 = 56
3 x 7 = 21	4 x 6 = 24	30 ÷ 5 = 6
9 x 5 = 45	45 ÷ 5 = 9	6 x 6 = 36
48 ÷ 6 = 8	8 x 5 = 40	42 ÷ 6 = 7
7 x 7 = 49	42 ÷ 6 = 7	9 x 5 = 45
3 x 9 = 27	7 x 4 = 28	49 ÷ 7 = 7
56 ÷ 8 = 7	35 ÷ 7 = 5	8 x 6 = 48
36 ÷ 4 = 9	9 x 3 = 27	72 ÷ 8 = 9
24 ÷ 3 = 8	24 ÷ 8 = 3	9 x 7 = 63
36 ÷ 9 = 4	8 x 2 = 16	54 ÷ 9 = 6
6 x 7 = 42	36 ÷ 9 = 4	7 x 6 = 42
4 x 4 = 16	6 x 10 = 60	10 ÷ 10 = 1
32 ÷ 8 = 4	80 ÷ 10 = 8	7 x 7 = 49
49 ÷ 7 = 7	6 x 9 = 54	16 ÷ 8 = 2
25 ÷ 5 = 5	16 ÷ 2 = 8	7 x 9 = 63
56 ÷ 7 = 8	54 ÷ 9 = 6	63 ÷ 7 = 9

Line of symmetry

If a plane figure is cut into two equal parts, the line of the cut is called a line of symmetry.

Draw as many lines of symmetry as you can find on each of these shapes.

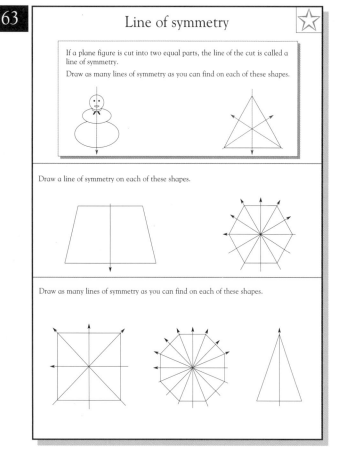

Draw a line of symmetry on each of these shapes.

Draw as many lines of symmetry as you can find on each of these shapes.

If children find it difficult to see where a line of symmetry falls, talk about where the shape could be folded so that both parts overlap exactly.

Ordering large numbers

Write these numbers in order, starting with the least.

256	654 327	39 214	147 243	9631
256	9631	39 214	147 243	654 327

Write these numbers in order, starting with the least.

72 463	730 241	261	5247	643 292
261	5247	72 463	643 292	730 241
641 471	260 453	59 372	657 473	4290
4290	59 372	260 453	641 471	657 473
327 914	647 212	47 900	3825	416
416	3825	47 900	327 914	647 212
593 103	761	374 239	91 761	1425
761	1425	91 761	374 239	593 103
600 200	500 200	5200	50 200	52 000
5200	50 200	52 000	500 200	600 200
6437	643	64 370	6430	643 000
643	6430	6437	64 370	643 000
9900	999	900 200	920 200	9 200 000
999	9900	900 200	920 200	9 200 000

In a country's election O'Neil got 900 550 votes, Schneider got 840 690 votes, Rojas got 8 406 900 votes, Marsalis got 7 964 201 votes and Samperi got 859 999 votes.

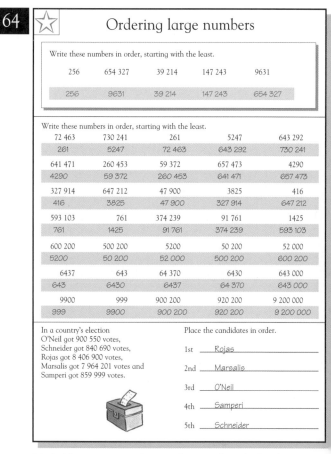

Place the candidates in order.

1st _Rojas_
2nd _Marsalis_
3rd _O'Neil_
4th _Samperi_
5th _Schneider_

If children are weak on place value, help them identify the significant digits when sorting a group of numbers. Take care when the same digits are used but with different place values.

Rounding whole numbers

Write these numbers to the nearest hundred.

529 **500**   1687 **1700**

If the place to the right of the place we are rounding is 5, round to the number above.

652 **700**

Round to the nearest hundred.

873 **900**	295 **300**	7348 **7300**	3561 **3600**
16 537 **16 500**	4855 **4900**	569 **600**	1200 **1200**
22 851 **22 900**	227 **200**	782 **800**	452 **500**

Round to the nearest ten-thousand.

23 478 **20 000**	418 700 **420 000**	58 397 **60 000**	351 899 **350 000**
109 544 **110 000**	31 059 **30 000**	67 414 **70 000**	33 500 **30 000**
89 388 **90 000**	801 821 **800 000**	134 800 **130 000**	45 010 **50 000**

Round to the nearest ten.

87 **90**	397 **400**	52 **50**	65 **70**
1392 **1390**	15 **20**	12 489 **12 490**	2861 **2860**
75 **80**	715 **720**	34 **30**	18 149 **18 150**

Round to the nearest thousand.

3284 **3000**	112 810 **113 000**	10 518 **11 000**	83 477 **83 000**
8499 **8000**	225 500 **226 000**	4500 **5000**	6112 **6000**
1059 **1000**	93 606 **94 000**	6752 **7000**	2550 **3000**

If children are confused about where to round, help them underline the rounding place and circle the digit to its right– that is the digit to compare to 5.

66

Choosing units of measure

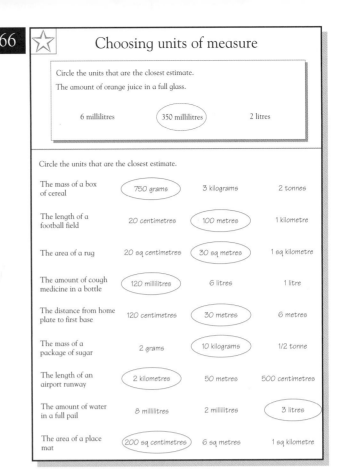

Circle the units that are the closest estimate.
The amount of orange juice in a full glass.

6 millilitres   (350 millilitres)   2 litres

Circle the units that are the closest estimate.

The mass of a box of cereal	(750 grams)	3 kilograms	2 tonnes
The length of a football field	20 centimetres	(100 metres)	1 kilometre
The area of a rug	20 sq centimetres	(30 sq metres)	1 sq kilometre
The amount of cough medicine in a bottle	(120 millilitres)	6 litres	1 litre
The distance from home plate to first base	120 centimetres	(30 metres)	6 metres
The mass of a package of sugar	2 grams	(10 kilograms)	1/2 tonne
The length of an airport runway	(2 kilometres)	50 metres	500 centimetres
The amount of water in a full pail	8 millilitres	2 millilitres	(3 litres)
The area of a place mat	(200 sq centimetres)	6 sq metres	1 sq kilometre

Children need mental benchmarks for each of the units in order to choose the best unit of measure. Suggest examples, such as the mass of a few raisins for grams and the mass of a pair of shoes for a kilogram.

67

Comparing fractions

Which is greater, $\frac{2}{3}$ or $\frac{3}{4}$? $\boxed{\frac{3}{4}}$

The common denominator of 3 and 4 is 12.

So $\frac{2}{3} = \frac{8}{12}$ and $\frac{3}{4} = \frac{9}{12}$

$\frac{3}{4}$ is greater.

Which is greater?

$\frac{1}{4}$ or $\frac{1}{3}$ $\boxed{\frac{1}{3}}$ $\frac{5}{6}$ or $\frac{7}{9}$ $\boxed{\frac{5}{6}}$ $\frac{1}{2}$ or $\frac{5}{8}$ $\boxed{\frac{5}{8}}$ $\frac{4}{9}$ or $\frac{1}{3}$ $\boxed{\frac{4}{9}}$

$\frac{2}{5}$ or $\frac{3}{8}$ $\boxed{\frac{2}{5}}$ $\frac{7}{10}$ or $\frac{8}{9}$ $\boxed{\frac{8}{9}}$ $\frac{8}{10}$ or $\frac{7}{8}$ $\boxed{\frac{7}{8}}$ $\frac{7}{12}$ or $\frac{2}{3}$ $\boxed{\frac{2}{3}}$

$\frac{2}{3}$ or $\frac{5}{8}$ $\boxed{\frac{2}{3}}$ $\frac{4}{15}$ or $\frac{1}{3}$ $\boxed{\frac{1}{3}}$ $\frac{3}{5}$ or $\frac{2}{3}$ $\boxed{\frac{2}{3}}$ $\frac{3}{8}$ or $\frac{1}{4}$ $\boxed{\frac{3}{8}}$

Which two fractions in each row are equal?

$\frac{1}{4}$ $\frac{3}{8}$ $\frac{4}{12}$ $\frac{3}{12}$ $\frac{7}{8}$ $\frac{5}{8}$ $\boxed{\frac{1}{4} \text{ and } \frac{3}{12}}$

$\frac{5}{8}$ $\frac{6}{9}$ $\frac{7}{10}$ $\frac{8}{12}$ $\frac{1}{2}$ $\frac{3}{4}$ $\boxed{\frac{6}{9} \text{ and } \frac{8}{12}}$

$\frac{7}{12}$ $\frac{6}{14}$ $\frac{7}{14}$ $\frac{3}{8}$ $\frac{4}{8}$ $\frac{9}{12}$ $\boxed{\frac{7}{14} \text{ and } \frac{4}{8}}$

$\frac{3}{8}$ $\frac{3}{9}$ $\frac{2}{6}$ $\frac{4}{7}$ $\frac{9}{10}$ $\frac{6}{7}$ $\boxed{\frac{3}{9} \text{ and } \frac{2}{6}}$

$\frac{3}{10}$ $\frac{5}{15}$ $\frac{2}{10}$ $\frac{3}{15}$ $\frac{4}{10}$ $\frac{7}{15}$ $\boxed{\frac{2}{10} \text{ and } \frac{3}{15}}$

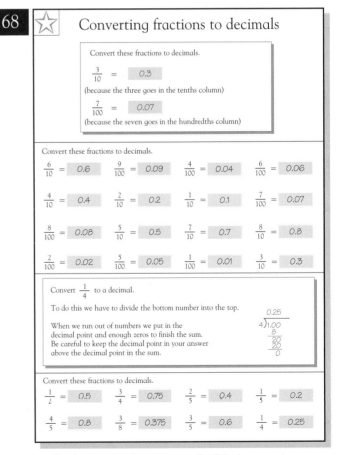

Put these fractions in order starting with the least.

$\frac{1}{2}$ $\frac{5}{6}$ $\frac{2}{3}$ $\boxed{\frac{1}{2} \quad \frac{2}{3} \quad \frac{5}{6}}$

$\frac{5}{8}$ $\frac{3}{4}$ $\frac{11}{12}$ $\boxed{\frac{5}{8} \quad \frac{3}{4} \quad \frac{11}{12}}$

$\frac{2}{3}$ $\frac{8}{15}$ $\frac{3}{5}$ $\boxed{\frac{8}{15} \quad \frac{3}{5} \quad \frac{2}{3}}$

Difficulty in finding a common denominator indicates a weakness in times tables knowledge. Children need to convert all the fractions in the later questions into a common form before answering the question. Be careful that they do not try to guess the answer.

Converting fractions to decimals

Convert these fractions to decimals.

$\frac{3}{10} = \boxed{0.3}$

(because the three goes in the tenths column)

$\frac{7}{100} = \boxed{0.07}$

(because the seven goes in the hundredths column)

Convert these fractions to decimals.

$\frac{6}{10} = \boxed{0.6}$ $\frac{9}{100} = \boxed{0.09}$ $\frac{4}{100} = \boxed{0.04}$ $\frac{6}{100} = \boxed{0.06}$

$\frac{4}{10} = \boxed{0.4}$ $\frac{2}{10} = \boxed{0.2}$ $\frac{1}{10} = \boxed{0.1}$ $\frac{7}{100} = \boxed{0.07}$

$\frac{8}{100} = \boxed{0.08}$ $\frac{5}{10} = \boxed{0.5}$ $\frac{7}{10} = \boxed{0.7}$ $\frac{8}{10} = \boxed{0.8}$

$\frac{2}{100} = \boxed{0.02}$ $\frac{5}{100} = \boxed{0.05}$ $\frac{1}{100} = \boxed{0.01}$ $\frac{3}{10} = \boxed{0.3}$

Convert $\frac{1}{4}$ to a decimal.

To do this we have to divide the bottom number into the top.

When we run out of numbers we put in the decimal point and enough zeros to finish the sum. Be careful to keep the decimal point in your answer above the decimal point in the sum.

$$\begin{array}{r} 0.25 \\ 4\overline{)1.00} \\ 8 \\ \overline{20} \\ 20 \\ \overline{0} \end{array}$$

Convert these fractions to decimals.

$\frac{1}{2} = \boxed{0.5}$ $\frac{3}{4} = \boxed{0.75}$ $\frac{2}{5} = \boxed{0.4}$ $\frac{1}{5} = \boxed{0.2}$

$\frac{4}{5} = \boxed{0.8}$ $\frac{3}{8} = \boxed{0.375}$ $\frac{3}{5} = \boxed{0.6}$ $\frac{1}{4} = \boxed{0.25}$

Difficulty in the first section highlights weakness in understanding place value to the first two decimal places. It may be necessary to reinforce understanding of 10ths and 100ths in decimals.

Adding fractions

Work out the answer to the problem.

$$\frac{1}{5}+\frac{3}{5}=\frac{4}{5} \qquad \frac{4}{9}+\frac{2}{9}=\frac{6}{9}=\frac{2}{3}$$

Remember to reduce to simplest form if you need to.

Work out the answer to each sum. Reduce to simplest form if you need to.

$\frac{2}{7}+\frac{3}{7}=\frac{5}{7}$ $\qquad$ $\frac{2}{9}+\frac{5}{9}=\frac{7}{9}$ $\qquad$ $\frac{1}{3}+\frac{1}{3}=\frac{2}{3}$

$\frac{3}{10}+\frac{4}{10}=\frac{7}{10}$ $\qquad$ $\frac{1}{8}+\frac{2}{8}=\frac{3}{8}$ $\qquad$ $\frac{2}{9}+\frac{3}{9}=\frac{5}{9}$

$\frac{2}{5}+\frac{1}{5}=\frac{3}{5}$ $\qquad$ $\frac{1}{7}+\frac{5}{7}=\frac{6}{7}$ $\qquad$ $\frac{4}{9}+\frac{1}{9}=\frac{5}{9}$

$\frac{3}{20}+\frac{4}{20}=\frac{7}{20}$ $\qquad$ $\frac{3}{100}+\frac{8}{100}=\frac{11}{100}$ $\qquad$ $\frac{7}{10}+\frac{2}{10}=\frac{9}{10}$

$\frac{1}{6}+\frac{2}{6}=\frac{3}{6}=\frac{1}{2}$ $\qquad$ $\frac{31}{100}+\frac{19}{100}=\frac{50}{100}=\frac{1}{2}$ $\qquad$ $\frac{11}{20}+\frac{4}{20}=\frac{15}{20}=\frac{3}{4}$

$\frac{3}{10}+\frac{3}{10}=\frac{6}{10}=\frac{3}{5}$ $\qquad$ $\frac{1}{12}+\frac{5}{12}=\frac{6}{12}=\frac{1}{2}$ $\qquad$ $\frac{2}{6}+\frac{2}{6}=\frac{4}{6}=\frac{2}{3}$

$\frac{3}{8}+\frac{3}{8}=\frac{6}{8}=\frac{3}{4}$ $\qquad$ $\frac{3}{8}+\frac{1}{8}=\frac{4}{8}=\frac{1}{2}$ $\qquad$ $\frac{5}{12}+\frac{3}{12}=\frac{8}{12}=\frac{2}{3}$

$\frac{1}{4}+\frac{1}{4}=\frac{2}{4}=\frac{1}{2}$ $\qquad$ $\frac{3}{20}+\frac{2}{20}=\frac{5}{20}=\frac{1}{4}$ $\qquad$ $\frac{2}{6}+\frac{2}{6}=\frac{4}{6}=\frac{2}{3}$

$\frac{2}{7}+\frac{4}{7}=\frac{6}{7}$ $\qquad$ $\frac{2}{9}+\frac{2}{9}=\frac{4}{9}$ $\qquad$ $\frac{13}{20}+\frac{5}{20}=\frac{18}{20}=\frac{9}{10}$

$\frac{81}{100}+\frac{9}{100}=\frac{90}{100}=\frac{9}{10}$ $\qquad$ $\frac{7}{20}+\frac{6}{20}=\frac{13}{20}$ $\qquad$ $\frac{3}{8}+\frac{2}{8}=\frac{5}{8}$

$\frac{6}{10}+\frac{2}{10}=\frac{8}{10}=\frac{4}{5}$ $\qquad$ $\frac{29}{100}+\frac{46}{100}=\frac{75}{100}=\frac{3}{4}$ $\qquad$ $\frac{73}{100}+\frac{17}{100}=\frac{90}{100}=\frac{9}{10}$

Difficulty in reducing a sum to a simpler form points to a weakness in finding the greatest common factor of the numerator and denominator. Children can reduce the answer in stages, first looking at whether 2 is a common factor, then 3, and so on.

70

Subtracting fractions

Write the answer to each problem.

$$\frac{4}{5}-\frac{2}{5}=\frac{2}{5} \qquad \frac{8}{9}-\frac{5}{9}=\frac{3}{9}=\frac{1}{3}$$

Reduce to simplest form if you need to.

Write the answer to each problem. Reduce to simplest form if you need to.

$\frac{3}{5}-\frac{1}{5}=\frac{2}{5}$ $\qquad$ $\frac{6}{7}-\frac{3}{7}=\frac{3}{7}$ $\qquad$ $\frac{9}{10}-\frac{6}{10}=\frac{3}{10}$

$\frac{7}{10}-\frac{4}{10}=\frac{3}{10}$ $\qquad$ $\frac{5}{9}-\frac{4}{9}=\frac{1}{9}$ $\qquad$ $\frac{2}{3}-\frac{1}{3}=\frac{1}{3}$

$\frac{7}{8}-\frac{3}{8}=\frac{4}{8}=\frac{1}{2}$ $\qquad$ $\frac{14}{20}-\frac{10}{20}=\frac{4}{20}=\frac{1}{5}$ $\qquad$ $\frac{5}{6}-\frac{1}{6}=\frac{4}{6}=\frac{2}{3}$

$\frac{11}{12}-\frac{5}{12}=\frac{6}{12}=\frac{1}{2}$ $\qquad$ $\frac{17}{20}-\frac{12}{20}=\frac{5}{20}=\frac{1}{4}$ $\qquad$ $\frac{9}{12}-\frac{3}{12}=\frac{6}{12}=\frac{1}{2}$

$\frac{8}{10}-\frac{6}{10}=\frac{2}{10}=\frac{1}{5}$ $\qquad$ $\frac{12}{12}-\frac{2}{12}=\frac{10}{12}=\frac{5}{6}$ $\qquad$ $\frac{9}{10}-\frac{3}{10}=\frac{6}{10}=\frac{3}{5}$

$\frac{8}{9}-\frac{2}{9}=\frac{6}{9}=\frac{2}{3}$ $\qquad$ $\frac{7}{8}-\frac{1}{8}=\frac{6}{8}=\frac{3}{4}$ $\qquad$ $\frac{9}{12}-\frac{5}{12}=\frac{4}{12}=\frac{1}{3}$

$\frac{3}{4}-\frac{2}{4}=\frac{1}{4}$ $\qquad$ $\frac{6}{8}-\frac{3}{8}=\frac{3}{8}$ $\qquad$ $\frac{18}{20}-\frac{8}{20}=\frac{10}{20}=\frac{1}{2}$

$\frac{4}{6}-\frac{2}{6}=\frac{2}{6}=\frac{1}{3}$ $\qquad$ $\frac{5}{12}-\frac{4}{12}=\frac{1}{12}$ $\qquad$ $\frac{3}{8}-\frac{2}{8}=\frac{1}{8}$

$\frac{5}{7}-\frac{1}{7}=\frac{4}{7}$ $\qquad$ $\frac{5}{16}-\frac{1}{16}=\frac{4}{16}=\frac{1}{4}$ $\qquad$ $\frac{90}{100}-\frac{80}{100}=\frac{10}{100}=\frac{1}{10}$

See the notes on page 69.

71

Adding fractions

Write the answer to each problem.

$$\frac{3}{8}+\frac{5}{8}=\frac{8}{8}=1 \qquad \frac{3}{4}+\frac{3}{4}=\frac{6}{4}=\frac{3}{2}=1\frac{1}{2}$$

Write the answer to each problem.

$\frac{7}{10}+\frac{6}{10}=\frac{13}{10}=1\frac{3}{10}$ $\qquad$ $\frac{6}{7}+\frac{5}{7}=\frac{11}{7}=1\frac{4}{7}$ $\qquad$ $\frac{2}{3}+\frac{2}{3}=\frac{4}{3}=1\frac{1}{3}$

$\frac{5}{10}+\frac{6}{10}=\frac{11}{10}=1\frac{1}{10}$ $\qquad$ $\frac{8}{13}+\frac{5}{13}=\frac{13}{13}=1$ $\qquad$ $\frac{7}{8}+\frac{4}{8}=\frac{11}{8}=1\frac{3}{8}$

$\frac{7}{8}+\frac{5}{8}=\frac{12}{8}=\frac{3}{2}=1\frac{1}{2}$ $\qquad$ $\frac{2}{5}+\frac{3}{5}=\frac{5}{5}=1$ $\qquad$ $\frac{5}{8}+\frac{5}{8}=\frac{10}{8}=\frac{5}{4}=1\frac{1}{4}$

$\frac{10}{20}+\frac{15}{20}=\frac{25}{20}=\frac{5}{4}=1\frac{1}{4}$ $\qquad$ $\frac{2}{3}+\frac{1}{3}=\frac{3}{3}=1$ $\qquad$ $\frac{5}{6}+\frac{5}{6}=\frac{10}{6}=\frac{5}{3}=1\frac{2}{3}$

$\frac{5}{6}+\frac{3}{6}=\frac{8}{6}=\frac{4}{3}=1\frac{1}{3}$ $\qquad$ $\frac{6}{12}+\frac{7}{12}=\frac{13}{12}=1\frac{1}{12}$ $\qquad$ $\frac{8}{10}+\frac{6}{10}=\frac{14}{10}=\frac{7}{5}=1\frac{2}{5}$

$\frac{12}{20}+\frac{10}{20}=\frac{22}{20}=\frac{11}{10}=1\frac{1}{10}$ $\qquad$ $\frac{3}{10}+\frac{7}{10}=\frac{10}{10}=1$ $\qquad$ $\frac{75}{100}+\frac{75}{100}=\frac{150}{100}=\frac{3}{2}=1\frac{1}{2}$

$\frac{10}{20}+\frac{16}{20}=\frac{26}{20}=\frac{13}{10}=1\frac{3}{10}$ $\qquad$ $\frac{4}{5}+\frac{4}{5}=\frac{8}{5}=1\frac{3}{5}$ $\qquad$ $\frac{11}{21}+\frac{17}{21}=\frac{28}{21}=\frac{4}{3}=1\frac{1}{3}$

If children leave the answer as a fraction or do not reduce it, they are completing only one of the two steps to finding the simplest form. Have them write the answer as a mixed number first, and then reduce the fraction part.

Adding fractions

Write the answer to each problem.

$$\frac{2}{3}+\frac{1}{6}=\frac{4}{6}+\frac{1}{6}=\frac{5}{6} \qquad \frac{3}{4}+\frac{5}{6}=\frac{9}{12}+\frac{10}{12}=\frac{19}{12}=1\frac{7}{12}$$

Work out the answer to each problem. Rename as a mixed number if you need to.

$\frac{2}{5}+\frac{7}{10}=\frac{4}{10}+\frac{7}{10}=\frac{11}{10}=1\frac{1}{10}$ $\qquad$ $\frac{3}{4}+\frac{7}{10}=\frac{15}{20}+\frac{14}{20}=\frac{29}{20}=1\frac{9}{20}$

$\frac{1}{4}+\frac{5}{6}=\frac{3}{12}+\frac{10}{12}=\frac{13}{12}=1\frac{1}{12}$ $\qquad$ $\frac{3}{4}+\frac{7}{8}=\frac{6}{8}+\frac{7}{8}=\frac{13}{8}=1\frac{5}{8}$

$\frac{2}{3}+\frac{1}{4}=\frac{8}{12}+\frac{3}{12}=\frac{11}{12}$ $\qquad$ $\frac{5}{6}+\frac{11}{12}=\frac{10}{12}+\frac{11}{12}=\frac{21}{12}=1\frac{3}{4}$

$\frac{5}{7}+\frac{3}{14}=\frac{10}{14}+\frac{3}{14}=\frac{13}{14}$ $\qquad$ $\frac{5}{8}+\frac{7}{10}=\frac{25}{40}+\frac{28}{40}=\frac{53}{40}=1\frac{13}{40}$

$\frac{3}{4}+\frac{3}{5}=\frac{15}{20}+\frac{12}{20}=\frac{27}{20}=1\frac{7}{20}$ $\qquad$ $\frac{1}{2}+\frac{5}{9}=\frac{9}{18}+\frac{10}{18}=\frac{19}{18}=1\frac{1}{18}$

$\frac{2}{3}+\frac{7}{9}=\frac{6}{9}+\frac{7}{9}=\frac{13}{9}=1\frac{4}{9}$ $\qquad$ $\frac{1}{3}+\frac{7}{8}=\frac{8}{24}+\frac{21}{24}=\frac{29}{24}=1\frac{5}{24}$

$\frac{3}{8}+\frac{1}{6}=\frac{9}{24}+\frac{4}{24}=\frac{13}{24}$ $\qquad$ $\frac{2}{3}+\frac{4}{5}=\frac{10}{15}+\frac{12}{15}=\frac{22}{15}=1\frac{7}{15}$

$\frac{4}{5}+\frac{5}{6}=\frac{24}{30}+\frac{25}{30}=\frac{49}{30}=1\frac{19}{30}$ $\qquad$ $\frac{2}{3}+\frac{3}{10}=\frac{20}{30}+\frac{9}{30}=\frac{29}{30}$

Difficulty in finding a common denominator indicates a weakness in finding the least common multiple of two numbers. Children can always find a common denominator by multiplying the given denominators.

73

Subtracting fractions ⭐

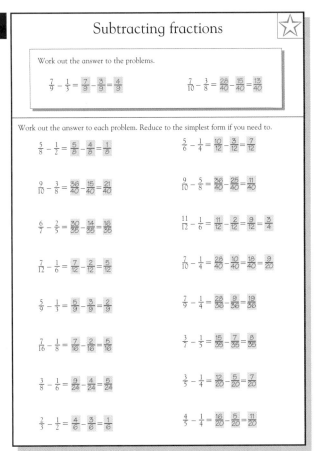

Work out the answer to the problems.

$$\frac{7}{9} - \frac{1}{3} = \frac{7}{9} - \frac{3}{9} = \frac{4}{9} \qquad \frac{7}{10} - \frac{3}{8} = \frac{28}{40} - \frac{15}{40} = \frac{13}{40}$$

Work out the answer to each problem. Reduce to the simplest form if you need to.

$$\frac{5}{8} - \frac{1}{2} = \frac{5}{8} - \frac{4}{8} = \frac{1}{8} \qquad\qquad \frac{5}{6} - \frac{1}{4} = \frac{10}{12} - \frac{3}{12} = \frac{7}{12}$$

$$\frac{9}{10} - \frac{3}{8} = \frac{36}{40} - \frac{15}{40} = \frac{21}{40} \qquad \frac{9}{10} - \frac{5}{8} = \frac{36}{40} - \frac{25}{40} = \frac{11}{40}$$

$$\frac{6}{7} - \frac{2}{5} = \frac{30}{35} - \frac{14}{35} = \frac{16}{35} \qquad \frac{11}{12} - \frac{1}{6} = \frac{11}{12} - \frac{2}{12} = \frac{9}{12} = \frac{3}{4}$$

$$\frac{7}{12} - \frac{1}{6} = \frac{7}{12} - \frac{2}{12} = \frac{5}{12} \qquad \frac{7}{10} - \frac{1}{4} = \frac{28}{40} - \frac{10}{40} = \frac{18}{40} = \frac{9}{20}$$

$$\frac{5}{9} - \frac{1}{3} = \frac{5}{9} - \frac{3}{9} = \frac{2}{9} \qquad \frac{7}{9} - \frac{1}{4} = \frac{28}{36} - \frac{9}{36} = \frac{19}{36}$$

$$\frac{7}{16} - \frac{1}{8} = \frac{7}{16} - \frac{2}{16} = \frac{5}{16} \qquad \frac{3}{7} - \frac{1}{5} = \frac{15}{35} - \frac{7}{35} = \frac{8}{35}$$

$$\frac{3}{8} - \frac{1}{6} = \frac{9}{24} - \frac{4}{24} = \frac{5}{24} \qquad \frac{3}{5} - \frac{1}{4} = \frac{12}{20} - \frac{5}{20} = \frac{7}{20}$$

$$\frac{2}{3} - \frac{1}{2} = \frac{4}{6} - \frac{3}{6} = \frac{1}{6} \qquad \frac{4}{5} - \frac{1}{4} = \frac{16}{20} - \frac{5}{20} = \frac{11}{20}$$

See the notes on page 72.

74

⭐ Adding mixed numbers

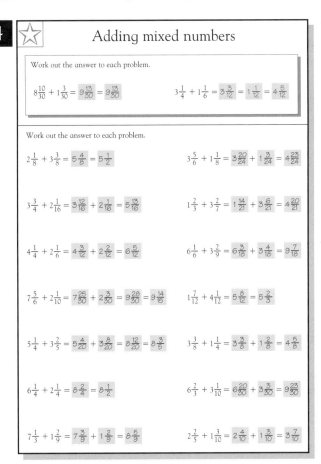

Work out the answer to each problem.

$$8\frac{10}{30} + 1\frac{3}{30} = 9\frac{13}{30} = 9\frac{13}{30} \qquad 3\frac{1}{4} + 1\frac{1}{6} = 3\frac{3}{12} = 1\frac{1}{12} = 4\frac{5}{12}$$

Work out the answer to each problem.

$$2\frac{1}{8} + 3\frac{3}{8} = 5\frac{4}{8} = 5\frac{1}{2} \qquad 3\frac{5}{6} + 1\frac{1}{8} = 3\frac{20}{24} + 1\frac{3}{24} = 4\frac{23}{24}$$

$$3\frac{3}{4} + 2\frac{1}{16} = 3\frac{12}{16} + 2\frac{1}{16} = 5\frac{13}{16} \qquad 1\frac{2}{3} + 3\frac{2}{7} = 1\frac{14}{21} + 3\frac{6}{21} = 4\frac{20}{21}$$

$$4\frac{1}{4} + 2\frac{1}{6} = 4\frac{3}{12} + 2\frac{2}{12} = 6\frac{5}{12} \qquad 6\frac{1}{6} + 3\frac{2}{9} = 6\frac{3}{18} + 3\frac{4}{18} = 9\frac{7}{18}$$

$$7\frac{5}{6} + 2\frac{1}{10} = 7\frac{25}{30} + 2\frac{3}{30} = 9\frac{28}{30} = 9\frac{14}{15} \qquad 1\frac{7}{12} + 4\frac{1}{12} = 5\frac{8}{12} = 5\frac{2}{3}$$

$$5\frac{1}{4} + 3\frac{2}{5} = 5\frac{4}{20} + 3\frac{8}{20} = 8\frac{12}{20} = 8\frac{3}{5} \qquad 3\frac{3}{8} + 1\frac{1}{4} = 3\frac{3}{8} + 1\frac{2}{8} = 4\frac{5}{8}$$

$$6\frac{1}{4} + 2\frac{1}{4} = 8\frac{2}{4} = 8\frac{1}{2} \qquad 6\frac{2}{3} + 3\frac{1}{10} = 6\frac{20}{30} + 3\frac{3}{30} = 9\frac{23}{30}$$

$$7\frac{1}{3} + 1\frac{2}{9} = 7\frac{3}{9} + 1\frac{2}{9} = 8\frac{5}{9} \qquad 2\frac{2}{5} + 1\frac{3}{10} = 2\frac{4}{10} + 1\frac{3}{10} = 3\frac{7}{10}$$

A common error is forgetting to recopy the whole number when renaming the mixed numbers. Children can recopy both whole numbers first, then rename the two fractions.

75

Subtracting mixed numbers ⭐

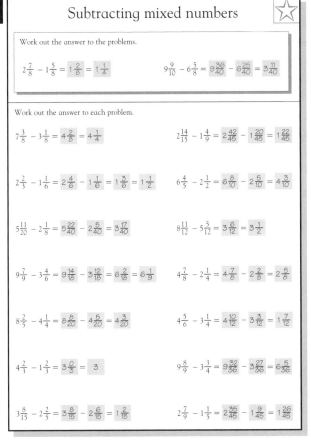

Work out the answer to the problems.

$$2\frac{7}{8} - 1\frac{5}{8} = 1\frac{2}{8} = 1\frac{1}{4} \qquad 9\frac{9}{10} - 6\frac{5}{8} = 9\frac{36}{40} - 6\frac{25}{40} = 3\frac{11}{40}$$

Work out the answer to each problem.

$$7\frac{3}{8} - 3\frac{1}{8} = 4\frac{2}{8} = 4\frac{1}{4} \qquad 2\frac{14}{15} - 1\frac{4}{9} = 2\frac{42}{45} - 1\frac{20}{45} = 1\frac{22}{45}$$

$$2\frac{2}{3} - 1\frac{1}{6} = 2\frac{4}{6} - 1\frac{1}{6} = 1\frac{3}{6} = 1\frac{1}{2} \qquad 6\frac{4}{5} - 2\frac{1}{2} = 6\frac{8}{10} - 2\frac{5}{10} = 4\frac{3}{10}$$

$$5\frac{11}{20} - 2\frac{1}{8} = 5\frac{22}{40} - 2\frac{5}{40} = 3\frac{17}{40} \qquad 8\frac{11}{12} - 5\frac{5}{12} = 3\frac{6}{12} = 3\frac{1}{2}$$

$$9\frac{7}{9} - 3\frac{4}{6} = 9\frac{14}{18} - 3\frac{12}{18} = 6\frac{2}{18} = 6\frac{1}{9} \qquad 4\frac{7}{8} - 2\frac{1}{4} = 4\frac{7}{8} - 2\frac{2}{8} = 2\frac{5}{8}$$

$$8\frac{2}{5} - 4\frac{1}{4} = 8\frac{8}{20} - 4\frac{5}{20} = 4\frac{3}{20} \qquad 4\frac{5}{6} - 3\frac{1}{4} = 4\frac{10}{12} - 3\frac{3}{12} = 1\frac{7}{12}$$

$$4\frac{2}{3} - 1\frac{2}{3} = 3\frac{0}{3} = 3 \qquad 9\frac{8}{9} - 3\frac{3}{4} = 9\frac{32}{36} - 3\frac{27}{36} = 6\frac{5}{36}$$

$$3\frac{8}{15} - 2\frac{2}{5} = 3\frac{8}{15} - 2\frac{6}{15} = 1\frac{2}{15} \qquad 2\frac{7}{9} - 1\frac{1}{5} = 2\frac{35}{45} - 1\frac{9}{45} = 1\frac{26}{45}$$

See the notes on page 74.

76

⭐ Adding mixed numbers and fractions

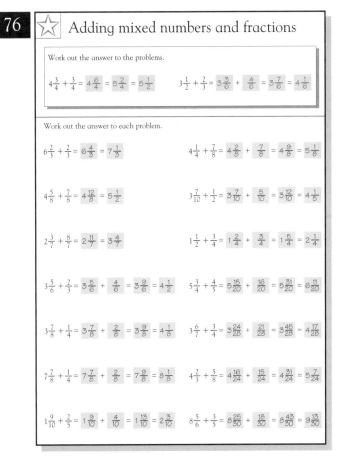

Work out the answer to the problems.

$$4\frac{3}{4} + \frac{3}{4} = 4\frac{6}{4} = 5\frac{2}{4} = 5\frac{1}{2} \qquad 3\frac{1}{2} + \frac{2}{3} = 3\frac{3}{6} + \frac{4}{6} = 3\frac{7}{6} = 4\frac{1}{6}$$

Work out the answer to each problem.

$$6\frac{2}{3} + \frac{2}{3} = 6\frac{4}{3} = 7\frac{1}{3} \qquad 4\frac{1}{4} + \frac{7}{8} = 4\frac{2}{8} + \frac{7}{8} = 4\frac{9}{8} = 5\frac{1}{8}$$

$$4\frac{5}{8} + \frac{7}{8} = 4\frac{12}{8} = 5\frac{1}{2} \qquad 3\frac{7}{10} + \frac{1}{2} = 3\frac{7}{10} + \frac{5}{10} = 3\frac{12}{10} = 4\frac{1}{5}$$

$$2\frac{3}{7} + \frac{8}{7} = 2\frac{11}{7} = 3\frac{4}{7} \qquad 1\frac{1}{2} + \frac{3}{4} = 1\frac{2}{4} + \frac{3}{4} = 1\frac{5}{4} = 2\frac{1}{4}$$

$$3\frac{5}{6} + \frac{2}{3} = 3\frac{5}{6} + \frac{4}{6} = 3\frac{9}{6} = 4\frac{1}{2} \qquad 5\frac{3}{4} + \frac{4}{5} = 5\frac{15}{20} + \frac{16}{20} = 5\frac{31}{20} = 6\frac{11}{20}$$

$$3\frac{7}{8} + \frac{1}{4} = 3\frac{7}{8} + \frac{2}{8} = 3\frac{9}{8} = 4\frac{1}{8} \qquad 3\frac{6}{7} + \frac{3}{4} = 3\frac{24}{28} + \frac{21}{28} = 3\frac{45}{28} = 4\frac{17}{28}$$

$$7\frac{7}{8} + \frac{1}{4} = 7\frac{7}{8} + \frac{2}{8} = 7\frac{9}{8} = 8\frac{1}{8} \qquad 4\frac{2}{3} + \frac{5}{8} = 4\frac{16}{24} + \frac{15}{24} = 4\frac{31}{24} = 5\frac{7}{24}$$

$$1\frac{9}{10} + \frac{2}{5} = 1\frac{9}{10} + \frac{4}{10} = 1\frac{13}{10} = 2\frac{3}{10} \qquad 8\frac{5}{6} + \frac{3}{5} = 8\frac{25}{30} + \frac{18}{30} = 8\frac{43}{30} = 9\frac{13}{30}$$

The most difficult step is renaming the answer as a proper mixed number. If children have trouble, get them to first rename the fractional part as a mixed number, and then add the 1 from this mixed number to the other whole number part.

77

Simple use of parentheses ⭐

Work out these problems.
$(4 + 6) - (2 + 1) =$ $10 - 3 = 7$
$(2 \times 5) + (10 - 4) =$ $10 + 6 = 16$
Remember to work out the parentheses first.

Work out these problems.

$(5 + 3) + (6 - 2) =$	12		$(3 - 1) + (12 - 1) =$	13
$(6 - 1) - (1 + 2) =$	2		$(9 + 5) - (3 + 6) =$	5
$(8 + 3) + (12 - 2) =$	21		$(14 + 12) - (9 + 4) =$	13
$(7 - 2) + (4 + 5) =$	14		$(9 - 3) - (4 + 2) =$	0

Now try these longer problems.

$(5 + 9) + (12 - 2) - (4 + 3) =$	17
$(10 + 5) - (2 + 4) + (9 + 6) =$	24
$(19 + 4) - (3 + 2) - (2 + 1) =$	15
$(24 - 5) - (3 + 7) - (5 - 2) =$	6
$(15 + 3) + (7 - 2) - (5 + 7) =$	11

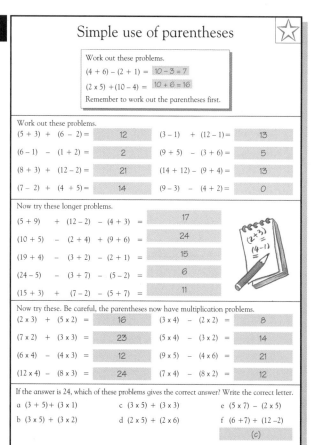

Now try these. Be careful, the parentheses now have multiplication problems.

$(2 \times 3) + (5 \times 2) =$	16		$(3 \times 4) - (2 \times 2) =$	8
$(7 \times 2) + (3 \times 3) =$	23		$(5 \times 4) - (3 \times 2) =$	14
$(6 \times 4) - (4 \times 3) =$	12		$(9 \times 5) - (4 \times 6) =$	21
$(12 \times 4) - (8 \times 3) =$	24		$(7 \times 4) - (8 \times 2) =$	12

If the answer is 24, which of these problems gives the correct answer? Write the correct letter.

a $(3 + 5) + (3 \times 1)$ c $(3 \times 5) + (3 \times 3)$ e $(5 \times 7) - (2 \times 5)$
b $(3 \times 5) + (3 \times 2)$ d $(2 \times 5) + (2 \times 6)$ f $(6 + 7) + (12 - 2)$

(c)

Errors on this page will most likely be the result of choosing the wrong order of operation. Remind children that they must work out the brackets first, before they add or subtract the results. Concentration and careful reading should prevent any problems.

78

⭐ ## Simple use of parentheses

Work out these problems.
$(3 + 2) \times (4 + 1) =$ $5 \times 5 = 25$
$(10 \times 5) \div (10 - 5) =$ $50 \div 5 = 10$
Remember to work out the parentheses first.

Work out these problems.

$(7 + 3) \times (8 - 4) =$	40		$(5 - 2) \times (8 - 1) =$	21
$(9 + 5) \div (1 + 6) =$	2		$(14 - 6) \times (4 + 3) =$	56
$(14 + 4) \div (12 - 6) =$	3		$(9 + 21) \div (8 - 5) =$	10
$(11 - 5) \times (7 + 5) =$	72		$(8 + 20) \div (12 - 10) =$	14
$(6 + 9) \div (8 - 3) =$	3		$(14 - 3) \times (6 + 1) =$	77
$(10 + 10) \div (2 + 3) =$	4		$(9 + 3) \times (2 + 4) =$	72

Now try these.

$(4 \times 3) \div (1 \times 2) =$	6		$(5 \times 4) \div (2 \times 2) =$	5
$(8 \times 5) \div (4 \times 1) =$	10		$(6 \times 4) \div (3 \times 4) =$	2
$(2 \times 4) \times (2 \times 3) =$	48		$(3 \times 5) \times (1 \times 2) =$	30
$(8 \times 4) \div (2 \times 2) =$	8		$(6 \times 4) \div (4 \times 2) =$	3

If the answer is 30, which of these problems gives the correct answer?
a $(3 \times 5) \times (2 \times 2)$ d $(20 \div 2) \times (12 \div 3)$
b $(4 \times 5) \times (5 \times 2)$ e $(5 \times 12) \div (2 \times 5)$
c $(12 \times 5) \div (8 \div 4)$ f $(9 \times 5) \div (10 \div 2)$ c

If the answer is 8, which of these problems gives the correct answer?
a $(16 \div 2) \div (2 \times 1)$ d $(24 \div 6) \times (8 \div 4)$
b $(9 \div 3) \times (3 \times 2)$ e $(8 \div 4) \times (8 \div 1)$
c $(12 \times 4) \div (6 \times 2)$ f $(16 \div 4) \times (20 \div 4)$ d

This page continues the work of the previous page, but the brackets are multiplied or divided. It may be necessary to remind children to read carefully, as several operations take place in each equation.

Simple use of parentheses ☆

Work out these problems.
$(5 + 3) + (9 - 2) =$ $8 + 7 = 15$
$(5 + 2) - (4 - 1) =$ $7 - 3 = 4$
$(4 + 2) \times (3 + 1) =$ $6 \times 4 = 24$
$(3 \times 5) \div (9 - 6) =$ $15 \div 3 = 5$
Remember to work out the parentheses first.

Work out these problems.

$(5 + 4) + (7 - 3) =$	13		$(9 - 2) + (6 + 4) =$	17
$(7 + 3) - (9 - 7) =$	8		$(15 - 5) + (2 + 3) =$	15
$(11 \times 2) - (3 \times 2) =$	16		$(15 \div 3) + (9 \times 2) =$	23
$(12 \times 2) - (3 \times 3) =$	15		$(6 \div 2) + (8 \times 2) =$	19
$(9 \times 3) - (7 \times 3) =$	6		$(15 \div 5) + (3 \times 4) =$	15
$(20 \div 5) - (8 \div 2) =$	0		$(5 \times 10) - (12 \times 4) =$	2

Now try these.

$(4 + 8) \div (3 \times 2) =$	2		$(6 \times 4) \div (3 \times 2) =$	4
$(9 + 5) \div (2 \times 1) =$	7		$(7 \times 4) \div (3 + 4) =$	4
$(3 + 6) \times (3 \times 3) =$	81		$(5 \times 5) \div (10 \div 2) =$	5
$(24 \div 2) \times (3 \times 2) =$	72		$(8 \times 6) \div (2 \times 12) =$	2

Write down the letters of all the problems that make 25.
a $(2 \times 5) \times (3 \times 2)$ d $(40 \div 2) + (10 \div 2)$
b $(5 \times 5) + (7 - 2)$ e $(10 \times 5) - (5 \times 5)$
c $(6 \times 5) - (10 \div 2)$ f $(10 \times 10) \div (10 - 6)$ c, d, e, f

Write down the letters of all the problems that make 20.
a $(10 \div 2) \times (4 \div 4)$ d $(20 \div 4) \times (8 \div 2)$
b $(7 \times 3) - (3 \div 3)$ e $(10 \div 2) + (20 \div 2)$
c $(8 \times 4) - (6 \times 2)$ f $(14 \div 2) + (2 \times 7)$ b, c

This page reinforces all the elements of the previous two pages. Again, the most likely cause of error will be lack of concentration.

☆ ## Multiplying decimals

Work out these problems.

$\overset{1}{4.6}$	$\overset{4}{3.9}$	$\overset{3}{8.4}$
$\times\ \ 3$	$\times\ \ 5$	$\times\ \ 8$
13.8	19.5	67.2

Work out these problems.

4.7 $\times\ 3$	9.1 $\times\ 3$	5.8 $\times\ 3$	1.7 $\times\ 2$	5.1 $\times\ 2$
14.1	27.3	17.4	3.4	10.2
7.4 $\times\ 2$	3.6 $\times\ 4$	6.5 $\times\ 4$	4.2 $\times\ 2$	3.8 $\times\ 2$
14.8	14.4	26.0	8.4	7.6
4.2 $\times\ 4$	4.7 $\times\ 4$	1.8 $\times\ 5$	3.4 $\times\ 5$	3.7 $\times\ 5$
16.8	18.8	9.0	17.0	18.5
2.5 $\times\ 5$	2.4 $\times\ 6$	5.3 $\times\ 7$	7.2 $\times\ 8$	5.1 $\times\ 9$
12.5	14.4	37.1	57.6	45.9
7.9 $\times\ 9$	8.6 $\times\ 9$	8.8 $\times\ 8$	7.5 $\times\ 8$	9.9 $\times\ 6$
71.1	77.4	70.4	60.0	59.4
6.8 $\times\ 7$	5.7 $\times\ 6$	6.9 $\times\ 7$	7.5 $\times\ 9$	8.4 $\times\ 9$
47.6	34.2	48.3	67.5	75.6
7.3 $\times\ 8$	2.8 $\times\ 7$	3.8 $\times\ 8$	7.7 $\times\ 7$	9.4 $\times\ 9$
58.4	19.6	30.4	53.9	84.6

Ensure that children work from right to left. Problems will highlight gaps in their knowledge of times tables. Remind them that the number they are multiplying has one decimal place, so their answer must have one decimal place also, and this can be put in at the end.

81

Multiplying decimals

Work out these problems.

¹ ¹	³ ¹	⁴ ²
37.5	26.2	65.3
x 2	x 5	x 9
75.0	131.0	587.7

Work out these problems.

53.3	93.2	51.4	34.6	35.2
x 2	x 2	x 2	x 3	x 3
106.6	186.4	102.8	103.8	105.6

46.5	25.8	16.4	47.1	37.4
x 4	x 4	x 3	x 5	x 5
186.0	103.2	49.2	235.5	187.0

12.4	46.3	17.5	36.5	72.4
x 5	x 5	x 6	x 6	x 7
62.0	231.5	105.0	219.0	506.8

37.5	20.3	73.4	92.6	47.9
x 7	x 7	x 7	x 6	x 6
262.5	142.1	513.8	555.6	287.4

53.9	75.6	28.8	79.4	99.9
x 8	x 8	x 8	x 8	x 9
431.2	604.8	230.4	635.2	899.1

37.9	14.8	35.4	46.8	27.2
x 9	x 9	x 9	x 8	x 7
341.1	133.2	318.6	374.4	190.4

39.5	84.2	68.5	73.2	47.6
x 6	x 9	x 8	x 9	x 6
237.0	757.8	548.0	658.8	285.6

This page further revises decimal multiplication, using larger numbers.

82

Real-life problems

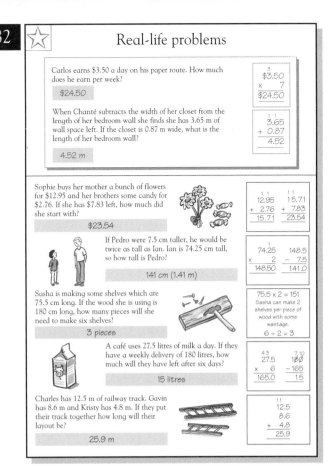

Carlos earns $3.50 a day on his paper route. How much does he earn per week?

$24.50

```
   3
  $3.50
 x    7
 $24.50
```

When Chanté subtracts the width of her closet from the length of her bedroom wall she finds she has 3.65 m of wall space left. If the closet is 0.87 m wide, what is the length of her bedroom wall?

4.52 m

```
  1 1
   3.65
 + 0.87
   4.52
```

Sophie buys her mother a bunch of flowers for $12.95 and her brothers some candy for $2.76. If she has $7.83 left, how much did she start with?

$23.54

```
  1 1       1 1
 12.95     15.71
 + 2.76    + 7.83
 15.71     23.54
```

If Pedro were 7.5 cm taller, he would be twice as tall as Ian. Ian is 74.25 cm tall, so how tall is Pedro?

141 cm (1.41 m)

```
  74.25     148.5
 x     2   -   7.5
 148.50     141.0
```

Sasha is making some shelves which are 75.5 cm long. If the wood she is using is 180 cm long, how many pieces will she need to make six shelves?

3 pieces

```
75.5 x 2 = 151
Sasha can make 2
shelves per piece of
wood with some
wastage.
  6 ÷ 2 = 3
```

A café uses 27.5 litres of milk a day. If they have a weekly delivery of 180 litres, how much will they have left after six days?

15 litres

```
  4 3       7 10
 27.5      1 8̸ 0̸
 x    6    - 165
 165.0      15
```

Charles has 12.5 m of railway track. Gavin has 8.6 m and Kristy has 4.8 m. If they put their track together how long will their layout be?

25.9 m

```
  1 1
  12.5
   8.6
 + 4.8
  25.9
```

This page provides an opportunity to apply math skills to real-life problems. Children will need to choose the operation carefully. Some questions require more than one operation.

83

Real-life problems

A novelist writes 9.5 pages of his book a day. How many pages will he write in nine days?

85.5 pages

```
   4
   9.5
 x   9
  85.5
```

After driving 147.7 km a driver stops at a service station. If he has another 115.4 km to go, how long will his trip be?

263.1 km

```
   1 1
  147.7
 + 115.4
  263.1
```

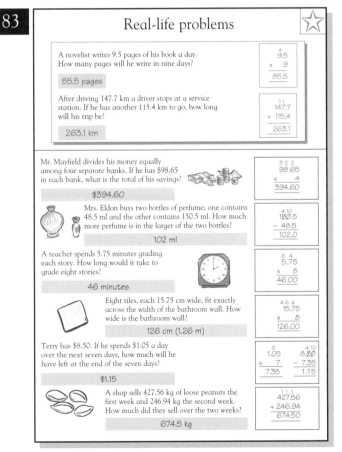

Mr. Mayfield divides his money equally among four separate banks. If he has $98.65 in each bank, what is the total of his savings?

$394.60

```
   3 2 2
  98.65
 x     4
 394.60
```

Mrs. Eldon buys two bottles of perfume; one contains 48.5 ml and the other contains 150.5 ml. How much more perfume is in the larger of the two bottles?

102 ml

```
  4 10
 15̸0̸.5
 - 48.5
 102.0
```

A teacher spends 5.75 minutes grading each story. How long would it take to grade eight stories?

46 minutes

```
   6 4
   5.75
 x    8
 46.00
```

Eight tiles, each 15.75 cm wide, fit exactly across the width of the bathroom wall. How wide is the bathroom wall?

126 cm (1.26 m)

```
   4 6 4
  15.75
 x     8
 126.00
```

Terry has $8.50. If he spends $1.05 a day over the next seven days, how much will he have left at the end of the seven days?

$1.15

```
   3        4 10
  1.05     8.5̸0̸
 x   7    - 7.35
  7.35     1.15
```

A shop sells 427.56 kg of loose peanuts the first week and 246.94 kg the second week. How much did they sell over the two weeks?

674.5 kg

```
  1 1 1
  427.56
 + 246.94
  674.50
```

This page also revises various operations applied to real-life situations.

Real-life problems

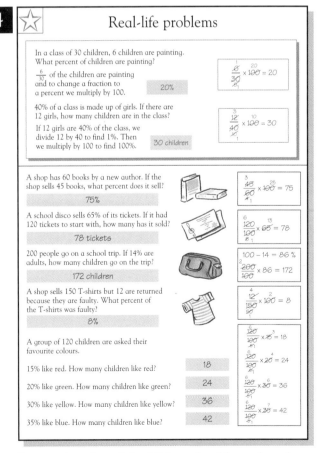

In a class of 30 children, 6 children are painting. What percent of children are painting?

$\frac{6}{30}$ of the children are painting and to change a fraction to a percent we multiply by 100.

20%

$$\frac{6̸}{3̸0̸} \times \overset{20}{1̸0̸0̸} = 20$$

40% of a class is made up of girls. If there are 12 girls, how many children are in the class?

If 12 girls are 40% of the class, we divide 12 by 40 to find 1%. Then we multiply by 100 to find 100%.

30 children

$$\frac{3}{12} \times \overset{10}{1̸0̸0̸} = 30$$

A shop has 60 books by a new author. If the shop sells 45 books, what percent does it sell?

75%

$$\frac{48}{6̸0̸} \times \overset{25}{1̸0̸0̸} = 75$$

A school disco sells 65% of its tickets. If it had 120 tickets to start with, how many has it sold?

78 tickets

$$\frac{\overset{6}{1̸2̸0̸}}{1̸0̸0̸} \times \overset{13}{65} = 78$$

200 people go on a school trip. If 14% are adults, how many children go on the trip?

172 children

100 − 14 = 86 %

$$\frac{\overset{2}{2̸0̸0̸}}{1̸0̸0̸} \times 86 = 172$$

A shop sells 150 T-shirts but 12 are returned because they are faulty. What percent of the T-shirts was faulty?

8%

$$\frac{\overset{4}{1̸2̸}}{1̸5̸0̸} \times \overset{2}{1̸0̸0̸} = 8$$

A group of 120 children are asked their favourite colours.

15% like red. How many children like red? — 18

$$\frac{1̸2̸0̸}{1̸0̸0̸} \times \overset{3}{1̸5̸} = 18$$

20% like green. How many children like green? — 24

$$\frac{1̸2̸0̸}{1̸0̸0̸} \times 20 = 24$$

30% like yellow. How many children like yellow? — 36

$$\frac{1̸2̸0̸}{1̸0̸0̸} \times 30 = 36$$

35% like blue. How many children like blue? — 42

$$\frac{1̸2̸0̸}{1̸0̸0̸} \times \overset{7}{3̸5̸} = 42$$

In questions 1 and 4, children should see that the answer can be expressed as a fraction, which can then be converted to a percentage by multiplying by 100.

Conversions: length ☆

Units of length	
10 millimetres	1 centimetre
1000 millimetres	1 metre
100 centimetres	1 metre
1000 metres	1 kilometre

This conversion table shows how to convert millimetres, centimetres, metres, and kilometres.

Neilika's rope is 3 metres long. How many millimetres long is it?

Brian's rope is 600 centimetres long. How many metres long is it?

$600 ÷ 100 = 6$ 6 metres

$3 × 100 = 300$ 300 centimetres long
$300 × 10 = 3000$ 3000 millimetres long

Convert each measurement to centimetres.

10 millimetres $10 ÷ 10 = 1$ 1 cm	200 millimetres $200 ÷ 10 = 20$ 20 cm	48 millimetres $48 ÷ 10 = 4.8$ 4.8 cm	72 millimetres $72 ÷ 10 = 7.2$ 7.2 cm

Convert each measurement to metres.

600 centimetres $600 ÷ 100 = 6$ 6 m	1200 centimetres $1200 ÷ 100 = 12$ 12 m	270 centimetres $270 ÷ 100 = 2.7$ 2.7 m	3600 centimetres $3600 ÷ 100 = 36$ 36 m

Convert each measurement to millimetres.

4 centimetres $4 × 10 = 40$ 40 millimetres	12 centimetres $12 × 10 = 120$ 120 millimetres	8 centimetres $8 × 10 = 80$ 80 millimetres	5 centimetres $5 × 10 = 50$ 50 millimetres

Convert each measurement to centimetres.

6 metres $6 × 100 = 600$ 600 cm	2 metres $2 × 100 = 200$ 200 cm	7 metres $7 × 100 = 700$ 700 cm	5 metres $5 × 100 = 500$ 500 cm

Convert each measurement.

4 metres $4 × 100 = 400$ 400 centimetres	5 kilometres $5 × 1000 = 5000$ 5000 metres	4 metres $4 × 100 = 400$ 400 centimetres	1 kilometre $1 × 100 000 = 100 000$ 100 000 centimetres
5840 centimetres $5840 ÷ 100 = 58.4$ 58.4 metres	31 680 centimetres $31 680 ÷ 100 000 = 3168$ .3168 kilometres	1760 metres $1760 ÷ 1000 = 1.76$ 1.76 kilometres	352 metres $352 ÷ 1000 = .352$ .352 kilometres

If children are confused whether to multiply or divide, have them think about whether the new unit is a longer or a shorter unit. If the unit is longer, there will be fewer of them, so division will be the appropriate operation to use.

86

☆ Conversions: capacity

Units of capacity	
1000 millilitres	1 litre

This conversion table shows how to convert millilitres and litres.

Katya's thermos holds 8 litres. How many millilitres does it hold?

Hannah's thermos holds 60 000 millilitres. How many litres does it hold?

$8 × 1000 = 8000$ 8000 millilitres

$60 000 ÷ 1000 = 60$ 60 litres

Convert each measurement to litres.

32 000 millilitres $32 000 ÷ 1000 = 32$ 32 litres	16 000 millilitres $16 000 ÷ 1000 = 16$ 16 litres	9600 millilitres $9600 ÷ 1000 = 9.6$ 9.6 litres	8000 millilitres $8000 ÷ 1000 = 8$ 8 litres

Convert each measurement to millilitres.

6 litres $6 × 1000 = 6000$ 6000 ml	12 litres $12 × 1000 = 12 000$ 12 000 ml	36 litres $36 × 1000 = 36 000$ 36 000 ml	50 litres $50 × 1000 = 50 000$ 50 000 ml
4 litres $4 × 1000 = 4000$ 4000 ml	12 litres $12 × 1000 = 12 000$ 12 000 ml	30 litres $30 × 1000 = 30 000$ 30 000 ml	16 litres $16 × 1000 = 16 000$ 16 000 ml

Convert each measurement to litres.

14 000 millilitres $14 000 ÷ 1000 = 14$ 14 litres	32 000 millilitres $32 000 ÷ 1000 = 32$ 32 litres	100 000 millilitres $100 000 ÷ 1000 = 100$ 100 litres	20 000 millilitres $20 000 ÷ 1000 = 20$ 20 litres

Convert each measurement.

3000 millilitres $3000 ÷ 1000 = 3$ 3 litres	5 litres $5 × 1000 = 5000$ 5000 millilitres	36 000 millilitres $36 000 ÷ 1000 = 36$ 36 litres	72 litres $72 × 1000 = 72 000$ 72 000 millilitres
1 litre $1 × 1000 = 1000$ 1000 millilitres	24 000 millilitres $24 000 ÷ 1000 = 24$ 24 litres	7 litres $7 × 1000 = 7000$ 7000 millilitres	11 000 millilitres $11 000 ÷ 1000 = 11$ 11 litres

See the notes for page 85.

87

Fraction of a number ☆

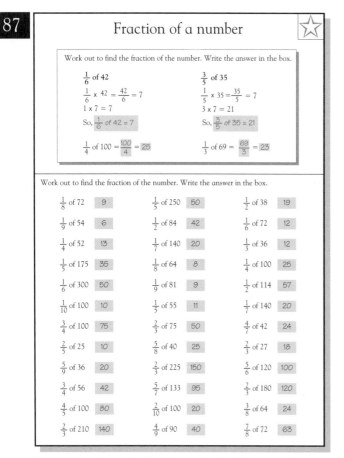

Work out to find the fraction of the number. Write the answer in the box.

$\frac{1}{6}$ of 42

$\frac{1}{6} × 42 = \frac{42}{6} = 7$

$1 × 7 = 7$

So, $\frac{1}{6}$ of $42 = 7$

$\frac{3}{5}$ of 35

$\frac{1}{5} × 35 = \frac{35}{5} = 7$

$3 × 7 = 21$

So, $\frac{3}{5}$ of $35 = 21$

$\frac{1}{4}$ of $100 = \frac{100}{4} = 25$

$\frac{1}{3}$ of $69 = \frac{69}{3} = 23$

Work out to find the fraction of the number. Write the answer in the box.

$\frac{1}{8}$ of 72	9	$\frac{1}{5}$ of 250	50	$\frac{1}{2}$ of 38	19
$\frac{1}{9}$ of 54	6	$\frac{1}{2}$ of 84	42	$\frac{1}{6}$ of 72	12
$\frac{1}{4}$ of 52	13	$\frac{1}{7}$ of 140	20	$\frac{1}{3}$ of 36	12
$\frac{1}{5}$ of 175	35	$\frac{1}{8}$ of 64	8	$\frac{1}{4}$ of 100	25
$\frac{1}{6}$ of 300	50	$\frac{1}{9}$ of 81	9	$\frac{1}{2}$ of 114	57
$\frac{1}{10}$ of 100	10	$\frac{1}{5}$ of 55	11	$\frac{1}{7}$ of 140	20
$\frac{3}{4}$ of 100	75	$\frac{2}{3}$ of 75	50	$\frac{4}{7}$ of 42	24
$\frac{2}{5}$ of 25	10	$\frac{5}{8}$ of 40	25	$\frac{2}{3}$ of 27	18
$\frac{5}{9}$ of 36	20	$\frac{2}{3}$ of 225	150	$\frac{5}{6}$ of 120	100
$\frac{3}{4}$ of 56	42	$\frac{5}{7}$ of 133	95	$\frac{2}{3}$ of 180	120
$\frac{4}{5}$ of 100	80	$\frac{2}{10}$ of 100	20	$\frac{3}{8}$ of 64	24
$\frac{2}{3}$ of 210	140	$\frac{4}{9}$ of 90	40	$\frac{7}{8}$ of 72	63

If children have difficulty with the first step, have them use long division to find the quotient.

☆ Showing decimals

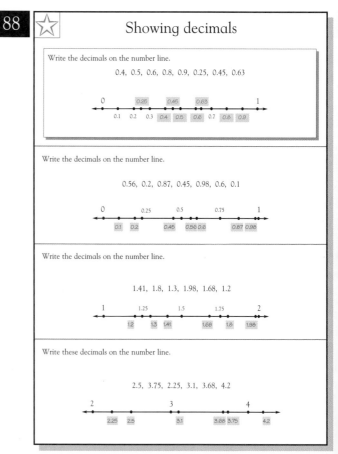

Write the decimals on the number line.

0.4, 0.5, 0.6, 0.8, 0.9, 0.25, 0.45, 0.63

Write the decimals on the number line.

0.56, 0.2, 0.87, 0.45, 0.98, 0.6, 0.1

Write the decimals on the number line.

1.41, 1.8, 1.3, 1.98, 1.68, 1.2

Write these decimals on the number line.

2.5, 3.75, 2.25, 3.1, 3.68, 4.2

If children are confused about where to place the decimals to hundredths, have them first fill in all of the tenths on the number line. Then ask which of those tenths the decimals to hundredths fall between.

89

Area of right-angled triangles ☆

Find the area of this right-angled triangle.

Because the area of this triangle is half the area of the rectangle shown, we can find the area of the rectangle and then divide it by two to find the area of the triangle.
So the area = (8 cm x 4 cm) ÷ 2
= 32 cm² ÷ 2 = 16 cm²

Area = 16 cm²

Find the area of these right-angled triangles.

5 cm, 12 cm — 30 cm²

3 cm, 10 cm — 15 cm²

9 cm, 2 cm — 9 cm²

4 cm, 14 cm — 28 cm²

5 cm, 6 cm — 15 cm²

6 cm, 8 cm — 24 cm²

6 cm, 12 cm — 36 cm²

20 cm — 30 cm²

3 cm, 7 cm, 4 cm — 14 cm²

The operation of multiplying the sides together and dividing by two should offer no serious difficulty to children, but make sure they are really clear about why they are doing this.

90

☆ Speed problems

How long would it take to travel 120 km at 8 km/h?
(Time = Distance ÷ Speed)

15 hours

$\frac{15}{8)120}$

If a bus takes 3 hours to travel 150 km, how fast is it going?
(Speed = Distance ÷ Time)

50 km/h

$\frac{50}{3)150}$

If a car travels at 60 km/h for 2 hours, how far has it gone?
(Distance = Speed × Time)

120 km

$\frac{60}{\times 2}{120}$

If a man walks for 6 kilometres at a steady speed of 3 km/h, how long will it take him?

2 hours

$\frac{6}{3} = 2$

A truck driver travels 120 km in 3 hours. If he drove at a steady speed, how fast was he going?

40 km/h

$\frac{40}{3)120}$

A car travels at a steady speed of 40 km/h. How far will it travel in 4 hours?

160 km

$\frac{40}{\times 4}{160}$

Shane walks 10 km at 4 km/h. Damien walks 12 km at 5 km/h. Which of them will take the longest?

Shane

Shane $4)10$ $2\frac{2}{4}=2\frac{1}{2}$
Damien $5)12$ $2\frac{2}{5}$
$2\frac{1}{2} > 2\frac{2}{5}$

Courtney drives for 30 minutes at 50 km/h and for 1 hour at 40 km/h. How far has he travelled altogether?

65 km

30 min = $\frac{1}{2}$ h
$\frac{25}{2)50}$
25 + 40 = 65

A racing car travels 340 km in 120 minutes. What speed is it travelling at?

170 km/h

120 min = 2 h
$\frac{170}{2)340}$

If children experience difficulty on this page, ask them what they need to find – speed, distance or time – and refer them to the necessary formula. Encourage them to develop simple examples that will help them to remember the formulas.

91

Conversion tables ☆

Draw a table to convert dollars to cents.

$	cents
1	100
2	200
3	300

Complete the conversion chart below.

Weeks	Days
1	7
2	14
3	21
4	28
5	35
6	42
7	49
8	56
9	63
10	70

Sunday
Monday
Tuesday
Wednesday
Thursday
Friday
Saturday

If there are 60 minutes in 1 hour, make a conversion chart for up to 10 hours.

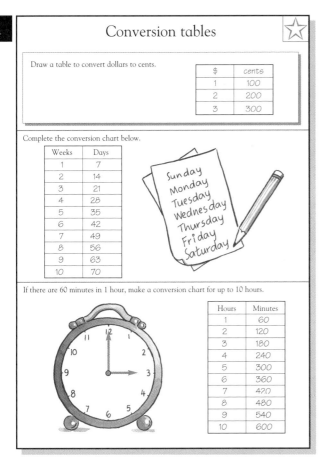

Hours	Minutes
1	60
2	120
3	180
4	240
5	300
6	360
7	420
8	480
9	540
10	600

Children will grasp that they are dealing with multiples of 7 and later, 60. Any problems will be due to weaknesses in tables or from missing out numbers as they work down the chart. Encourage care and concentration.

☆ Reading bar graphs

Look at this graph.

Ted's savings deposits

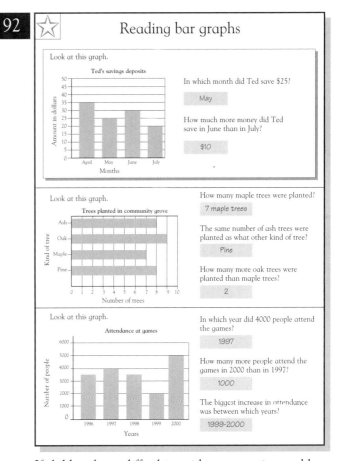

In which month did Ted save $25?

May

How much more money did Ted save in June than in July?

$10

Look at this graph.

Trees planted in community grove

How many maple trees were planted?

7 maple trees

The same number of ash trees were planted as what other kind of tree?

Pine

How many more oak trees were planted than maple trees?

2

Look at this graph.

Attendance at games

In which year did 4000 people attend the games?

1997

How many more people attend the games in 2000 than in 1997?

1000

The biggest increase in attendance was between which years?

1999-2000

If children have difficulties with computation problems, have them write down each of the numbers they read off the graph before computing with them.

Expanded form

What is the value of 3 in 2308?   300

Write 32 084 in expanded form.   30 000 + 2000 + 80 + 4

What is the value of 6 in these numbers?

26	6	162	60	36 904	6000
12 612	600	6130	6000	567 902	60 000
13 036	6	9764	60	17 632	600

What is the value of 4 in these numbers?

14 300	4000	942	40	8764	4
10 408	400	1043	40	45 987	40 000
6045	40	804 001	4000	694	4

Circle the numbers that have a 7 with the value of seventy thousand.

457 682   67 924   (870 234)   (372 987)

(171 345)   767 707   (79 835)   16 757

Write the numbers in expanded form.

34 897	30 000 + 4000 + 800 + 90 + 7
508 061	500 000 + 8000 + 60 + 1
50 810	50 000 + 800 + 10
8945	8000 + 900 + 40 + 5
60 098	60 000 + 90 + 8

Some children are confused about how to represent the zeros in a number. Be sure they know to skip those terms when they write the expanded form.

94

Cubes of small numbers

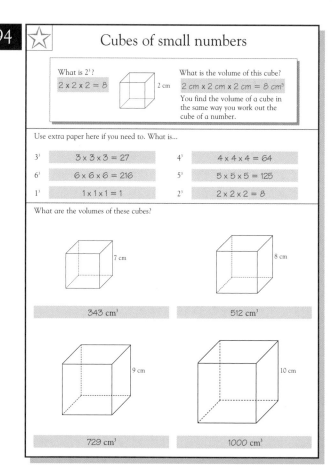

What is 2^3? $2 \times 2 \times 2 = 8$

What is the volume of this cube? $2\ cm \times 2\ cm \times 2\ cm = 8\ cm^3$

You find the volume of a cube in the same way you work out the cube of a number.

Use extra paper here if you need to. What is...

3^3	$3 \times 3 \times 3 = 27$	4^3	$4 \times 4 \times 4 = 64$
6^3	$6 \times 6 \times 6 = 216$	5^3	$5 \times 5 \times 5 = 125$
1^3	$1 \times 1 \times 1 = 1$	2^3	$2 \times 2 \times 2 = 8$

What are the volumes of these cubes?

7 cm   343 cm³

8 cm   512 cm³

9 cm   729 cm³

10 cm   1000 cm³

The most common mistake children make is confusing three cubed with three times three, especially when they are working quickly through the examples. It is necessary to reinforce the concept of cubing a number. Children may need some paper for their working out.

95

Multiplying fractions

Write the product.

$$\frac{3}{8} \times \frac{4}{7} = \frac{3}{14}$$ $$\frac{1}{5} \times \frac{3}{10} = \frac{3}{2} = 1\frac{1}{2}$$

Write the product.

$\frac{1}{4} \times \frac{1}{4} = \frac{1}{16}$ $\frac{3}{10} \times \frac{2}{6} = \frac{1}{10}$ $6 \times \frac{3}{4} = \frac{9}{2} = 4\frac{1}{2}$

$8 \times \frac{1}{4} = 2$ $\frac{2}{5} \times \frac{5}{7} = \frac{2}{7}$ $\frac{2}{5} \times \frac{5}{6} = \frac{1}{3}$

$\frac{2}{5} \times \frac{2}{3} = \frac{4}{15}$ $4 \times \frac{3}{16} = \frac{3}{4}$ $\frac{3}{8} \times 10 = \frac{15}{4} = 3\frac{3}{4}$

$\frac{1}{3} \times 15 = 5$ $\frac{5}{9} \times \frac{1}{5} = \frac{1}{9}$ $\frac{3}{4} \times \frac{4}{9} = \frac{1}{3}$

$\frac{1}{4} \times \frac{2}{7} = \frac{1}{14}$ $\frac{2}{9} \times \frac{3}{4} = \frac{1}{6}$ $12 \times \frac{3}{10} = \frac{18}{5} = 3\frac{3}{5}$

$\frac{2}{3} \times \frac{1}{3} = \frac{2}{9}$ $\frac{1}{12} \times 2 = \frac{1}{6}$ $\frac{3}{4} \times \frac{1}{4} = \frac{3}{16}$

$\frac{5}{6} \times 8 = \frac{20}{3} = 6\frac{2}{3}$ $7 \times \frac{1}{8} = \frac{7}{8}$ $\frac{1}{6} \times \frac{5}{6} = \frac{5}{36}$

$\frac{1}{2} \times 25 = \frac{25}{2} = 12\frac{1}{2}$ $\frac{7}{10} \times \frac{5}{7} = \frac{1}{2}$ $4 \times \frac{3}{4} = 3$

Some children are confused about how to multiply a fraction by a whole number. Remind them that any whole number is also a fraction with 1 as the denominator.

More complex fraction problems

Find $\frac{3}{5}$ of $30.00.

Find $\frac{1}{5}$: $30 ÷ 5 = $6
$6 × 3 = $18
So, $\frac{3}{5}$ of $30 is $18

Find $\frac{7}{10}$ of 60 cm

Find $\frac{1}{10}$: 60 cm ÷ 10 = 6 cm
6 cm × 7 = 42 cm
So, $\frac{7}{10}$ of 60 cm is 42 cm

Find $\frac{3}{5}$ of these amounts.

40 cm	$50	$10.50
40 cm ÷ 5 = 8 cm	$50 ÷ 5 = $10	$10.50 ÷ 5 = $2.10
3 × 8 cm = 24 cm	3 × $10 = $30	3 × $2.10 = $6.30
So, $\frac{3}{5}$ of 40 in. is 24 cm	So, $\frac{3}{5}$ of $50 is $30	So, $\frac{3}{5}$ of $10.50 is $6.30

80 m	75 ml	45 kg
80 m ÷ 5 = 16 m	75 ml ÷ 5 = 15 ml	45 kg ÷ 5 = 9 kg
3 × 16 m = 48 m	3 × 15 ml = 45 ml	3 × 9 kg = 27 kg
So, $\frac{3}{5}$ of 80 m is 48 m	So, $\frac{3}{5}$ of 75 ml is 45 ml	So, $\frac{3}{5}$ of 45 kg is 27 kg

Find $\frac{7}{10}$ of these amounts.

48 m	$98.00	75 km
48 m ÷ 10 = 4.8 m	$98 ÷ 10 = $9.80	75 km ÷ 10 = 7.5 km
7 × 4.8 m = 33.6 m	7 × $9.80 = $68.60	7 × 7.5 km = 52.5 km
So, $\frac{7}{10}$ of 48 m is 33.6 m	So, $\frac{7}{10}$ of $98 is $68.60	So, $\frac{7}{10}$ of 75 km is 52.5 km

Find $\frac{2}{3}$ of these amounts.

48 m	120 kg	$24.00
48 cm ÷ 3 = 16 cm	120 kg ÷ 3 = 40 kg	$24 ÷ 3 = $8
2 × 16 cm = 32 cm	2 × 40 kg = 80 kg	2 × $8 = $16
So, $\frac{2}{3}$ of 48 cm is 32 cm	So, $\frac{2}{3}$ of 120 kg is 80 kg	So, $\frac{2}{3}$ of $24 is $16

Ensure that children are dividing the amount by the denominator and multiplying the result by the numerator. You could explain that we divide by the bottom to find one part and multiply by the top to find the number of parts we want.

Finding percentages ☆

Find 30% of 140. $\frac{14\cancel{0}}{10\cancel{0}} \times 30 = 42$ (Divide by 100 to find 1% and then multiply by 30 to find 30%.)

Find 12% of 75. $\frac{75^3}{10\cancel{0}} \times 12^3 = 9$ (Divide by 100 to find 1% and then multiply by 12 to find 12%.)

Find 30% of these numbers.

620   $\frac{620}{100} \times 30 = 186$ 240 $\frac{240}{100} \times 30 = 72$

80   $\frac{80}{100} \times 30 = 24$ 160 $\frac{160}{100} \times 30 = 48$

Find 60% of these numbers.

60   $\frac{60}{100} \times 60 = 36$ 100 $\frac{100}{100} \times 60 = 60$

160   $\frac{160}{100} \times 60 = 96$ 580 $\frac{580}{100} \times 60 = 348$

Find 45% of these numbers.

80 g $\frac{80}{100} \times 45 = 36$ g   40 cm $\frac{40}{100} \times 45 = 18$ cm

240 ml $\frac{240}{100} \times 45 = 108$ ml   600 km $\frac{600}{100} \times 45 = 270$ km

Find 12% of these numbers.

$150 $\frac{150}{100} \times 12 = 18 $600 $\frac{600}{100} \times 12 = 72

125 m $\frac{125}{100} \times 12 = 15$ m   775 m $\frac{775}{100} \times 12 = 93$ m

The most common error when finding percentages is to reverse the operation, i.e. to divide by the percentage required and multiply by 100. Explain again that if the whole is 100% we divide the number by 100 to find 1% and then multiply by the percentage we want.

98

☆ Addition

Work out the answer to each problem.

```
  1 1            1 3 1
   634           1472
  4812             96
+ 1428           8391
------          + 564
  6874          ------
               10 523
```

Remember to regroup if you need to.

Find each sum.

```
  5 831      3 724      9 994        524
  8 375      9 942      7 358       7034
+   219    +   623    +   471     +   95
-------    -------    -------     ------
 14 425     14 289     17 823       7653
```

```
  7 341      9 328      7159        208
    299        347        39       4943
+ 5 143    + 8 222    +  748     +   55
-------    -------    ------     ------
 12 783     17 897     7946        5206
```

Find each sum.

```
  8 594      7 362      3041       7 641
    629        843       571         93
  9 878      4 732      5210      8 521
+    96    +    53    +   71     +  843
-------    -------    ------     ------
 19 197     12 990     8893       17 098
```

```
  8 795      6 043        27        146
    659          4       153       3714
  3 212        147      8612         26
+   961    + 8 948    +  127     + 5003
-------    -------    ------     ------
 13 627     15 142     8919        8889
```

This page should be fairly straightforward, but errors may creep in as the lists get longer towards the end. Errors will most likely be mistakes in adding the longer lists, adding across place value, or a failure to carry.

99

More addition ☆

Work out the answer to each problem.

```
 1 1   1        1 2 1
 23 714         11 541
  9 024           861
+   348         29 652
-------         +     5
 33 086         -------
                 42 059
```

Remember to regroup if you need to.

Find each sum.

```
 17 203     29 521     65 214     25 046
    112      6 211        973         15
+ 5 608    +    58    + 1 291    +   263
-------    -------    -------    -------
 22 923     35 790     67 478     25 324
```

```
  6 958     73 009     11 536     87 019
     71          3         48        127
+16 911    +   581    + 2 435    + 5 652
-------    -------    -------    -------
 23 940     73 593     14 019     92 798
```

Find each sum.

```
 79 622     64 599      6 940     72 148
  8 011        122        936        999
 47 391      6 375     58 274      7 481
+     7    +    91    +    36    + 21 685
-------    -------    -------    --------
135 031     71 187     66 186    102 313
```

```
 58 975     36 403          8         23
    858         73     22 849     99 951
  8 423        712        502        358
+    27    + 6 229    + 4 034    + 6 231
-------    -------    -------    -------
 68 283     43 417     27 393    106 563
```

Any problems on this page will be similar to those encountered on the previous page. As the numbers get larger, errors are more likely to occur.

☆ Dividing by ones

$477 \div 2$ can be written in two ways:

$238\frac{1}{2}$ or $238 \text{ r } 1$
$2\overline{)477}$ $2\overline{)477}$

Work out the answers to these problems. Use fraction remainders.

```
 239 1/2        215 3/4        115 4/5        122 6/7
 ------         ------         ------         ------
   239            215            115            122
2)479          4)863          5)579          7)860
  4              8              5              7
  -              -              -              -
  7              6              7              16
  6              4              5              14
  19             23             29             20
  18             20             25             14
  --             --             --             --
  1              3              4              6
```

```
  87 1/2         55 2/3         50 7/9         97 2/7
  -----          -----          -----          -----
    87             55             50             97
 2)175          3)167          9)457          3)293
   16             15             45             27
   --             --             --             --
   15             17             7              23
   14             15                            21
   --             --                            --
   1              2                             2
```

Work out the answers to these problems. Use unit remainders.

```
 352 r 1        127 r 2         82 r 2        131 r 4
 ------         ------          -----         ------
   352            127             82            131
2)705          5)637           4)330         7)921
  6              5               32            7
  --             --              --            --
  10             13              10            22
  10             10              8             21
  --             --              --            --
  5              37              2             11
  4              35                            7
  --             --                            --
  1              2                             4
```

Children may think that the two types of division represent different procedures. Point out that the only difference is in how to write the remainder.

Dividing by ones

361 ÷ 2 can be written in two ways:

$180\frac{1}{2}$ or   180 r 1

2) 361   2) 361

Work out the answers to these problems. Use fraction remainders.

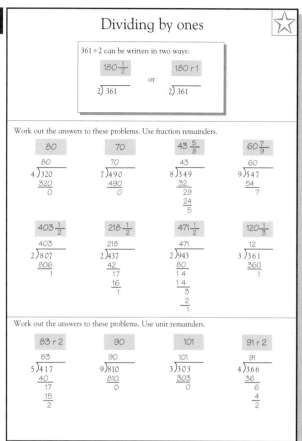

80	70	$43\frac{5}{8}$	$60\frac{7}{9}$

```
   80           70           43           60
4)320        7)490        8)349        9)547
  320          490          32           54
    0            0          29            7
                           24
                            5
```

$403\frac{1}{2}$	$218\frac{1}{2}$	$471\frac{1}{2}$	$120\frac{1}{3}$

```
  403          218          471          12
2)807        2)437        2)943        3)361
  806          42           80          360
    1          17           14            1
               16           14
                1            3
                            2
                            1
```

Work out the answers to these problems. Use unit remainders.

83 r 2	90	101	91 r 2

```
   83           90          101           91
5)417        9)810        3)303        4)366
  40           810          303           36
  17             0            0            6
  15                                       4
   2                                       2
```

Children may have trouble deciding where to place digits in the quotient. Have them place the digit directly above the number being subtracted in that step.

102

Dividing

589 ÷ 5 can be written in two ways:

$117\frac{4}{5}$ or   117 r 4

5) 589   5) 589

Work out the answers to these problems. Use fractions remainders.

$54\frac{3}{8}$	$39\frac{8}{9}$	$64\frac{4}{7}$	$113\frac{1}{7}$

```
   54           39           64           11
8)435        9)359        7)452        7)792
  40           27           42            7
  35           89           32           09
  32           81           28            7
   3            8            4           22
                                         21
                                          1
```

$117\frac{1}{8}$	$114\frac{1}{7}$	$32\frac{1}{9}$	$142\frac{1}{3}$

```
  117          114           32          142
8)937        7)799        9)289        6)854
  8            7            27           60
  13           09           19           25
   8            7           18           24
  57           29            1           14
  56           28                        12
   1            1                         2
```

Work out the answers to these problems. Use unit remainders.

72 r 5	136 r 1	119	68 r 3

```
   72          136          119           68
9)653        4)545        8)952        6)411
  63           4            8            36
  23           14           15           51
  18           12            8           48
   5           25           72            3
               24           72
                1            0
```

See the notes for page 101.

103

Everyday problems

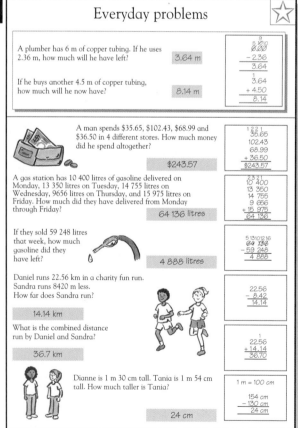

A plumber has 6 m of copper tubing. If he uses 2.36 m, how much will he have left?

3.64 m

```
    9
  5.10 10
  6.00
- 2.36
  3.64
```

If he buys another 4.5 m of copper tubing, how much will he now have?

8.14 m

```
    1
  3.64
+ 4.50
  8.14
```

A man spends $35.65, $102.43, $68.99 and $36.50 in 4 different stores. How much money did he spend altogether?

$243.57

```
  1 2 2 1
   35.65
  102.43
   68.99
+  36.50
 $243.57
```

A gas station has 10 400 litres of gasoline delivered on Monday, 13 350 litres on Tuesday, 14 755 litres on Wednesday, 9656 litres on Thursday, and 15 975 litres on Friday. How much did they have delivered from Monday through Friday?

64 136 litres

```
  2 3 2 1
  10 400
  13 350
  14 755
   9 656
+ 15 975
  64 136
```

If they sold 59 248 litres that week, how much gasoline did they have left?

4 888 litres

```
  5 13 10 12 16
  64 136
- 59 248
   4 888
```

Daniel runs 22.56 km in a charity fun run. Sandra runs 8420 m less. How far does Sandra run?

14.14 km

```
  22.56
-  8.42
  14.14
```

What is the combined distance run by Daniel and Sandra?

36.7 km

```
     1
  22.56
+ 14.14
  36.70
```

Dianne is 1 m 30 cm tall. Tania is 1 m 54 cm tall. How much taller is Tania?

24 cm

```
  1 m = 100 cm

   154 cm
 - 130 cm
    24 cm
```

Children will apply subtraction and addition skills to real-life problems. If they are unsure about which operation to use, discuss whether the answer will be larger (addition) or smaller (subtraction). Take care when units of measurement need to be converted.

104

Real-life problems

A man walks 18.34 km on Saturday and 16.57 km on Sunday. How far did he walk that weekend?

34.91 km

```
  1  1
  18.34
+ 16.57
  34.91
```

How much farther did he walk on Saturday?

1.77 km

```
     7  12
   1    14
  18.34
- 16.57
   1.77
```

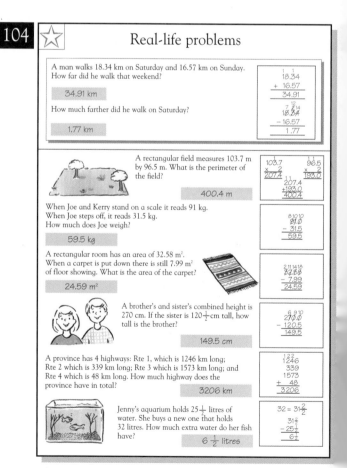

A rectangular field measures 103.7 m by 96.5 m. What is the perimeter of the field?

400.4 m

```
  103.7        96.5
 x    2       x    2
  207.4       193.0

  207.4
+ 193.0
  400.4
```

When Joe and Kerry stand on a scale it reads 91 kg. When Joe steps off, it reads 31.5 kg. How much does Joe weigh?

59.5 kg

```
  8 10 10
  91.0
- 31.5
  59.5
```

A rectangular room has an area of 32.58 m². When a carpet is put down there is still 7.99 m² of floor showing. What is the area of the carpet?

24.59 m²

```
  2 11 14 18
  32.58
-  7.99
  24.59
```

A brother's and sister's combined height is 270 cm. If the sister is $120\frac{1}{2}$ cm tall, how tall is the brother?

149.5 cm

```
  6 9 10
  270.0
- 120.5
  149.5
```

A province has 4 highways: Rte 1, which is 1246 km long; Rte 2 which is 339 km long; Rte 3 which is 1573 km long; and Rte 4 which is 48 km long. How much highway does the province have in total?

3206 km

```
  1 2 2
  1246
   339
  1573
+   48
  3206
```

Jenny's aquarium holds $25\frac{1}{2}$ litres of water. She buys a new one that holds 32 litres. How much extra water do her fish have?

$6\frac{1}{2}$ litres

```
  32 = 31 2/2

  31 2/2
- 25 1/2
   6 1/2
```

This page once again tests the skills of children in real-life problems. In the first question, make sure that they are finding the perimeter and not the area.

105 — Real-life problems

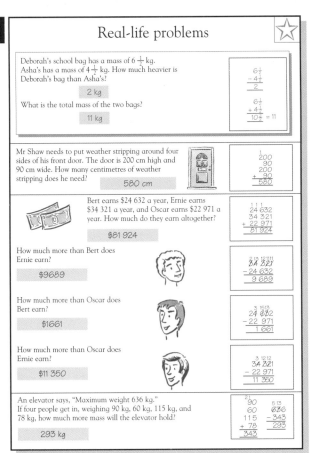

Deborah's school bag has a mass of $6\frac{1}{2}$ kg.
Asha's has a mass of $4\frac{1}{2}$ kg. How much heavier is
Deborah's bag than Asha's?

2 kg

$$\begin{array}{r} 6\frac{1}{2} \\ -4\frac{1}{2} \\ \hline 2 \end{array}$$

What is the total mass of the two bags?

11 kg

$$\begin{array}{r} 6\frac{1}{2} \\ +4\frac{1}{2} \\ \hline 10\frac{2}{2}=11 \end{array}$$

Mr Shaw needs to put weather stripping around four
sides of his front door. The door is 200 cm high and
90 cm wide. How many centimetres of weather
stripping does he need?

580 cm

$$\begin{array}{r} 200 \\ 90 \\ 200 \\ +\ 90 \\ \hline 580 \end{array}$$

Bert earns \$24 632 a year, Ernie earns
\$34 321 a year, and Oscar earns \$22 971 a
year. How much do they earn altogether?

\$81 924

$$\begin{array}{r} {}^{1\ 1\ 1} \\ 24\ 632 \\ 34\ 321 \\ +22\ 971 \\ \hline 81\ 924 \end{array}$$

How much more than Bert does
Ernie earn?

\$9689

$$\begin{array}{r} {}^{2\ 12\ 12\ 11\ 11} \\ 3\!\!\!/4\ 3\!\!\!/2\!\!\!/1 \\ -24\ 632 \\ \hline 9\ 689 \end{array}$$

How much more than Oscar does
Bert earn?

\$1661

$$\begin{array}{r} {}^{3\ \ \ 15\ 13} \\ 24\ 6\!\!\!/3\!\!\!/2 \\ -22\ 971 \\ \hline 1\ 661 \end{array}$$

How much more than Oscar does
Ernie earn?

\$11 350

$$\begin{array}{r} {}^{3\ \ 12\ 12} \\ 3\!\!\!/4\ 3\!\!\!/2\!\!\!/1 \\ -22\ 971 \\ \hline 11\ 350 \end{array}$$

An elevator says, "Maximum weight 636 kg."
If four people get in, weighing 90 kg, 60 kg, 115 kg, and
78 kg, how much more mass will the elevator hold?

293 kg

$$\begin{array}{r} {}^{2\ 1} \\ 90 \\ 60 \\ 115 \\ +78 \\ \hline 343 \end{array} \qquad \begin{array}{r} {}^{5\ 13} \\ 6\!\!\!/3\!\!\!/6 \\ -343 \\ \hline 293 \end{array}$$

See the notes for page 104.

106 — Multiplication by 2-digit numbers

Work out the answer to each problem.

$$\begin{array}{r} 27 \\ \times\ 76 \\ \hline 162 \\ 1890 \\ \hline 2052 \end{array} \qquad \begin{array}{r} 34 \\ \times\ 58 \\ \hline 272 \\ 1700 \\ \hline 1972 \end{array}$$

Work out the answer to each problem.

$$\begin{array}{r} 26 \\ \times\ 84 \\ \hline 104 \\ 2080 \\ \hline 2184 \end{array} \quad \begin{array}{r} 95 \\ \times\ 65 \\ \hline 475 \\ 5700 \\ \hline 6175 \end{array} \quad \begin{array}{r} 32 \\ \times\ 39 \\ \hline 288 \\ 960 \\ \hline 1248 \end{array} \quad \begin{array}{r} 78 \\ \times\ 49 \\ \hline 702 \\ 3120 \\ \hline 3822 \end{array}$$

$$\begin{array}{r} 97 \\ \times\ 46 \\ \hline 582 \\ 3880 \\ \hline 4462 \end{array} \quad \begin{array}{r} 94 \\ \times\ 37 \\ \hline 658 \\ 2820 \\ \hline 3478 \end{array} \quad \begin{array}{r} 32 \\ \times\ 64 \\ \hline 128 \\ 1920 \\ \hline 2048 \end{array} \quad \begin{array}{r} 47 \\ \times\ 75 \\ \hline 235 \\ 3290 \\ \hline 3525 \end{array}$$

$$\begin{array}{r} 28 \\ \times\ 95 \\ \hline 140 \\ 2520 \\ \hline 2660 \end{array} \quad \begin{array}{r} 47 \\ \times\ 62 \\ \hline 94 \\ 2820 \\ \hline 2914 \end{array} \quad \begin{array}{r} 36 \\ \times\ 87 \\ \hline 252 \\ 2880 \\ \hline 3132 \end{array} \quad \begin{array}{r} 45 \\ \times\ 33 \\ \hline 135 \\ 1350 \\ \hline 1485 \end{array}$$

$$\begin{array}{r} 46 \\ \times\ 85 \\ \hline 230 \\ 3680 \\ \hline 3910 \end{array} \quad \begin{array}{r} 29 \\ \times\ 72 \\ \hline 58 \\ 2030 \\ \hline 2088 \end{array} \quad \begin{array}{r} 85 \\ \times\ 29 \\ \hline 765 \\ 1700 \\ \hline 2465 \end{array} \quad \begin{array}{r} 63 \\ \times\ 84 \\ \hline 252 \\ 5040 \\ \hline 5292 \end{array}$$

Explain that multiplying by 84 means multiplying by
80, then by 4, and then adding the answers together.
Multiplying by 10 (or 80) means adding a zero and
multiplying by 1 (or 8). Multiplying by the tens digit
first, saves having to remember to put the zero later.

107 — Division by ones

$47 \div 2$ can be written in two ways:

$$2\overline{)47}\ \begin{array}{r} 23 \\ \underline{4} \\ 7 \\ \underline{6} \\ 1 \end{array} \quad 23\frac{1}{2} \qquad \text{or} \qquad 2\overline{)47}\ \begin{array}{r} 23 \\ \underline{4} \\ 7 \\ \underline{6} \\ 1 \end{array} \quad 23\ r\ 1$$

Write the quotients for these problems with fraction remainders.

$$\begin{array}{r} 8\frac{1}{2} \\ 2\overline{)17}\ \begin{array}{r} 8 \\ \underline{16} \\ 1 \end{array} \end{array} \quad \begin{array}{r} 4\frac{3}{4} \\ 4\overline{)19}\ \begin{array}{r} 4 \\ \underline{16} \\ 3 \end{array} \end{array} \quad \begin{array}{r} 5\frac{1}{3} \\ 3\overline{)16}\ \begin{array}{r} 5 \\ \underline{15} \\ 1 \end{array} \end{array} \quad \begin{array}{r} 9\frac{1}{4} \\ 4\overline{)37}\ \begin{array}{r} 9 \\ \underline{36} \\ 1 \end{array} \end{array}$$

$$\begin{array}{r} 9\frac{2}{3} \\ 3\overline{)29}\ \begin{array}{r} 9 \\ \underline{27} \\ 2 \end{array} \end{array} \quad \begin{array}{r} 22\frac{1}{2} \\ 2\overline{)45}\ \begin{array}{r} 22 \\ \underline{4} \\ 5 \\ \underline{4} \\ 1 \end{array} \end{array} \quad \begin{array}{r} 17\frac{2}{5} \\ 5\overline{)87}\ \begin{array}{r} 17 \\ \underline{5} \\ 37 \\ \underline{35} \\ 1 \end{array} \end{array} \quad \begin{array}{r} 9\frac{4}{5} \\ 5\overline{)49}\ \begin{array}{r} 9 \\ \underline{45} \\ 4 \end{array} \end{array}$$

Write the quotients for these problems with unit remainders.

$$\begin{array}{r} 36\ r\ 1 \\ 2\overline{)73}\ \begin{array}{r} 36 \\ \underline{6} \\ 13 \\ \underline{12} \\ 1 \end{array} \end{array} \quad \begin{array}{r} 42\ r\ 1 \\ 2\overline{)85}\ \begin{array}{r} 42 \\ \underline{4} \\ 5 \\ \underline{4} \\ 1 \end{array} \end{array} \quad \begin{array}{r} 19\ r\ 1 \\ 2\overline{)39}\ \begin{array}{r} 19 \\ \underline{2} \\ 19 \\ \underline{18} \\ 1 \end{array} \end{array} \quad \begin{array}{r} 14\ r\ 3 \\ 4\overline{)59}\ \begin{array}{r} 14 \\ \underline{4} \\ 19 \\ \underline{16} \\ 3 \end{array} \end{array}$$

$$\begin{array}{r} 17\ r\ 3 \\ 4\overline{)71}\ \begin{array}{r} 17 \\ \underline{4} \\ 31 \\ \underline{28} \\ 3 \end{array} \end{array} \quad \begin{array}{r} 20\ r\ 3 \\ 4\overline{)83}\ \begin{array}{r} 20 \\ \underline{8} \\ 3 \\ \underline{0} \\ 3 \end{array} \end{array} \quad \begin{array}{r} 5\ r\ 4 \\ 5\overline{)29}\ \begin{array}{r} 5 \\ \underline{25} \\ 4 \end{array} \end{array} \quad \begin{array}{r} 9\ r\ 2 \\ 5\overline{)47}\ \begin{array}{r} 9 \\ \underline{45} \\ 2 \end{array} \end{array}$$

By now children will be comfortable with remainders.
In the second section, they have to place a decimal
point after the number being divided and add one or
two zeros. Encourage them to use the last section as
practice for the operation they found most difficult.

108 — Dividing

$646 \div 3$ can be written in two ways:

$$3\overline{)646}\quad 215\frac{1}{3} \qquad \text{or} \qquad 3\overline{)646}\quad 215\ r\ 1$$

Work out the answer to each problem. Use fraction remainders.

$$\begin{array}{r} 94\frac{1}{4} \\ 4\overline{)377}\ \begin{array}{r} 94 \\ \underline{36} \\ 17 \\ \underline{16} \\ 1 \end{array} \end{array} \quad \begin{array}{r} 84\frac{1}{2} \\ 2\overline{)169}\ \begin{array}{r} 84 \\ \underline{16} \\ 09 \\ \underline{8} \\ 1 \end{array} \end{array} \quad \begin{array}{r} 22\frac{4}{7} \\ 7\overline{)158}\ \begin{array}{r} 22 \\ \underline{14} \\ 18 \\ \underline{14} \\ 4 \end{array} \end{array} \quad \begin{array}{r} 92 \\ 4\overline{)368}\ \begin{array}{r} 92 \\ \underline{36} \\ 08 \\ \underline{8} \\ 0 \end{array} \end{array}$$

$$\begin{array}{r} 39\frac{2}{5} \\ 5\overline{)197}\ \begin{array}{r} 39 \\ \underline{15} \\ 47 \\ \underline{45} \\ 2 \end{array} \end{array} \quad \begin{array}{r} 70\frac{6}{9} \\ 9\overline{)636}\ \begin{array}{r} 70 \\ \underline{63} \\ 06 \\ \underline{0} \\ 6 \end{array} \end{array} \quad \begin{array}{r} 162\frac{1}{2} \\ 2\overline{)325}\ \begin{array}{r} 162 \\ \underline{2} \\ 12 \\ \underline{12} \\ 05 \\ \underline{4} \\ 1 \end{array} \end{array} \quad \begin{array}{r} 196\frac{3}{14} \\ 4\overline{)787}\ \begin{array}{r} 196 \\ \underline{4} \\ 38 \\ \underline{36} \\ 27 \\ \underline{24} \\ 3 \end{array} \end{array}$$

Work out the answer to each problem. Use unit remainders.

$$\begin{array}{r} 189\ r\ 2 \\ 5\overline{)947}\ \begin{array}{r} 189 \\ \underline{5} \\ 44 \\ \underline{40} \\ 47 \\ \underline{45} \\ 2 \end{array} \end{array} \quad \begin{array}{r} 243\ r\ 2 \\ 3\overline{)731}\ \begin{array}{r} 243 \\ \underline{6} \\ 13 \\ \underline{12} \\ 11 \\ \underline{9} \\ 2 \end{array} \end{array} \quad \begin{array}{r} 125\ r\ 3 \\ 7\overline{)878}\ \begin{array}{r} 125 \\ \underline{7} \\ 17 \\ \underline{14} \\ 38 \\ \underline{35} \\ 3 \end{array} \end{array} \quad \begin{array}{r} 97\ r\ 2 \\ 9\overline{)875}\ \begin{array}{r} 97 \\ \underline{81} \\ 65 \\ \underline{63} \\ 2 \end{array} \end{array}$$

See the notes on page 101.

109

Division of 3-digit decimal numbers ☆

Work out these division sums.

```
    0.89              0.74
3)2.67            4)2.96
  24                28
  27                16
  27                16
   0   0.89          0   0.74
```

Work out these division problems.

```
  1.47          1.83          1.53          1.62
2)2.94        4)7.32        4)6.12        2)3.24
  2             4             4             2
  9             33            21            12
  8             32            20            12
  14            12            12            04
  14            12            12            4
  0             0             0             0
```

```
  4.99          3.24          1.56          1.87
2)9.98        3)9.72        4)6.24        4)7.48
  8             9             4             4
  19            07            22            34
  18            6             20            32
  18            12            24            28
  18            12            24            28
  0             0             0             0
```

```
  0.56          0.74          0.75          0.87
4)2.24        3)2.22        3)2.25        3)2.61
  20            21            21            24
  24            12            15            21
  24            12            15            21
  0             0             0             0
```

On this page, the decimal point has been incorporated into the middle of the number being divided. After the previous two pages, carrying across the decimal point should be familiar to children. No additional zeros need to be added on in this section.

110

☆ Division of 3-digit decimal numbers

Work out these division problems.

```
    1.99              1.61
5)9.95            6)9.66
  5                 6
  49                36
  45                36
  45                6
  45   1.99          6   1.61
   0                 0
```

Work out these division problems.

```
  1.63          1.85          1.27          1.52
5)8.15        5)9.25        5)6.35        6)9.12
  5             5             5             6
  31            42            13            31
  30            40            10            30
  15            25            35            12
  15            25            35            12
  0             0             0             0
```

```
  0.36          1.26          0.69          0.74
6)2.16        7)8.82        7)4.83        8)5.92
  18            7             42            56
  36            18            63            32
  36            14            63            32
  0             42            0             0
                42
                0
```

```
  1.09          0.91          0.63          1.06
8)8.72        9)8.19        9)5.67        6)6.36
  8             81            54            6
  72            9             27            36
  72            9             27            36
  0             0             0             0
```

The comments on the previous page also apply to this one, but as the dividing numbers are larger any weakness in multiplication facts for 6, 7, 8, and 9 times tables will show up.

111

Real-life problems ☆

A builder uses 1600 kg of sand a day. How much will he use in 5 days?

8000 kg

```
  3
1600
x  5
8000
```

If he uses 9500 kg the next week, how much more has he used than the week before?

1500 kg

```
9500
- 8000
1500
```

An electrician uses 184 m of cable while working on four houses. If he uses the same amount on each house, how much does he use on one house?

46 m

```
  46
4)184
  16
  24
  24
  0
```

A family looks at vacations in two different resorts. The first one costs $846.95. The second costs $932. How much will the family save if they choose the cheaper resort?

$85.05

```
  8 2 11 9 10
  932.00
- 846.95
  85.05
```

Doris has 5 sections of fence, each 96 cm wide. If she puts them together, how much of her yard can she fence off?

480 cm

```
  3
  96
x  5
480
```

Shula goes on a sponsored walk and collects $15.95 from her mother, $8.36 from her uncle, $4.65 from her brother, and $2.75 from her aunt. How much does she collect altogether?

$31.71

```
  2 2 2
  15.95
   8.36
   4.65
+  2.75
  31.71
```

A taxi company has 9 cars. If each car holds 40.4 litres of gasoline, how many litres will it take to fill all of the cars?

363.6 litres

```
  3
  40.4
x    9
363.6
```

This page provides an opportunity to apply the skills practiced. Children will need to select the operation necessary. If they are unsure about which operation to use, discuss whether the answer will be larger or smaller, which narrows down the options.

☆ Rounding money

Round to the nearest dollar.

$3.95 rounds to **$4**

$2.25 rounds to **$2**

Round to the nearest ten dollars.

$15.50 rounds to **$20**

$14.40 rounds to **$10**

Round to the nearest dollar.

$2.60 rounds to **$3** $8.49 rounds to **$8** $3.39 rounds to **$3**

$9.55 rounds to **$10** $1.75 rounds to **$2** $4.30 rounds to **$4**

$7.15 rounds to **$7** $6.95 rounds to **$7** $2.53 rounds to **$3**

Round to the nearest ten dollars.

$37.34 rounds to **$40** $21.75 rounds to **$20** $85.03 rounds to **$90**

$71.99 rounds to **$70** $66.89 rounds to **$70** $52.99 rounds to **$50**

$55.31 rounds to **$60** $12.79 rounds to **$10** $15.00 rounds to **$20**

Round to the nearest hundred dollars.

$307.12 rounds to **$300** $175.50 rounds to **$200** $115.99 rounds to **$100**

$860.55 rounds to **$900** $417.13 rounds to **$400** $650.15 rounds to **$700**

$739.10 rounds to **$700** $249.66 rounds to **$200** $367.50 rounds to **$400**

If children have difficulty, have them decide which are the two nearest hundred dollars, and which is closest to the number.

Estimating sums of money ⭐

Round to the leading digit. Estimate the sum.

$3.26 → $3	$68.53 → $70
+ $4.82 → + $5	+ $34.60 → + $30
is about $8	is about $100

Round to the leading digit. Estimate the sum.

$52.61 → $50
+ $27.95 → + $30
is about $80

$19.20 → $20
+ $22.13 → + $20
is about $40

$70.75 → $70
+ $12.49 → + $10
is about $80

$701.34 → $700
+ $100.80 → + $100
is about $800

$339.50 → $300
+ $422.13 → + $400
is about $700

$160.07 → $200
+ $230.89 → + $200
is about $400

$25.61 → $30
+ $72.51 → + $70
is about $100

$61.39 → $60
+ $19.50 → + $20
is about $80

$18.32 → $20
+ $13.90 → + $10
is about $30

$587.35 → $600
+ $251.89 → + $300
is about $900

$109.98 → $100
+ $210.09 → + $200
is about $300

$470.02 → $500
+ $203.17 → + $200
is about $700

Round to the leading digit. Estimate the sum.

$75.95 + $17.95 → $100

$41.67 + $20.35 → $60

$49.19 + $38.70 → $90

$784.65 + $101.05 → $900

$516.50 + $290.69 → $800

$58.78 + $33.25 → $90

$82.90 + $11.79 → $90

$90.09 + $14.50 → $100

In section 2, children need to estimate by rounding mentally. If they have trouble, have them write the rounded numbers above the originals first, and then add them.

114

Estimating differences of money

Round the numbers to the leading digit. Estimate the differences.

$8.75 → $9
− $5.10 → − $5
is about $4

$61.47 → $60
− $35.64 → − $40
is about $20

Round the numbers to the leading digit. Estimate the differences.

$17.90 → $20
− $12.30 → − $10
is about $10

$6.40 → $6
− $3.75 → − $4
is about $2

$87.45 → $90
− $54.99 → − $50
is about $40

$34.90 → $30
− $12.60 → − $10
is about $20

$8.68 → $9
− $4.39 → − $4
is about $5

$363.24 → $400
− $127.66 → − $100
is about $300

$78.75 → $80
− $24.99 → − $20
is about $60

$64.21 → $60
− $28.56 → − $30
is about $30

$723.34 → $700
− $487.12 → − $500
is about $200

Round the numbers to the leading digit. Estimate the differences.

$8.12 − $1.35
→ $8 − $1 = $7

$49.63 − $27.85
→ $50 − $30 = $20

$7.50 − $3.15
→ $8 − $3 = $5

$85.15 − $42.99
→ $90 − $40 = $50

$5.85 − $4.75
→ $6 − $5 = $1

$634.60 − $267.25
→ $600 − $300 = $300

$37.35 − $16.99
→ $40 − $20 = $20

$842.17 − $169.54
→ $800 − $200 = $600

$56.95 − $20.58
→ $60 − $20 = $40

$628.37 − $252.11
→ $600 − $300 = $300

See the comments on page 113.

115

Estimating sums and differences ⭐

Round the numbers to the leading digit. Estimate the sum or difference.

3576 → 4000
+ 1307 → +1000
is about 5000

198 248 → 200 000
− 116 431 → − 100 000
is about 100 000

Round the numbers to the leading digit. Estimate the sum or difference.

685 → 700
+ 489 → + 500
is about 1200

21 481 → 20 000
− 12 500 → − 10 000
is about 10 000

7834 → 8 000
+ 3106 → + 3 000
is about 11 000

682 778 → 700 000
+ 130 001 → + 100 000
is about 800 000

58 499 → 60 000
− 22 135 → − 20 000
is about 40 000

902 276 → 900 000
− 615 999 → − 600 000
is about 300 000

46 801 → 50 000
+ 34 700 → + 30 000
is about 80 000

9734 → 10 000
− 8306 → − 8 000
is about 2 000

65 606 → 70 000
+ 85 943 → + 90 000
is about 160 000

5218 → 5000
− 3673 → − 4000
is about 1000

745 → 700
+ 451 → + 500
is about 1200

337 297 → 300 000
− 168 931 → − 200 000
is about 100 000

Write < or > for each problem.

329 + 495 > 800

11 569 − 6146 < 6000

563 − 317 < 300

8193 − 6668 > 1000

41 924 − 12 445 < 50 000

634 577 + 192 556 > 800 000

18 885 + 12 691 > 30 000

713 096 − 321 667 < 400 000

In section 2, children need to think about their estimates more carefully if the estimate is very close to the number on the right side of the equation. Have them look at the numbers in the next place to the right to adjust their estimates up or down.

Estimating products

Round to the leading digit. Estimate the product.

3456 x 6
3000 x 6 = 18 000

73 x 46
70 x 50 = 3500

Round to the leading digit. Estimate the sum.

1908 x 8
2000 x 8 = 16 000

5 x 6099
5 x 6000 = 30 000

7 x 1108
7 x 1000 = 7000

5239 x 9
5000 x 9 = 45 000

81 x 32
80 x 30 = 2400

19 x 62
20 x 60 = 1200

39 x 44
40 x 40 = 1600

94 x 12
90 x 10 = 900

Estimate the product.

6 x 7243	42 000	4785 x 4	20 000	3 x 8924	27 000
2785 x 5	15 000	6298 x 4	24 000	7 x 7105	49 000
8 x 2870	24 000	4176 x 7	28 000	5 x 4803	25 000
6777 x 9	63 000	6 x 8022	48 000	3785 x 4	16 000
42 x 51	2000	54 x 28	1500	23 x 75	1600
16 x 32	600	47 x 54	2500	59 x 52	3000
17 x 74	1400	33 x 22	600	81 x 18	1600
31 x 91	2700	38 x 87	3600	46 x 77	4000

Have children try to estimate the answer mentally. If they have trouble, have them write the rounded numbers first.

Estimating quotients

Round to compatible numbers. Estimate the quotient.

$3156 \div 6$
$3000 \div 6 =$ 500

$2159 \div 5$
$2500 \div 5 =$ 500

Round to compatible numbers. Estimate the quotient.

$1934 \div 8$
$1600 \div 8 = 200$

$4066 \div 5$
$4000 \div 5 = 800$

$1108 \div 4$
$1200 \div 4 = 300$

$5657 \div 9$
$5400 \div 9 = 600$

$3998 \div 6$
$4200 \div 6 = 700$

$5525 \div 7$
$5600 \div 7 = 800$

$1701 \div 3$
$1500 \div 3 = 500$

$1304 \div 2$
$1200 \div 2 = 600$

Estimate the quotient.

$4798 \div 7$ 700	$8205 \div 9$ 900	$5022 \div 5$ 1000
$3785 \div 4$ 900	$5528 \div 6$ 900	$2375 \div 8$ 300
$1632 \div 3$ 500	$4251 \div 4$ 1000	$4754 \div 9$ 500
$7352 \div 8$ 900	$1774 \div 2$ 900	$3322 \div 7$ 500
$3591 \div 6$ 600	$2887 \div 5$ 600	$5746 \div 2$ 3000
$3703 \div 3$ 1200	$2392 \div 6$ 400	$6621 \div 8$ 800

Children should round the dividend to a nearby number that can easily be divided by the divisor. Compatible numbers are ones that are just multiples of the divisor. Knowledge of basic division facts should allow these estimations to be done mentally.

118

Rounding mixed numbers

Round to the closest whole number.

$2\frac{5}{6}$

$\frac{5}{6}$ is more than $\frac{1}{2}$, so, $2\frac{5}{6}$ rounds up to 3.

$3\frac{2}{5}$

$\frac{2}{5}$ is less than $\frac{1}{2}$, so, $3\frac{2}{5}$ rounds down to 3.

Circle the fractions that are more than $\frac{1}{2}$.

$\frac{3}{7}$ $\frac{2}{9}$ $\left(\frac{6}{7}\right)$ $\left(\frac{5}{9}\right)$ $\frac{3}{8}$ $\frac{1}{7}$ $\left(\frac{2}{3}\right)$ $\left(\frac{4}{7}\right)$

$\left(\frac{7}{10}\right)$ $\frac{2}{5}$ $\frac{1}{3}$ $\left(\frac{5}{6}\right)$ $\left(\frac{3}{4}\right)$ $\frac{2}{9}$ $\left(\frac{5}{8}\right)$ $\left(\frac{3}{5}\right)$

Circle the fractions that are less than $\frac{1}{2}$.

$\left(\frac{1}{8}\right)$ $\left(\frac{3}{9}\right)$ $\frac{4}{5}$ $\left(\frac{2}{7}\right)$ $\frac{3}{5}$ $\left(\frac{2}{5}\right)$ $\frac{7}{10}$ $\left(\frac{2}{9}\right)$

$\frac{3}{4}$ $\left(\frac{1}{3}\right)$ $\left(\frac{4}{9}\right)$ $\left(\frac{3}{10}\right)$ $\frac{5}{6}$ $\left(\frac{1}{4}\right)$ $\left(\frac{3}{7}\right)$ $\frac{5}{9}$

Round to the closest whole number.

$4\frac{3}{8}$ 4	$2\frac{6}{7}$ 3	$5\frac{3}{4}$ 6	$3\frac{2}{9}$ 3
$2\frac{5}{6}$ 3	$1\frac{7}{8}$ 2	$2\frac{2}{5}$ 2	$5\frac{1}{7}$ 5
$3\frac{1}{6}$ 3	$5\frac{3}{8}$ 5	$3\frac{3}{5}$ 4	$7\frac{8}{13}$ 8
$6\frac{3}{5}$ 7	$1\frac{1}{4}$ 1	$4\frac{5}{6}$ 5	$9\frac{3}{4}$ 10
$5\frac{2}{3}$ 6	$3\frac{3}{7}$ 3	$1\frac{6}{7}$ 2	$6\frac{3}{4}$ 7

If children have trouble rounding, explain that if the numerator is less than half as big as the denominator, the fraction is less than one-half.

119

Calculate the mean

What is the mean of 6 and 10? $(6+10) \div 2 = 8$

David is 9, Asha is 10, and Daniel is 5. What is their mean age? $(9 + 10 + 5) \div 3 = 8$ years

Calculate the mean of these amounts.

9 and 5	7	6 and 8	7
5 and 7	6	11 and 7	9
8 and 12	10	13 and 15	14
19 and 21	20	40 and 60	50

Calculate the mean of these amounts.

5, 7, and 3	5	11, 9, and 7	9
14, 10, and 6	10	12, 8, and 4	8
7, 3, 5, and 9	6	$1, $1.50, $2.50, and $3	$2
16¢, 9¢, 12¢, and 3¢	10¢	5 g, 7 g, 8 g, and 8 g	7 g

Calculate these answers.

The mean of two numbers is 7. If one of the numbers is 6, what is the other number?   8

The mean of three numbers is 4. If two of the numbers are 4 and 5, what is the third number?   3

The mean of four numbers is 12. If three of the numbers are 9, 15, and 8, what is the fourth number?   16

Two children record their last five spelling-test scores.

| Gayle | 17 | 18 | 16 | 14 | 15 |
| Sally | 19 | 20 | 12 | 13 | 11 |

Which child has the best mean score?   Gayle

The average of a number list is known as the 'mean'. Children should add the list and divide by the amount of numbers. In part 3, explain that if the mean is 7, the total must have been 14, so if they take away the number given they will find the number required.

Mean, median, and mode

Sian throws a dice 7 times. Here are her results:
4, 2, 1, 2, 4, 2, 6

What is the mean? $(4 + 2 + 1 + 2 + 4 + 2 + 6) \div 7 = 3$

What is the median? Put the numbers in order of size and find the middle number, example, 1, 2, 2, 2, 4, 4, 6.

The median is 2.

What is the mode?   The most common result, which is 2.

A school soccer team scores the following number of goals in their first 9 matches:
2, 2, 1, 3, 2, 1, 2, 4, 1

What is the mean score?   2

What is the median score?   2

Write down the mode for their results.   2

The ages of the local hockey players are:
17, 15, 16, 19, 17, 19, 22, 17, 18, 21, 17

What is the mean of their ages?   18

What is their median age?   17

Write down the mode for their ages.   17

The results of Susan's last 11 spelling tests were:
15, 12, 15, 17, 11, 16, 19, 11, 3, 11, 13

What is the mean of her scores?   13

What is her median score?   13

Write down the mode for her scores.   11

The work on this page leads on from previous work on the mean, but also expands it to the median and the mode. The biggest problem children may have is remembering which is which. Encourage them to develop a system that works for them.

Line graphs

Look at this graph.

Luis's Bike Trip

How many kilometres did Luis ride during the first hour of his trip?
6 kilometres

How many hours did Luis's trip take?
6 hours

How far did he travel in all?
20 kilometres

Luis stopped for lunch for one hour. What time did he stop?
11 A.M.

Did Luis cover more distance between 12 and 1 or between 1 and 2?
between 12 and 1

Between which two hours did Luis travel 4 kilometres?
between 10 and 11

During which hours did Luis ride the fastest?
between 9 and 10 and between 12 and 1

Did Luis travel farther before or after his lunch break?
he travelled the same distance: 10 kilometres

How much longer did it take Luis to ride 10 kilometres after lunch?
1 hour longer

Children may have trouble deciding how far Luis travelled between two times. Have them find the distance at the starting and ending times, and then subtract to get the answer.

122

Coordinates

Write the coordinates of:

A (2, 4)
B (3, 1)
C (1, 1)

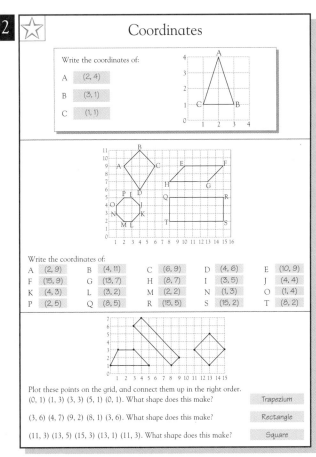

Write the coordinates of:

A	(2, 9)	B	(4, 11)	C	(6, 9)	D	(4, 6)	E	(10, 9)
F	(15, 9)	G	(13, 7)	H	(8, 7)	I	(3, 5)	J	(4, 4)
K	(4, 3)	L	(3, 2)	M	(2, 2)	N	(1, 3)	O	(1, 4)
P	(2, 5)	Q	(8, 5)	R	(15, 5)	S	(15, 2)	T	(8, 2)

Plot these points on the grid, and connect them up in the right order.
(0, 1) (1, 3) (3, 3) (5, 1) (0, 1). What shape does this make?
Trapezium

(3, 6) (4, 7) (9, 2) (8, 1) (3, 6). What shape does this make?
Rectangle

(11, 3) (13, 5) (15, 3) (13, 1) (11, 3). What shape does this make?
Square

Children should remember to read off the horizontal coordinate first. In the second section, it is important that they join the coordinates in the order in which they are written, to produce the shape intended.

123

Drawing angles

Acute angles are between 0° and 90°.   Obtuse angles are between 90° and 180°.

When you get to 180° you have a straight line.

Use a protractor to draw these angles. Remember to mark the angle you have drawn.

150°

135°

45°

110°

10°

20°

To do the work on this page and the next, children require a 360° protractor. Check that they read the protractor from the right direction. Remind children to mark the angles. This is important to avoid confusion when drawing reflex angles.

Reading and writing numbers

264 346 in words is Two hundred sixty-four thousand three hundred forty-six

One million three hundred twelve thousand five hundred two is 1 312 502

Write each of these numbers in words.

326 208   Three hundred twenty-six thousand two hundred eight

704 543   Seven hundred four thousand five hundred forty-three

240 701   Two hundred forty thousand seven hundred one

278 520   Two hundred seventy-eight thousand five hundred twenty

Write each of these in numbers.

Five hundred seventeen thousand forty-two   517 042

Six hundred ninety-four thousand seven hundred eleven   694 711

Eight hundred nine thousand two hundred three   809 203

Nine hundred thousand four hundred four   900 404

Write each of these numbers in words.

9 307 012   Nine million three hundred seven thousand twelve

5 042 390   Five million forty-two thousand three hundred ninety

9 908 434   Nine million nine hundred eight thousand four hundred thirty-four

8 400 642   Eight million four hundred thousand six hundred forty-two

Write each of these in numbers.

Eight million two hundred fifty-one   8 000 251

Two million forty thousand four hundred four   2 040 404

Seven million three hundred two thousand one hundred one   7 302 101

Two million five hundred forty-one thousand five   2 541 005

Children may use zeros incorrectly in numbers. In word form, zeros are omitted, but children should take care to include them when writing numbers in standard form.

Multiplying and dividing by 10

Write the answer in the box.

26 x 10 = 260

40 ÷ 10 = 4

Write the answer in the box.

76 x 10 = 760   43 x 10 = 430   93 x 10 = 930

66 x 10 = 660   13 x 10 = 130   47 x 10 = 470

147 x 10 = 1470   936 x 10 = 9360   284 x 10 = 2840

364 x 10 = 3640   821 x 10 = 8210   473 x 10 = 4730

Write the answer in the box.

30 ÷ 10 = 3   20 ÷ 10 = 2   70 ÷ 10 = 7

60 ÷ 10 = 6   50 ÷ 10 = 5   580 ÷ 10 = 58

310 ÷ 10 = 31   270 ÷ 10 = 27   100 ÷ 10 = 10

540 ÷ 10 = 54   890 ÷ 10 = 89   710 ÷ 10 = 71

Write the number that has been multiplied by 10.

37 x 10 = 370   64 x 10 = 640   74 x 10 = 740

81 x 10 = 810   10 x 10 = 100   83 x 10 = 830

714 x 10 = 7140   307 x 10 = 3070   529 x 10 = 5290

264 x 10 = 2640   829 x 10 = 8290   648 x 10 = 6480

Write the number that has been divided by 10.

30 ÷ 10 = 3   20 ÷ 10 = 2   90 ÷ 10 = 9

420 ÷ 10 = 42   930 ÷ 10 = 93   740 ÷ 10 = 74

570 ÷ 10 = 57   380 ÷ 10 = 38   860 ÷ 10 = 86

Children should realize that multiplying a whole number by 10 means writing a zero at the end. To divide a multiple of ten by 10, simply take the final zero off the number. In the two final sections, the inverse operation is used for solving the problems.

126

Identifying patterns

Continue each pattern.

Steps of 9:   5   14   23   32   41   50

Steps of 14:   20   34   48   62   76   90

Continue each pattern.

21	38	55	72	89	106	123	140
13	37	61	85	109	133	157	181
7	25	43	61	79	97	115	133
32	48	64	80	96	112	128	144
12	31	50	69	88	107	126	145
32	54	76	98	120	142	164	186
24	64	104	144	184	224	264	304
4	34	64	94	124	154	184	214
36	126	216	306?	396	486	576	666
12	72	132	192	252	312	372	432
25	45	65	85	105	125	145	165
22	72	122	172	222	272	322	372
25	100	175	250	325	400	475	550
60	165	270	375	480	585	690	795
8	107	206	305	404	503	602	701
10	61	112	163	214	265	316	367
26	127	228	329	430	531	632	733
48	100	152	204	256	308	360	412

Children should determine what number to add to the first number to make the second number, and check to make sure that adding the same number turns the second number into the third. They can then continue the pattern.

127

Recognizing multiples of 6, 7, and 8

Circle the multiples of 6.

8   (12)   15   (18)   20   (24)

Circle the multiples of 6.

8   22   14   (18)   (36)   40

16   38   44   25   (30)   (60)

(6)   21   19   (54)   56   (24)

(12)   (48)   10   20   35   26

(42)   39   23   28   (36)   32

Circle the multiples of 7.

(7)   17   24   59   (42)   55

15   20   (21)   46   12   (70)

(14)   27   69   36   47   (49)

65   19   57   (28)   38   (63)

33   34   (35)   37   60   (56)

Circle the multiples of 8.

(40)   26   15   25   38   (56)

26   (8)   73   41   (64)   12

75   58   62   (24)   31   (72)

12   (80)   (32)   46   38   78

(16)   42   66   28   (48)   68

Circle the number that is a multiple of 6 and 7.

18   54   (42)   21   28   63

Circle the numbers that are multiples of 6 and 8.

16   (24)   36   (48)   54   42

Circle the number that is a multiple of 7 and 8.

24   32   40   28   42   (56)

Success on this page will basically depend on a knowledge of multiplication tables. Where children experience difficulties, multiplication table practice should be encouraged.

Factors of numbers from 1 to 30

The factors of 10 are   1   2   5   10

Circle the factors of 4.   (1)   (2)   3   (4)

Write all the factors of each number.

The factors of 26 are   1, 2, 13, 26

The factors of 30 are   1, 2, 3, 5, 6, 10, 15, 30

The factors of 9 are   1, 3, 9

The factors of 12 are   1, 2, 3, 4, 6, 12

The factors of 15 are   1, 3, 5, 15

The factors of 22 are   1, 2, 11, 22

The factors of 20 are   1, 2, 4, 5, 10, 20

The factors of 21 are   1, 3, 7, 21

The factors of 24 are   1, 2, 3, 4, 6, 8, 12, 24

Circle all the factors of each number.

Which numbers are factors of 14?   (1)(2) 3   5   (7) 9   12 (14)

Which numbers are factors of 13?   (1) 2   3   4   5   6   7   8   9   10   11 (13)

Which numbers are factors of 7?   (1) 2   3   4   5   6 (7)

Which numbers are factors of 11?   (1) 2   3   4   5   6   7   8   9   10 (11)

Which numbers are factors of 6?   (1)(2)(3) 4   5 (6)

Which numbers are factors of 8?   (1)(2) 3 (4) 5   6   7 (8)

Which numbers are factors of 17?   (1) 2   5   7   12   14   16 (17)

Which numbers are factors of 18?   (1)(2)(3) 4   5 (6) 8 (9)10   12 (18)

Some numbers only have factors of 1 and themselves. They are called prime numbers. Write down all the prime numbers that are less than 30 in the box.

2, 3, 5, 7, 11, 13, 17, 19, 23, 29

Encourage a systematic approach such as starting and working forward to the number that is half of number in question. Children often forget that 1 a the number itself are factors of a given number. Yo may need to point out that 1 is not a prime numbe

Recognizing equivalent fractions ☆

Make each pair of fractions equal by writing a number in the box.

$\frac{1}{2} = \frac{2}{4}$ $\frac{1}{3} = \frac{2}{6}$

Make each pair of fractions equal by writing a number in the box.

$\frac{1}{2} = \frac{5}{10}$ $\frac{3}{4} = \frac{6}{8}$ $\frac{1}{3} = \frac{3}{9}$

$\frac{2}{3} = \frac{8}{12}$ $\frac{6}{12} = \frac{3}{6}$ $\frac{4}{8} = \frac{1}{2}$

$\frac{1}{5} = \frac{2}{10}$ $\frac{4}{12} = \frac{2}{6}$ $\frac{3}{5} = \frac{6}{10}$

$\frac{1}{4} = \frac{2}{8}$ $\frac{6}{18} = \frac{1}{3}$ $\frac{3}{12} = \frac{1}{4}$

$\frac{3}{9} = \frac{1}{3}$ $\frac{4}{10} = \frac{2}{5}$ $\frac{3}{4} = \frac{9}{12}$

$\frac{4}{16} = \frac{1}{4}$ $\frac{15}{20} = \frac{3}{4}$ $\frac{6}{12} = \frac{1}{2}$

$\frac{3}{5} = \frac{6}{10}$ $\frac{3}{6} = \frac{1}{2}$ $\frac{9}{12} = \frac{3}{4}$

Make each row of fractions equal by writing a number in each box.

$\frac{1}{2} = \frac{2}{4} = \frac{3}{6} = \frac{4}{8} = \frac{5}{10} = \frac{6}{12}$

$\frac{1}{4} = \frac{2}{8} = \frac{3}{12} = \frac{4}{16} = \frac{5}{20} = \frac{6}{24}$

$\frac{3}{4} = \frac{6}{8} = \frac{9}{12} = \frac{12}{16} = \frac{15}{20} = \frac{18}{24}$

$\frac{1}{3} = \frac{2}{6} = \frac{3}{9} = \frac{4}{12} = \frac{5}{15} = \frac{12}{36}$

$\frac{1}{5} = \frac{2}{10} = \frac{3}{15} = \frac{4}{20} = \frac{5}{25} = \frac{6}{30}$

$\frac{2}{3} = \frac{4}{6} = \frac{6}{9} = \frac{8}{12} = \frac{10}{15} = \frac{14}{21}$

If children have problems with this page, point out that fractions remain the same as long as you multiply both the numerator and denominator by the same number, or divide the numerator and denominator by the same number.

130

☆ Rounding decimals

Round each decimal to the nearest whole number.

3.4   3

5.7   6

4.5   5

If the whole number has 5 after it, round it to the whole number above.

Round each decimal to the nearest whole number.

6.2	6	2.5	3	1.5	2	3.8	4
5.5	6	2.8	3	3.2	3	8.5	9
5.4	5	7.9	8	3.7	4	2.3	2
1.1	1	8.6	9	8.3	8	9.2	9
4.7	5	6.3	6	7.3	7	8.7	9

Round each decimal to the nearest whole number.

14.4	14	42.3	42	74.1	74	59.7	60
29.9	30	32.6	33	63.5	64	96.4	96
18.2	18	37.5	38	39.6	40	76.3	76
40.1	40	28.7	29	26.9	27	12.5	13
29.5	30	38.5	39	87.2	87	41.6	42

Round each decimal to the nearest whole number.

137.6	138	423.5	424	426.2	426	111.8	112
641.6	642	333.5	334	805.2	805	246.8	247
119.5	120	799.6	800	562.3	562	410.2	410
682.4	682	759.6	760	531.5	532	829.9	830
743.4	743	831.1	831	276.7	277	649.3	649

If children experience difficulties, you might want to use a number line showing tenths. Errors often occur when a number with 9 in the ones column is rounded up. Children also often neglect to alter the tens digit in a number such as 19.7.

131

Real-life problems ☆

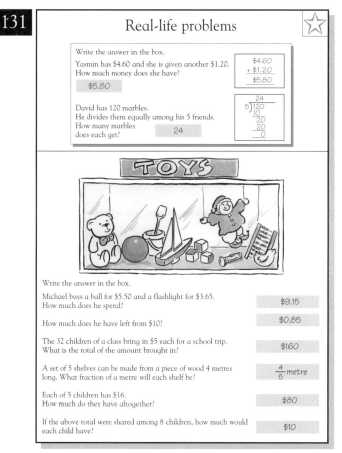

Write the answer in the box.

Yasmin has $4.60 and she is given another $1.20. How much money does she have?

$5.80

$\begin{array}{r} \$4.60 \\ + \$1.20 \\ \hline \$5.80 \end{array}$

David has 120 marbles. He divides them equally among his 5 friends. How many marbles does each get?   24

$\begin{array}{r} 24 \\ 5)\overline{120} \\ \underline{10} \\ 20 \\ \underline{20} \\ 0 \end{array}$

Write the answer in the box.

Michael buys a ball for $5.50 and a flashlight for $3.65. How much does he spend? $9.15

How much does he have left from $10? $0.85

The 32 children of a class bring in $5 each for a school trip. What is the total of the amount brought in? $160

A set of 5 shelves can be made from a piece of wood 4 metres long. What fraction of a metre will each shelf be? $\frac{4}{5}$ metre

Each of 5 children has $16. How much do they have altogether? $80

If the above total were shared among 8 children, how much would each child have? $10

This page tests children's ability to choose the operation required to solve real-life problems, mostly involving money. Discussing whether the answer will be larger or smaller than the question will help children decide on their choice of operation.

132

☆ Real-life problems

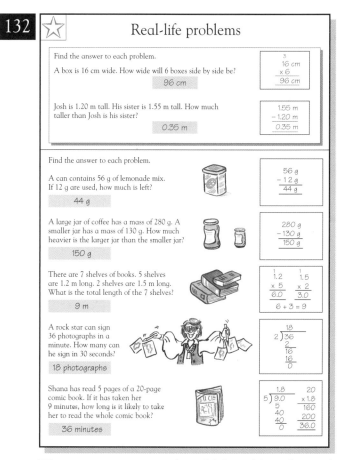

Find the answer to each problem.

A box is 16 cm wide. How wide will 6 boxes side by side be?   96 cm

$\begin{array}{r} \overset{3}{16} \text{ cm} \\ \times 6 \\ \hline 96 \text{ cm} \end{array}$

Josh is 1.20 m tall. His sister is 1.55 m tall. How much taller than Josh is his sister?   0.35 m

$\begin{array}{r} 1.55 \text{ m} \\ - 1.20 \text{ m} \\ \hline 0.35 \text{ m} \end{array}$

Find the answer to each problem.

A can contains 56 g of lemonade mix. If 12 g are used, how much is left?   44 g

$\begin{array}{r} 56 \text{ g} \\ - 12 \text{ g} \\ \hline 44 \text{ g} \end{array}$

A large jar of coffee has a mass of 280 g. A smaller jar has a mass of 130 g. How much heavier is the larger jar than the smaller jar?   150 g

$\begin{array}{r} 280 \text{ g} \\ - 130 \text{ g} \\ \hline 150 \text{ g} \end{array}$

There are 7 shelves of books. 5 shelves are 1.2 m long. 2 shelves are 1.5 m long. What is the total length of the 7 shelves?   9 m

$\begin{array}{r} 1.2 \\ \times 5 \\ \hline 6.0 \end{array}$ $\begin{array}{r} 1.5 \\ \times 2 \\ \hline 3.0 \end{array}$

$6 + 3 = 9$

A rock star can sign 36 photographs in a minute. How many can he sign in 30 seconds?   18 photographs

$\begin{array}{r} 18 \\ 2)\overline{36} \\ \underline{2} \\ 16 \\ \underline{16} \\ 0 \end{array}$

Shana has read 5 pages of a 20-page comic book. If it has taken her 9 minutes, how long is it likely to take her to read the whole comic book?   36 minutes

$\begin{array}{r} 1.8 \\ 5)\overline{9.0} \\ \underline{5} \\ 40 \\ \underline{40} \\ 0 \end{array}$ $\begin{array}{r} 20 \\ \times 1.8 \\ \hline 160 \\ 200 \\ \hline 36.0 \end{array}$

This page continues with real-life problems but with units other than money. Note that children must perform three operations to solve the third problem.

Problems involving time

Find the answer to this problem.

A train leaves the station at 7:30 A.M. and arrives at the end of the line at 10:45 A.M. How long did the journey take?

3 hours 15 minutes

7:30 → 10:30 = 3 h
10:30 → 10:45 = 15 min
Total = 3 h 15 min

Find the answer to each problem.

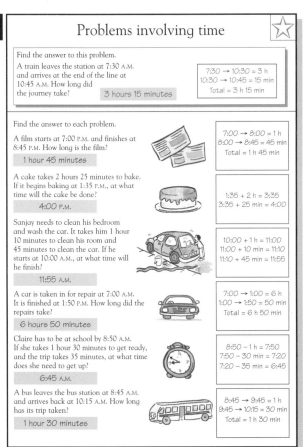

A film starts at 7:00 P.M. and finishes at 8:45 P.M. How long is the film?

1 hour 45 minutes

7:00 → 8:00 = 1 h
8:00 → 8:45 = 45 min
Total = 1 h 45 min

A cake takes 2 hours 25 minutes to bake. If it begins baking at 1:35 P.M., at what time will the cake be done?

4:00 P.M.

1:35 + 2 h = 3:35
3:35 + 25 min = 4:00

Sanjay needs to clean his bedroom and wash the car. It takes him 1 hour 10 minutes to clean his room and 45 minutes to clean the car. If he starts at 10:00 A.M., at what time will he finish?

11:55 A.M.

10:00 + 1 h = 11:00
11:00 + 10 min = 11:10
11:10 + 45 min = 11:55

A car is taken in for repair at 7:00 A.M. It is finished at 1:50 P.M. How long did the repairs take?

6 hours 50 minutes

7:00 → 1:00 = 6 h
1:00 → 1:50 = 50 min
Total = 6 h 50 min

Claire has to be at school by 8:50 A.M. If she takes 1 hour 30 minutes to get ready, and the trip takes 35 minutes, at what time does she need to get up?

6:45 A.M.

8:50 − 1 h = 7:50
7:50 − 30 min = 7:20
7:20 − 35 min = 6:45

A bus leaves the bus station at 8:45 A.M. and arrives back at 10:15 A.M. How long has its trip taken?

1 hour 30 minutes

8:45 → 9:45 = 1 h
9:45 → 10:15 = 30 min
Total = 1 h 30 min

Children must remember that hours are based on units of 60 rather than of 10, so when they regroup, they will add 60 to the minutes instead of the 10 they would add when regrouping numbers.

Elapsed time

Write the answer in the box.

10:40   11:40   12:40   1:20

1 hour → 1 hour → 40 minutes →

Carmen's gymnastics class starts at 10:40 A.M. and ends at 1:20 P.M. How long does it last?

2 hours and 40 minutes

Write the answer in the box.

The ferry leaves the mainland at 11:00 A.M. and docks on the island at 3 P.M. How long is the ride?

4 hours

11:00 A.M. to 12:00 P.M. = 1 h
12:00 P.M. to 3:00 P.M. = 3 h
Total 1 + 3 = 4

The movie starts at 6:05 P.M. and ends at 9:17 P.M. How long is it?

3 hours 12 minutes

6:05 + 3 hours = 9:05
9:05 + 12 min = 9:17
Total 3 h 12 min

Pat works an 8-hour shift at the fairgrounds. If he starts work at 9 A.M., at what time is he finished?

5 P.M.

9 A.M. + 3 h = 12 P.M.
12 P.M. + 5 h = 5 P.M.

Keesha wants to videotape a program that starts at 11:30 P.M. It lasts 1 hour and 45 minutes. What time will it end?

1:15 A.M.

11:30 P.M. + 1 h = 12:30 A.M.
12:30 A.M. + 45 min = 1:15 A.M.

Mai finished painting her porch at 4:25 P.M. The instructions said she should wait at least 15 hours to paint the trim. What is the earliest time when she could start painting the trim?

7:25 A.M.

4:25 P.M. + 12 h = 4:25 A.M.
4:25 A.M. + 3 h = 7:25 A.M.

If children have trouble keeping track of the changes in hours or minutes, have them write down each step as in the diagram.

Recognizing multiples

Circle the multiples of 10.

14   (20)   25   (30)   47   (60)

Circle the multiples of 6.

20   (48)   56   (72)   25   35
1   3   (6)   16   26   (36)

Circle the multiples of 7.

(14)   24   (35)   27   47   (49)
(63)   (42)   52   37   64   71

Circle the multiples of 8.

25   31   (48)   84   (32)   (8)
18   54   (64)   35   (72)   28

Circle the multiples of 9.

17   (81)   (27)   35   92   106
(45)   53   (108)   (90)   33   95
64   (9)   28   (18)   (36)   98

Circle the multiples of 10.

15   35   (20)   46   (90)   (100)
44   37   (30)   29   (50)   45

Circle the multiples of 11.

24   (110)   123   54   (66)   90
45   (33)   87   98   (99)   (121)
43   (44)   65   (55)   21   (22)

Circle the multiples of 12.

136   134   (144)   109   (108)   (132)
(24)   34   58   68   (48)   (60)
35   29   (72)   74   (84)   94

Success on this page basically depends on knowledge of multiplication tables. Where children experience difficulties, it may be necessary to reinforce multiplication tables.

Bar graphs

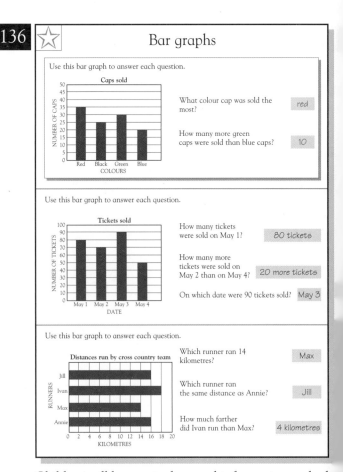

Use this bar graph to answer each question.

What colour cap was sold the most?   red

How many more green caps were sold than blue caps?   10

Use this bar graph to answer each question.

How many tickets were sold on May 1?   80 tickets

How many more tickets were sold on May 2 than on May 4?   20 more tickets

On which date were 90 tickets sold?   May 3

Use this bar graph to answer each question.

Which runner ran 14 kilometres?   Max

Which runner ran the same distance as Annie?   Jill

How much farther did Ivan run than Max?   4 kilometres

Children will be required to read information, to look [for] specific information, and to manipulate the information they read on a bar graph, to answer the questions. They may need to be reassured that a horizontal bar graph [can] be read in much the same way as a vertical bar graph.

Triangles

Look at these different triangles.

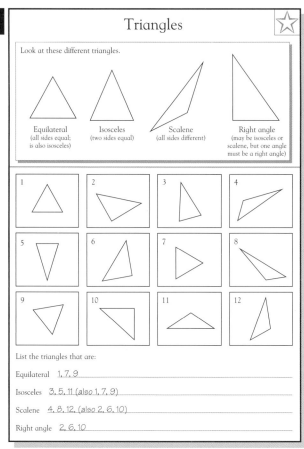

Equilateral
(all sides equal;
is also isosceles)

Isosceles
(two sides equal)

Scalene
(all sides different)

Right angle
(may be isosceles or
scalene, but one angle
must be a right angle)

1 2 3 4

5 6 7 8

9 10 11 12

List the triangles that are:

Equilateral 1, 7, 9

Isosceles 3, 5, 11 (also 1, 7, 9)

Scalene 4, 8, 12, (also 2, 6, 10)

Right angle 2, 6, 10

This page will highlight any gaps in children's ability to recognize and name triangles. Make sure that children can identify the triangles that have been rotated.

Place value to 10 000 000

| How many hundreds are there in 7000? | 70 | hundreds (70 x 100 = 7000) |
| What is the value of the 9 in 694? | 90 | (because the 9 is in the tens column) |

Write how many tens there are in:

400	40	tens	600	60	tens	900	90	tens
200	20	tens	1300	130	tens	4700	470	tens
4800	480	tens	1240	124	tens	1320	132	tens
2630	263	tens	5920	592	tens	4350	435	tens

What is the value of the 7 in these numbers?

| 76 | 70 | | 720 | 700 | | 137 | 7 |
| 7122 | 7000 | | 74 301 | 70 000 | | 724 | 700 |

What is the value of the 3 in these numbers?

| 324 126 | 300 000 | 3 927 141 | 3 000 000 | 214 623 | 3 |
| 8 254 320 | 300 | 3 711 999 | 3 000 000 | 124 372 | 300 |

Write how many hundreds there are in:

6400	64	hundreds	8500	85	hundreds
19 900	199	hundreds	36 200	362	hundreds
524 600	5246	hundreds	712 400	7124	hundreds

What is the value of the 8 in these numbers?

| 8 214 631 | 8 000 000 | 2 398 147 | 8000 | 463 846 | 800 |
| 287 034 | 80 000 | 8 110 927 | 8 000 000 | 105 428 | 8 |

Explain to children that finding how many tens there are in a number is the same as dividing by 10. In the number 400, for example, there are 40 tens, because 400 divided by 10 is 40.

Multiplying and dividing by 10

Write the answer in the box.

37 x 10 = 370   58 ÷ 10 = 5.8

Write the product in the box.

94 x 10 =	940	13 x 10 =	130	37 x 10 =	370
36 x 10 =	360	47 x 10 =	470	54 x 10 =	540
236 x 10 =	2360	419 x 10 =	4190	262 x 10 =	2620
531 x 10 =	5310	674 x 10 =	6740	801 x 10 =	8010

Write the quotient in the box.

92 ÷ 10 =	9.2	48 ÷ 10 =	4.8	37 ÷ 10 =	3.7
18 ÷ 10 =	1.8	29 ÷ 10 =	2.9	54 ÷ 10 =	5.4
345 ÷ 10 =	34.5	354 ÷ 10 =	35.4	723 ÷ 10 =	72.3
531 ÷ 10 =	53.1	262 ÷ 10 =	26.2	419 ÷ 10 =	41.9

Find the missing factor.

23	x 10 = 230	75	x 10 = 750	99	x 10 = 990
48	x 10 = 480	13	x 10 = 130	25	x 10 = 250
52	x 10 = 520	39	x 10 = 390	27	x 10 = 270
62	x 10 = 620	86	x 10 = 860	17	x 10 = 170

Find the dividend.

47	÷ 10 = 4.7	68	÷ 10 = 6.8	124	÷ 10 = 12.4
257	÷ 10 = 25.7	362	÷ 10 = 36.2	314	÷ 10 = 31.4
408	÷ 10 = 40.8	672	÷ 10 = 67.2	809	÷ 10 = 80.9
924	÷ 10 = 92.4	327	÷ 10 = 32.7	563	÷ 10 = 56.3

Remind children that multiplying by 10 adds a 0 to the original figure. Dividing by 10 moves the decimal one place to the left. Whole numbers can be written with a decimal point (e.g. 16 as 16.0). Inverse operations in the later sections give the number that begins the equation.

Appropriate units of measure

Choose the best units to measure the length of each item.

millimetres   centimetres   metres

desk   tooth   swimming pool

centimetres   millimetres   metres

Choose the best units to measure the length of each item.

centimetres   metres   kilometres

bed	bicycle	toothbrush	football field
centimetres	centimetres	centimetres	metres
shoe	driveway	sailboat	highway
centimetres	metres	metres	kilometres

The height of a door is about 2 metres .

The length of a pencil is about 17 centimetres.

The height of a flagpole is about 7 metres .

Choose the best units to measure the mass of each item.

grams   kilograms   tonnes

train	kitten	watermelon	tennis ball
tonnes	grams	kilograms	grams
shoe	bag of potatoes	elephant	washing machine
grams	kilograms	tonnes	kilograms

The mass of a hamburger is about 26 grams .

The mass of a bag of apples is about 2 kilograms .

The mass of a truck is about 4 tonnes .

Children might come up with their own examples of items that measure about 1 centimetre, 1 metre, and 1 kilometre, as well as items that have a mass of about 1 gram, 1 kilogram, and 1 tonne. They can use these as benchmarks to find the appropriate unit .

141 Identifying patterns

Continue each pattern.

Intervals of 6:	1	7	13	19	25	31	37
Intervals of 3:	27	24	21	18	15	12	9

Continue each pattern.

0	10	20	30	40	50	60
15	20	25	30	35	40	45
5	7	9	11	13	15	17
2	9	16	23	30	37	44
4	7	10	13	16	19	22
2	10	18	26	34	42	50

Continue each pattern.

44	38	32	26	20	14	8
33	29	25	21	17	13	9
27	23	19	15	11	7	3
56	48	40	32	24	16	8
49	42	35	28	21	14	7
28	25	22	19	16	13	10

Continue each pattern.

36	30	24	18	12	6	0
5	14	23	32	41	50	59
3	8	13	18	23	28	33
47	40	33	26	19	12	5
1	4	7	10	13	16	19

Point out that some of the patterns show an increase and some a decrease. Children should see what operation turns the first number into the second, and that the same operation turns the second number into the third. They can then continue the pattern.

142 Factors of numbers from 31 to 65

The factors of 40 are 1 2 4 5 8 10 20 40

Circle the factors of 56.

(1) (2) 3 (4) 5 6 (7) (8) (14) (28) 32 (56)

Find all the factors of each number.

The factors of 31 are 1, 31

The factors of 47 are 1, 47

The factors of 60 are 1, 2, 3, 4, 5, 6, 10, 12, 15, 20, 30, 60

The factors of 50 are 1, 2, 5, 10, 25, 50

The factors of 42 are 1, 2, 3, 6, 7, 14, 21, 42

The factors of 32 are 1, 2, 4, 8, 16, 32

The factors of 48 are 1, 2, 3, 4, 6, 8, 12, 16, 24, 48

The factors of 35 are 1, 5, 7, 35

The factors of 52 are 1, 2, 4, 13, 26, 52

Circle all the factors of each number.

Which numbers are factors of 39?

(1) 2 (3) 4 5 8 9 10 (13) 14 15 20 25 (39)

Which numbers are factors of 45?

(1) (3) 4 (5) 8 (9) 12 (15) 16 21 24 36 40 44 (45)

Which numbers are factors of 61?

(1) 3 4 5 6 10 15 16 18 20 26 31 40 (61)

Which numbers are factors of 65?

(1) 2 4 (5) 6 8 9 10 12 (13) 14 15 30 60 (65)

Some numbers have only factors of 1 and themselves. They are called prime numbers.
Write all the prime numbers between 31 and 65 in the box.

31, 37, 41, 43, 47, 53, 59, 61

Children often miss some of the factors of a number, especially when the number is large. Encourage a systematic method of finding factors. Children may forget that 1 and the number itself are factors of the number. If needed, discuss prime numbers with them.

143 Greatest common factor

Circle the common factors.
Write the greatest common factor (GCF).

24: (1), (2), (3), 4, (6), 8, 12, 24

60: (1), (2), (3), 4, 5, (6), 8, 10, 12, 60 The GCF is 6

42: (1), (2), (3), (6), 7, 14

Find the factors. Circle the common factors.

45: (1), (3), 5, (9), 15, 45

36: (1), 2, (3), 4, 6, 8, (9), 12, 18, 36

28: (1), (2), 4, 7, 14, 28

54: (1), (2), 3, 6, 9, 18, 54

Find the factors. Write the GCF.

35: (1), (5), 7, 35

The GCF is 5

80: (1), 2, 4, (5), 8, 10, 20, 40, 80

32: (1), (2), (4), (8), (16), (32)

The GCF is 32

64: (1), (2), (4), (8), (16), (32), 64

12: (1), 2, (3), 4, 6, 12

24: (1), 2, (3), 4, 6, 8, 12, 24

15: (1), (3), 5, 15

The GCF is 3

54: (1), (2), (3), (6), (9), (18), 27, 54

72: (1), (2), (3), 4, (6), 8, (9), 12, (18), 24, 36

18: (1), (2), (3), (6), (9), (18)

The GCF is 18

It is common for children to skip some of the factors of a number. Have them test factors systematically, beginning with 2, and then 3, and so on.

144 Writing equivalent fractions

Make these fractions equal by writing the missing number.

$\frac{20}{100} = \frac{2}{10} = \frac{1}{5}$

$\frac{5}{15} = \frac{1}{3}$

Make these fractions equal by writing a number in the box.

$\frac{10}{100} = \frac{1}{10}$	$\frac{8}{100} = \frac{2}{25}$	$\frac{4}{100} = \frac{1}{25}$
$\frac{2}{20} = \frac{1}{10}$	$\frac{5}{100} = \frac{1}{20}$	$\frac{6}{20} = \frac{3}{10}$
$\frac{3}{5} = \frac{12}{20}$	$\frac{5}{6} = \frac{10}{12}$	$\frac{2}{8} = \frac{6}{24}$
$\frac{2}{3} = \frac{16}{24}$	$\frac{2}{18} = \frac{1}{9}$	$\frac{4}{50} = \frac{2}{25}$
$\frac{11}{12} = \frac{33}{36}$	$\frac{12}{15} = \frac{4}{5}$	$\frac{8}{20} = \frac{2}{5}$
$\frac{2}{12} = \frac{1}{6}$	$\frac{5}{20} = \frac{1}{4}$	$\frac{5}{8} = \frac{10}{16}$
$\frac{7}{8} = \frac{21}{24}$	$\frac{15}{100} = \frac{3}{20}$	$\frac{6}{24} = \frac{1}{4}$
$\frac{5}{25} = \frac{1}{5}$	$\frac{8}{20} = \frac{2}{5}$	$\frac{15}{20} = \frac{3}{4}$
$\frac{5}{30} = \frac{1}{6}$	$\frac{12}{14} = \frac{6}{7}$	$\frac{1}{5} = \frac{4}{20}$
$\frac{9}{18} = \frac{1}{2}$	$\frac{24}{30} = \frac{4}{5}$	$\frac{25}{30} = \frac{5}{6}$

$\frac{1}{8} = \frac{2}{16} = \frac{3}{24} = \frac{4}{32} = \frac{5}{40} = \frac{6}{48}$

$\frac{20}{100} = \frac{5}{25} = \frac{2}{10} = \frac{1}{5} = \frac{10}{50} = \frac{40}{200}$

$\frac{2}{5} = \frac{6}{15} = \frac{8}{20} = \frac{10}{25} = \frac{20}{50} = \frac{40}{100}$

$\frac{1}{6} = \frac{2}{12} = \frac{3}{18} = \frac{4}{24} = \frac{5}{30} = \frac{6}{36}$

$\frac{2}{3} = \frac{16}{24} = \frac{24}{36} = \frac{14}{21} = \frac{6}{9} = \frac{200}{300}$

Remind children that fractions retain the same value if you multiply both the numerator and denominator by the same number or divide the numerator and denominator by the same number.

Fraction models

Write the missing numbers to show what part is shaded.

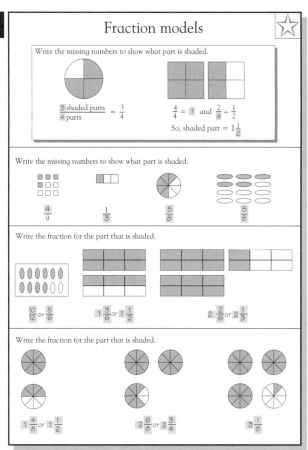

$\frac{3}{4}$ shaded parts $= \frac{3}{4}$
4 parts

$\frac{4}{4} = 1$ and $\frac{2}{4} = \frac{1}{2}$

So, shaded part $= 1\frac{1}{2}$

Write the missing numbers to show what part is shaded.

$\frac{4}{9}$ $\frac{1}{3}$ $\frac{5}{8}$ $\frac{5}{8}$

Write the fraction for the part that is shaded.

$\frac{10}{12}$ or $\frac{5}{6}$ $1\frac{3}{6}$ or $1\frac{1}{2}$ $2\frac{2}{6}$ or $2\frac{1}{3}$

Write the fraction for the part that is shaded.

$1\frac{4}{8}$ or $1\frac{1}{2}$ $2\frac{6}{8}$ or $2\frac{3}{4}$ $3\frac{1}{8}$

Some children may need further explanation of the models of mixed numbers. Point out that when all the parts of a model are shaded, the model shows the number 1.

Multiplying by one-digit numbers

Find each product. Remember to regroup.

$\overset{1\,1}{465}$ $\times\ 3$	$\overset{3}{391}$ $\times\ 4$	$\overset{3\,4}{278}$ $\times\ 5$
1395	1564	1390

Find each product.

563 $\times\ 3$	910 $\times\ 2$	437 $\times\ 3$	812 $\times\ 2$
1689	1820	1311	1624

572 $\times\ 4$	831 $\times\ 3$	406 $\times\ 5$	394 $\times\ 6$
2288	2493	2030	2364

Find each product.

318 $\times\ 3$	223 $\times\ 4$	542 $\times\ 4$	217 $\times\ 3$
954	892	2168	651

127 $\times\ 4$	275 $\times\ 5$	798 $\times\ 6$	365 $\times\ 6$
508	1375	4788	2190

100 $\times\ 5$	372 $\times\ 4$	881 $\times\ 4$	953 $\times\ 3$
500	1488	3524	2859

Solve each problem.

A middle school has 255 students. A high school has 6 times as many students. How many children are there at the high school?

1530 students

$\overset{3\,3}{255}$ $\times\ 6$ = 1530

A train can carry 365 passengers. How many could it carry on

four trips?   1460 passengers

six trips?   2190 passengers

$\overset{2\,2}{365}$ $\times\ 4$ = 1460 $\overset{3\,3}{365}$ $\times\ 6$ = 2190

Make sure children understand the convention of multiplication, i.e. multiply the ones first and work left. Problems on this page may result from gaps in knowledge of the 2, 3, 4, 5, and 6 times tables. Errors will also occur if children neglect to regroup.

Multiplying by one-digit numbers

Find each product. Remember to regroup.

$\overset{3\,3}{456}$ $\times\ 6$	$\overset{1\,2}{823}$ $\times\ 8$	$\overset{4\,4}{755}$ $\times\ 9$
2736	6584	6795

Find each product.

394 $\times\ 7$	736 $\times\ 7$	827 $\times\ 8$	943 $\times\ 9$
2758	5152	6616	8487

643 $\times\ 6$	199 $\times\ 6$	821 $\times\ 7$	547 $\times\ 8$
3858	1194	5747	4376

501 $\times\ 7$	377 $\times\ 8$	843 $\times\ 8$	222 $\times\ 9$
3507	3016	6744	1998

471 $\times\ 9$	223 $\times\ 8$	606 $\times\ 6$	513 $\times\ 7$
4239	1784	3636	3591

500 $\times\ 9$	800 $\times\ 9$	900 $\times\ 8$	200 $\times\ 9$
4500	7200	7200	1800

Solve each problem.

A crate holds 550 apples. How many apples are there in 8 crates?

4400 apples

$\overset{4}{550}$ $\times\ 8$ = 4400

Keyshawn swims 760 laps each week. How many laps does he swim in 5 weeks?

3800 people

$\overset{3}{760}$ $\times\ 5$ = 3800

Problems encountered will be similar to the previous page. Gaps in knowledge of the 6, 7, 8, and 9 times table will result in children's errors.

Real-life problems

Find the answer to each problem.

Jacob spent $4.68 at the store and had $4.77 left. How much did he have to start with?

$9.45

$\overset{1\ 1}{4.77}$ $+\ 4.68$ = 9.45

Tracy receives a weekly allowance of $3.00 a week. How much will she have if she saves all of it for 8 weeks?

$24.00

3.00 $\times\ 8$ = 24.00

Find the answer to each problem.

A theater charges $4 for each matinee ticket. If it sells 360 tickets for a matinee performance, how much does it take in?

$1440

$\overset{2}{360}$ $\times\ 4$ = 1440

David has saved $9.59. His sister has $3.24 less. How much does she have?

$6.35

9.59 $-\ 3.24$ = 6.35

The cost for 9 children to go to a theme park is $72. How much does each child pay? If only 6 children go, what will the cost be?

$8 per child
$48 for 6 children

$9\overline{)72}$ = 8

$6 \times 8 = 48$

Paul has $3.69. His sister gives him another $5.25, and he goes out and buys a CD single for $3.99. How much does he have left?

$4.95

$\overset{1}{3.69}$ $+\ 5.25$ = 8.94 $\overset{7\ 18}{8.94}$ $-\ 3.99$ = 4.95

Ian has $20 in savings. He decides to spend $\frac{1}{4}$ of it. How much will he have left?

$15

$20 \div 4 = 5$

$20 - 5 = 15$

This page and the next provide children an opportunity to apply the skills they have practiced. They will need to select the appropriate operation. If they are unsure, discuss whether the answer should be larger or smaller. This can help them decide on the operation.

Real-life problems ★

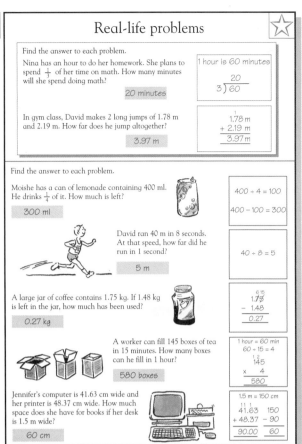

Find the answer to each problem.

Nina has an hour to do her homework. She plans to spend $\frac{1}{3}$ of her time on math. How many minutes will she spend doing math?

20 minutes

$$1 \text{ hour is } 60 \text{ minutes}$$
$$\begin{array}{r} 20 \\ 3\overline{)60} \end{array}$$

In gym class, David makes 2 long jumps of 1.78 m and 2.19 m. How far does he jump altogether?

3.97 m

$$\begin{array}{r} 1.78 \text{ m} \\ + 2.19 \text{ m} \\ \hline 3.97 \text{ m} \end{array}$$

Find the answer to each problem.

Moishe has a can of lemonade containing 400 ml. He drinks $\frac{1}{4}$ of it. How much is left?

300 ml

$$400 \div 4 = 100$$
$$400 - 100 = 300$$

David ran 40 m in 8 seconds. At that speed, how far did he run in 1 second?

5 m

$$40 \div 8 = 5$$

A large jar of coffee contains 1.75 kg. If 1.48 kg is left in the jar, how much has been used?

0.27 kg

$$\begin{array}{r} \overset{6}{1}.\overset{15}{7}5 \\ - 1.48 \\ \hline 0.27 \end{array}$$

A worker can fill 145 boxes of tea in 15 minutes. How many boxes can he fill in 1 hour?

580 boxes

$$1 \text{ hour} = 60 \text{ min}$$
$$60 \div 15 = 4$$
$$\begin{array}{r} \overset{1}{1}\overset{2}{4}5 \\ \times \quad 4 \\ \hline 580 \end{array}$$

Jennifer's computer is 41.63 cm wide and her printer is 48.37 cm wide. How much space does she have for books if her desk is 1.5 m wide?

60 cm

$$1.5 \text{ m} = 150 \text{ cm}$$
$$\begin{array}{r} \overset{1}{4}1.63 \\ + 48.37 \\ \hline 90.00 \end{array} \quad \begin{array}{r} 150 \\ - 90 \\ \hline 60 \end{array}$$

This page deals with units other than money. Note that solving the final problem requires two operations.

★ Problems involving time

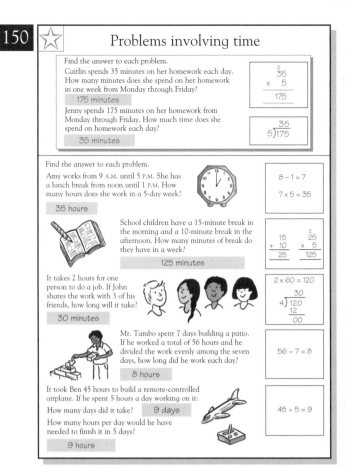

Find the answer to each problem.

Caitlin spends 35 minutes on her homework each day. How many minutes does she spend on her homework in one week from Monday through Friday?

175 minutes

$$\begin{array}{r} \overset{2}{3}5 \\ \times \quad 5 \\ \hline 175 \end{array}$$

Jenny spends 175 minutes on her homework from Monday through Friday. How much time does she spend on homework each day?

35 minutes

$$\begin{array}{r} 35 \\ 5\overline{)175} \end{array}$$

Find the answer to each problem.

Amy works from 9 A.M. until 5 P.M. She has a lunch break from noon until 1 P.M. How many hours does she work in a 5-day week?

35 hours

$$8 - 1 = 7$$
$$7 \times 5 = 35$$

School children have a 15-minute break in the morning and a 10-minute break in the afternoon. How many minutes of break do they have in a week?

125 minutes

$$\begin{array}{r} 15 \\ + 10 \\ \hline 25 \end{array} \quad \begin{array}{r} \overset{2}{2}5 \\ \times \quad 5 \\ \hline 125 \end{array}$$

It takes 2 hours for one person to do a job. If John shares the work with 3 of his friends, how long will it take?

30 minutes

$$2 \times 60 = 120$$
$$\begin{array}{r} 30 \\ 4\overline{)120} \\ 12 \\ \hline 00 \end{array}$$

Mr. Tambo spent 7 days building a patio. If he worked a total of 56 hours and he divided the work evenly among the seven days, how long did he work each day?

8 hours

$$56 \div 7 = 8$$

It took Ben 45 hours to build a remote-controlled airplane. If he spent 5 hours a day working on it:
How many days did it take? **9 days**
How many hours per day would he have needed to finish it in 5 days?

9 hours

$$45 \div 5 = 9$$

For the second problem, children should realize that a school week is 5 days. For the third problem, check that children divide by 4 rather than 3.

Multiplying and dividing ★

Write the answer in the box.

26 x 10 = **260**		26 x 100 = **2600**	
400 ÷ 10 = **40**		400 ÷ 100 = **4**	

Write the product in the box.

33 x 10 = **330**	21 x 10 = **210**	42 x 10 = **420**
94 x 100 = **9400**	36 x 100 = **3600**	81 x 100 = **8100**
416 x 10 = **4160**	204 x 10 = **2040**	513 x 10 = **5130**
767 x 100 = **76 700**	821 x 100 = **82 100**	245 x 100 = **24 500**

Write the quotient in the box.

120 ÷ 10 = **12**	260 ÷ 10 = **26**	470 ÷ 10 = **47**
300 ÷ 100 = **3**	800 ÷ 100 = **8**	400 ÷ 100 = **4**
20 ÷ 10 = **2**	30 ÷ 10 = **3**	70 ÷ 10 = **7**
500 ÷ 100 = **5**	100 ÷ 100 = **1**	900 ÷ 100 = **9**

Write the number that has been multiplied by 100.

59 x 100 = 5900	**714** x 100 = 71 400
721 x 100 = 72 100	**234** x 100 = 23 400
11 x 100 = 1100	**470** x 100 = 47 000
84 x 100 = 8400	**441** x 100 = 44 100

Write the number that has been divided by 100.

200 ÷ 100 = 2	**800** ÷ 100 = 8
2100 ÷ 100 = 21	**1800** ÷ 100 = 18
8600 ÷ 100 = 86	**2100** ÷ 100 = 21
1000 ÷ 100 = 10	**5900** ÷ 100 = 59

Children should realize that multiplying a whole number by 10 or 100 means writing one or two zeros at the end of the number. To divide a multiple of ten by 10, simply take the final zero off. In the two final sections, solve by using the inverse operation.

★ Identifying patterns

Continue each pattern.

Steps of 2: $\frac{1}{2}$	$2\frac{1}{2}$	$4\frac{1}{2}$	**$6\frac{1}{2}$**	**$8\frac{1}{2}$**	**$10\frac{1}{2}$**
Steps of 5: 3.5	8.5	13.5	**18.5**	**23.5**	**28.5**

Continue each pattern.

$5\frac{1}{2}$	$10\frac{1}{2}$	$15\frac{1}{2}$	**$20\frac{1}{2}$**	**$25\frac{1}{2}$**	**$30\frac{1}{2}$**
$1\frac{1}{4}$	$3\frac{1}{4}$	$5\frac{1}{4}$	**$7\frac{1}{4}$**	**$9\frac{1}{4}$**	**$11\frac{1}{4}$**
$8\frac{1}{3}$	$9\frac{1}{3}$	$10\frac{1}{3}$	**$11\frac{1}{3}$**	**$12\frac{1}{3}$**	**$13\frac{1}{3}$**
$55\frac{3}{4}$	$45\frac{3}{4}$	$35\frac{3}{4}$	**$25\frac{3}{4}$**	**$15\frac{3}{4}$**	**$5\frac{3}{4}$**
$42\frac{1}{2}$	$38\frac{1}{2}$	$34\frac{1}{2}$	**$30\frac{1}{2}$**	**$26\frac{1}{2}$**	**$22\frac{1}{2}$**
7.5	6.5	5.5	**4.5**	**3.5**	**2.5**
28.4	25.4	22.4	**19.4**	**16.4**	**13.4**
81.6	73.6	65.6	**57.6**	**49.6**	**41.6**
6.3	10.3	14.3	**18.3**	**22.3**	**26.3**
12.1	13.1	14.1	**15.1**	**16.1**	17.1
14.6	21.6	28.6	**35.6**	**42.6**	**49.6**
$11\frac{1}{2}$	$10\frac{1}{2}$	$9\frac{1}{2}$	**$8\frac{1}{2}$**	**$7\frac{1}{2}$**	**$6\frac{1}{2}$**
8.4	11.4	14.4	**17.4**	**20.4**	**23.4**
$7\frac{3}{4}$	$13\frac{3}{4}$	$19\frac{3}{4}$	**$25\frac{3}{4}$**	**$31\frac{3}{4}$**	**$37\frac{3}{4}$**
57.5	48.5	39.5	**30.5**	**21.5**	**12.5**

The patterns on this page are formed by adding or subtracting whole numbers but the items in each row mixed numbers or decimals. Children should see who operation turns the first number into the second, and second into the third, and then continue the pattern

153 — Products with odd and even numbers ☆

Find the products of these numbers.

3 and 4 — The product of 3 and 4 is 12. 6 and 8 — The product of 6 and 8 is 48.

Find the products of these odd and even numbers.

5 and 6 — The product of 5 and 6 is 30. 3 and 2 — The product of 3 and 2 is 6.

7 and 4 — The product of 7 and 4 is 28. 8 and 3 — The product of 8 and 3 is 24.

6 and 3 — The product of 6 and 3 is 18. 2 and 9 — The product of 2 and 9 is 18.

10 and 3 — The product of 10 and 3 is 30. 12 and 5 — The product of 12 and 5 is 60.

What do you notice about your answers? _The product of odd and even numbers is always an even number._

Find the products of these odd numbers.

5 and 7 — The product of 5 and 7 is 35. 3 and 9 — The product of 3 and 9 is 27.

5 and 11 — The product of 5 and 11 is 55. 7 and 3 — The product of 7 and 3 is 21.

9 and 5 — The product of 9 and 5 is 45. 11 and 7 — The product of 11 and 7 is 77.

13 and 3 — The product of 13 and 3 is 39. 1 and 5 — The product of 1 and 5 is 5.

What do you notice about your answers? _The product of two odd numbers is always an odd number._

Find the products of these even numbers.

2 and 4 — The product of 2 and 4 is 8. 4 and 6 — The product of 4 and 6 is 24.

6 and 2 — The product of 6 and 2 is 12. 4 and 8 — The product of 4 and 8 is 32.

10 and 2 — The product of 10 and 2 is 20. 4 and 10 — The product of 4 and 10 is 40.

6 and 10 — The product of 6 and 10 is 60. 6 and 8 — The product of 6 and 8 is 48.

What do you notice about your answers? _The product of two even numbers is always an even number._

Can you write a rule for the products with odd and even numbers?
The product of two numbers will always be even unless both numbers are odd.

Children may need help answering the questions on what they notice about the products. Accept any rule about products that children write, as long as it indicates that they have grasped the concept.

154 — ☆ Factors of numbers from 66 to 100

The factors of 66 are   1   2   3   6   11   22   33   66

Circle the factors of 94. (1) (2) 28 32 43 (47) 71 86 (94)

Write the factors of each number in the box.

The factors of 70 are — 1, 2, 5, 7, 10, 14, 35, 70

The factors of 85 are — 1, 5, 17, 85

The factors of 69 are — 1, 3, 23, 69

The factors of 83 are — 1, 83

The factors of 75 are — 1, 3, 5, 15, 25, 75

The factors of 96 are — 1, 2, 3, 4, 6, 8, 12, 16, 24, 32, 48, 96

The factors of 63 are — 1, 3, 7, 9, 21, 63

The factors of 99 are — 1, 3, 9, 11, 33, 99

The factors of 72 are — 1, 2, 3, 4, 6, 8, 9, 12, 18, 24, 36, 72

Circle the factors of 68.
(1) (2) 3 (4) 5 6 7 8 9 11 12 (17) (34) 35 62 (68)

Circle the factors of 95.
(1) 2 3 4 (5) 15 16 17 (19) 24 37 85 90 (95) 96

Circle the factors of 88.
(1) (2) 3 (4) 5 6 (8) 10 (11) 15 (22) 25 27 (44) 87 (88)

Circle the factors of 73.
(1) 2 4 5 6 8 9 10 12 13 14 15 30 60 (73)

A prime number only has two factors, 1 and itself.
Write all the prime numbers between 66 and 100 in the box.

67, 71, 73, 79, 83, 89, 97

Children often miss some of the factors of a number, especially for large numbers. Encourage a systematic method of finding factors. Children may forget that 1 and the number itself are factors of a number.
If necessary, discuss prime numbers with children.

155 — Multiplying by two-digit numbers ☆

Write the product for each problem.

```
   1          2
   1          1
  56         45
x 32       x 43
 112        135
1680       1800
1792       1935
```

Write the product for each problem.

```
  56         23         47         84
x 23       x 24       x 25       x 22
 168         92        235        168
1120        460        940       1680
1288        552       1175       1848

  73         52         64         51
x 34       x 35       x 33       x 32
 292        260        192        102
2190       1560       1920       1530
2482       1820       2112       1632
```

Write the product for each problem.

```
  41         65         72         84
x 62       x 54       x 68       x 71
  82        260        576         84
2460       3250       4320       5880
2542       3510       4896       5964

  92         57         38         26
x 63       x 82       x 94       x 75
 276        114        152        130
5520       4560       3420       1820
5796       4674       3572       1950
```

Children should understand that multiplying a number by 32 is the same as multiplying the number by 2 and then by 30, and adding the two products.

156 — ☆ Multiplying by two-digit numbers

Write the product for each problem.

```
   7          7
   6          6
  39         68
x 87       x 98
 273        544
3120       6120
3393       6664
```

Write the product for each problem.

```
  87         76         99         85
x 98       x 78       x 69       x 98
 696        608        891        680
7830       5320       5940       7650
8526       5928       6831       8330

  88         67         94         89
x 95       x 76       x 69       x 47
 440        402        846        623
7920       4690       5640       3560
8360       5092       6486       4183
```

Write the product for each problem.

```
  87         46         58         73
x 79       x 67       x 59       x 98
 783        322        522        584
6090       2760       2900       6570
6873       3082       3422       7154

  95         58         78         96
x 67       x 88       x 97       x 79
 665        464        546        864
5700       4640       7020       6720
6365       5104       7566       7584
```

This page gives further practice of multiplication as on the previous page. Make sure that children do not neglect to regroup when necessary.

Extra Practice

Answer Section
with Parents' Notes

This section provides answers for the Extra Practice section on pages 158–201. There are also notes for each page, indicating the skills being developed, pointing out potential issues, or providing ideas for extra activities and ways to help children.

When checking the answers with children, encourage them to explain their reasoning. This will allow you to understand how they are thinking and where the stumbling blocks may be. Occasionally, you may find that a particular problem is slightly beyond your child's capabilities. Offer as much help and support as needed, and encourage them to reason out the solutions to the best of their abilities.

Around the home, continue to provide opportunities for practical use of measuring equipment and appropriate tools, such as calculators, weighing scales, timetables, and computer programs. This will help children to visualize situations when answering math problems.

Build your child's confidence with words of praise. If they are getting answers wrong, encourage them to return to try again another time. Good luck, and remember to have fun!

★ Place value

Write each of these using numbers.

Fifteen thousand seven hundred twenty-nine	15 729
Six hundred eighteen thousand two hundred forty-three	618 243
Six hundred thousand four	600 004
One hundred seven thousand two hundred fifty-six	107 256
Three hundred thousand two hundred eighteen	300 218
Eight hundred six thousand one hundred seven	806 107
Three hundred twenty-one thousand five hundred fifty-nine	321 559
Nine hundred ninety-nine thousand nine hundred ninety-nine	999 999
Two thousand one hundred sixty-nine	2169
Eight hundred five thousand four hundred one	805 401

Write each row in order, starting with the smallest number.

21 358	13 560	34 078	100 000
13 560	21 358	34 078	100 000

99 000	9999	10 000	9009
9009	9999	10 000	99 000

Write each number using words.

1502   One thousand five hundred two

2416   Two thousand four hundred sixteen

Children need practice to understand very large numbers. Sometimes children can be confused when a 0 is a placeholder as with 7401, for example, where they might say "seven thousand forty-one." Watch out for this.

Multiply and divide by 10 and 100 ★

Write the answers.

269 x 10 =	2690	7650 ÷ 10 =	765
845 x 10 =	8450	52 430 ÷ 10 =	5243
1564 x 10 =	15 640	76 400 ÷ 10 =	7640
7405 x 10 =	74 050	6000 ÷ 10 =	600
7420 x 10 =	74 200	5290 ÷ 10 =	529
15 645 x 10 =	156 450	1350 ÷ 10 =	135
23 785 x 10 =	237 850	5500 ÷ 10 =	550
54 866 x 10 =	548 660	12 600 ÷ 10 =	1260
9400 x 10 =	94 000	1000 ÷ 10 =	100
4545 x 10 =	45 450	6800 ÷ 100 =	68
5212 x 10 =	52 120	6000 ÷ 100 =	60
2867 x 100 =	286 700	5000 ÷ 100 =	50
6734 x 100 =	673 400	5500 ÷ 100 =	55
5089 x 100 =	508 900	60 200 ÷ 100 =	602
967 x 100 =	96 700	40 000 ÷ 100 =	400
3000 x 100 =	300 000	66 000 ÷ 100 =	660

Although it is simple to tell children to "add a 0 when multiplying by 10," it is important they understand the principle that each number becomes 10 times larger.

★ Ordering sets of amounts

Write each row in order, starting with the smallest number.

7 m	690 cm	1.6 km	900 m	1700 m
690 cm	7 m	900 m	1.6 km	1700 m

23 cm	240 mm	180 mm	20 cm	0.21 m
180 mm	20 cm	0.21 m	23 cm	240 mm

2.8 km	3000 m	2.5 km	2600 m	1.9 km
1.9 km	2.5 km	2600 m	2.8 km	3000 m

678 g	0.5 kg	2.3 kg	1400 g	0.95 kg
0.5 kg	678 g	0.95 kg	1400 g	2.3 kg

1200 mL	1.6 L	0.9 L	850 mL	1400 mL
850 mL	0.9 L	1200 mL	1400 mL	1.6 L

$5.50	280 ¢	$0.75	600 ¢	$3.90
$0.75	280 ¢	$3.90	$5.50	600 ¢

12 L	11 000 mL	8.5 L	110.45 mL	6.85 L
110.45 mL	6.85 L	8.5 L	11 000 mL	12 L

150 seconds	3 minutes	1 hour	130 minutes	600 seconds
150 seconds	3 minutes	600 seconds	1 hour	130 minutes

$\frac{1}{2}$ L	$\frac{3}{5}$ L	1.2 L	0.25 L	2 L
0.25 L	$\frac{1}{2}$ L	$\frac{3}{5}$ L	1.2 L	2 L

2 hours	50 minutes	$3\frac{1}{2}$ hours	100 minutes	$1\frac{1}{2}$ hours
50 minutes	$1\frac{1}{2}$ hours	100 minutes	2 hours	$3\frac{1}{2}$ hours

Within each row the units have been mixed up, so effectively these questions are not just about ordering by size but also enabling children to convert between units, as well as between decimal and fractional amounts.

Constant steps ★

Continue each sequence.

1.6	2.2	2.8	3.4	4.0	4.6	5.2	5.8
3.7	4.2	4.7	5.2	5.7	6.2	6.7	7.2
$1\frac{1}{2}$	$4\frac{1}{2}$	$7\frac{1}{2}$	$10\frac{1}{2}$	$13\frac{1}{2}$	$16\frac{1}{2}$	$19\frac{1}{2}$	$22\frac{1}{2}$
35	28	21	14	7	0	-7	-14
5.9	4.9	3.9	2.9	1.9	0.9	-0.1	-1.1
$6\frac{1}{4}$	$5\frac{3}{4}$	$5\frac{1}{4}$	$4\frac{3}{4}$	$4\frac{1}{4}$	$3\frac{3}{4}$	$3\frac{1}{4}$	$2\frac{3}{4}$
-6.5	-5.6	-4.7	-3.8	-2.9	-2.0	-1.1	-0.2
34	45	56	67	78	89	100	111
8.6	9.2	9.8	10.4	11.0	11.6	12.2	12.8
30	45	60	75	90	105	120	135
-50	-44	-38	-32	-26	-20	-14	-8
0.6	1.1	1.6	2.1	2.6	3.1	3.6	4.1
4.6	7.6	10.6	13.6	16.6	19.6	22.6	25.6
14.4	13.9	13.4	12.9	12.4	11.9	11.4	10.9
7.3	6.3	5.3	4.3	3.3	2.3	1.3	0.3

Children should manage well with these questions as long as they spot how the numbers are changing and then correctly calculate the next in the sequence. The sequences that go from positive to negative numbers can be a bit trickier.

★ Negative numbers

Write each row in order, beginning with the lowest number.

8	4	–3	–7	0	9	–5
–7	–5	–3	0	4	8	9

–10	5	10	0	–5	12	14
–10	–5	0	5	10	12	14

7	–3	9	–4	–6	6	5
–6	–4	–3	5	6	7	9

0	5	–5	4	–4	3	–3
–5	–4	–3	0	3	4	5

0.5	1.5	–0.5	0	–1.5	–0.2	0.2
–1.5	–0.5	–0.2	0	0.2	0.5	1.5

14	8	0	9	–3	12	–20
–20	–3	0	8	9	12	14

–8	–6	–10	0	–4	–1	6
–10	–8	–6	–4	–1	0	6

30	0	50	–60	–30	20	–10
–60	–30	–10	0	20	30	50

–5	12	–20	30	40	–10	50
–20	–10	–5	12	30	40	50

$\frac{1}{2}$	$\frac{1}{3}$	$\frac{1}{4}$	$\frac{9}{10}$	$-\frac{1}{4}$	–1	–2
–2	–1	$-\frac{1}{4}$	$\frac{1}{4}$	$\frac{1}{3}$	$\frac{1}{2}$	$\frac{9}{10}$

Answering these correctly will show that children have a good understanding of the way positive and negative numbers work.

Calculating temperature ★

Use the thermometer to count the number of degrees from one temperature to another to answer these questions.

What is the difference in temperatures?

5°C and 12°C	7°C	10°C and 3°C	7°C
1°C and 14°C	13°C	4°C and 0°C	4°C
8°C and 20°C	12°C	18°C and 30°C	12°C
15°C and 25°C	10°C	10°C and 14°C	4°C
19°C and 12°C	7°C	5°C and –2°C	7°C
–3°C and 7°C	10°C	8°C and –1°C	9°C
–4°C and 4°C	8°C	9°C and 0°C	9°C
6°C and –3°C	9°C	–8°C and 3°C	11°C
10°C and –3°C	13°C	–5°C and 12°C	17°C
–3°C and –4°C	1°C	–6°C and –8°C	2°C
0°C and –5°C	5°C	0°C and –20°C	20°C
–10°C and –30°C	20°C	–4°C and –12°C	8°C

The temperature in Calgary, Alberta is 5°C but the temperature in Moscow, Russia is 8°C colder. What is the temperature in Moscow? → –3°C

The temperature in Madrid, Spain is 12°C warmer than the temperature in Toronto, Ontario. The temperature in Toronto is –3°C. What is the temperature in Madrid? → 9°C

The temperature in Paris, France is 7°C and in Montreal, Quebec is –4°C. What is the difference in temperature between Paris and Montreal? → 11°C

If children are having any doubts over this type of work, encourage them to draw a simple number line going from a positive value such as 20 to a negative number such as –20.

★ Ordering decimals

Write each row in order, starting with the smallest number.

3.89	9.83	8.93	9.38	3.98
3.89	3.98	8.93	9.38	9.83

0.67	7.06	6.7	7.6	6.07
0.67	6.07	6.7	7.06	7.6

12.65	16.52	26.51	62.15	26.25
12.65	16.52	26.25	26.51	62.15

30.06	36.0	6.03	63.0	30.6
6.03	30.06	30.6	36.0	63.0

3.16	3.61	0.36	36.01	3.06
0.36	3.06	3.16	3.61	36.01

3.42 cm	4.85 cm	1.65 cm	2.33 cm	3.76 cm
1.65 cm	2.33 cm	3.42 cm	3.76 cm	4.85 cm

5.23 m	12.08 m	3.76 m	11.82 m	9.65 m
3.76 m	5.23 m	9.65 m	11.82 m	12.08 m

4.56 mm	3.88 mm	1.26 mm	6.07 mm	4.5 mm
1.26 mm	3.88 mm	4.5 mm	4.56 mm	6.07 mm

10.08 L	9.45 L	3.45 L	6.5 L	5.1 L
3.45 L	5.1 L	6.5 L	9.45 L	10.08 L

7 km	6.8 km	7.03 km	5 km	7.34 km
5 km	6.8 km	7 km	7.03 km	7.34 km

If children find this work difficult, help them by suggesting they look first at the whole numbers and sort those, and then move to sorting the numbers in the first decimal place and so on.

Rounding decimals ★

Round each number to the nearest whole number.

3.65	1.87	4.52	6.3	2.01	5.45
4	2	5	6	2	5

4.88	5.5	7.43	9.09	4.83	6.21
5	6	7	9	5	6

4.86 mm	5.23 m	7.6 km	4.9 mm	8.28 m	7.06 cm
5 mm	5 m	8 km	5 mm	8 m	7 cm

0.69 g	7.26 cm	5.46 g	27.06 mL	9.99 g	46.34 kg
1 g	7 cm	5 g	27 mL	10 g	46 kg

Round each amount to the nearest whole dollar.

$2.58	$1.60	$4.12	$5.85	$16.17	$8.30
$3	$2	$4	$6	$16	$8

$1.56	$9.45	$6.01	$8.51	$21.76	$79.90
$2	$9	$6	$9	$22	$80

Round each number to the nearest tenth.

12.42	11.76	12.38	14.75	17.48	5.69
12.4	11.8	12.4	14.8	17.5	5.7

3.47	4.92	13.31	24.44	18.09	15.63
3.5	4.9	13.3	24.4	18.1	15.6

2.31	2.85	3.65	8.12	19.49	6.10
2.3	2.9	3.7	8.1	19.5	6.1

5.67	14.67	5.55	0.78	0.50	1.46
5.7	14.7	5.6	0.8	0.5	1.5

For children who are still grappling with decimal amounts some of these can be tricky, and it would be useful if an adult sat alongside them to help out on any that are causing difficulty.

★ Equivalent fractions

Write five fractions that are equivalent to $\frac{1}{2}$. Answers may vary.

$\frac{1}{2}$ $\frac{2}{4}$ $\frac{3}{6}$ $\frac{4}{8}$ $\frac{5}{10}$ $\frac{6}{12}$

Write five fractions that are equivalent to $\frac{1}{5}$. Answers may vary.

$\frac{1}{5}$ $\frac{2}{10}$ $\frac{3}{15}$ $\frac{4}{20}$ $\frac{5}{25}$ $\frac{6}{30}$

Write five fractions that are equivalent to $\frac{3}{5}$. Answers may vary.

$\frac{3}{5}$ $\frac{6}{10}$ $\frac{9}{15}$ $\frac{12}{20}$ $\frac{15}{25}$ $\frac{18}{30}$

Write five fractions that are equivalent to $\frac{1}{10}$. Answers may vary.

$\frac{1}{10}$ $\frac{2}{20}$ $\frac{3}{30}$ $\frac{4}{40}$ $\frac{5}{50}$ $\frac{6}{60}$

Write five fractions that are equivalent to $\frac{3}{4}$. Answers may vary.

$\frac{3}{4}$ $\frac{6}{8}$ $\frac{9}{12}$ $\frac{12}{16}$ $\frac{15}{20}$ $\frac{18}{24}$

Write five fractions that are equivalent to $\frac{3}{10}$. Answers may vary.

$\frac{3}{10}$ $\frac{6}{20}$ $\frac{9}{30}$ $\frac{12}{40}$ $\frac{15}{50}$ $\frac{18}{60}$

Write five fractions that are equivalent to $\frac{2}{3}$. Answers may vary.

$\frac{2}{3}$ $\frac{4}{6}$ $\frac{6}{9}$ $\frac{8}{12}$ $\frac{10}{15}$ $\frac{12}{18}$

166

Each fraction has an infinite number of equivalents so not all are given in the answers.

Fractions of amounts ★

What is one-quarter ($\frac{1}{4}$) of each amount?

12 ¢ — 3 ¢   40 ¢ — 10 ¢   60 ¢ — 15 ¢ $1.00 — 25 ¢ $8.00 — $2

24 cm — 6 cm   36 cm — 9 cm   4 m — 1 m   16 cm — 4 cm   240 cm — 60 cm

8 kg — 2 kg   28 mL — 7 mL   44 g — 11 g   52 kg — 13 kg   120 mL — 30 mL

What is two-thirds ($\frac{2}{3}$) of each amount?

21 km — 14 km   27 kg — 18 kg   15 ¢ — 10 ¢ $30 — $20   18 cm — 12 cm

12 litres — 8 litres   9 cm — 6 cm   30 m — 20 m   45 kg — 30 kg   60 mm — 40 mm

24 mL — 16 mL   36 m — 24 m   90 km — 60 km   48 cm — 32 cm $120 — $80

What is three-quarters ($\frac{3}{4}$) of each amount?

$1.00 — 75 ¢ $1.60 — $1.20 $1.12 — 84 ¢ $1.40 — $1.05 $10.00 — $7.50

96 ¢ — 72 ¢   84 ¢ — 63 ¢   72 ¢ — 54 ¢   56 ¢ — 42 ¢   104 ¢ — 78 ¢

240 m — 180 m   400 m — 300 m   600 m — 450 m   480 m — 360 m   220 m — 165 m

What is four-fifths ($\frac{4}{5}$) of each amount?

350 mL — 280 mL   8 m — 6.4 m $5 — $4   15 km — 12 km   20 m — 16 m

100 mm — 80 mm   80 m — 64 m   60 ¢ — 48 ¢   90 cm — 72 cm   30 ¢ — 24 ¢

500 km — 400 km $2 — $1.60   250 ¢ — 200 ¢ $120 — $96   900 m — 720 m

167

Children should be able to work unitary fractions ($\frac{1}{2}, \frac{1}{3}, \frac{1}{4}$) fairly easily. For other fractions ($\frac{2}{3}, \frac{3}{4}, \frac{4}{5}$) the simplest method is to work out one part, for example one-third, and then multiply by whatever is needed.

★ Fractions to decimals

Write each fraction in its decimal form.

$\frac{1}{2}$ — 0.5 $\frac{1}{4}$ — 0.25 $\frac{3}{4}$ — 0.75 $\frac{1}{5}$ — 0.2 $\frac{2}{5}$ — 0.4

$\frac{3}{5}$ — 0.6 $\frac{4}{5}$ — 0.8 $\frac{1}{3}$ — 0.33 $\frac{2}{3}$ — 0.66 $\frac{1}{10}$ — 0.1

$\frac{2}{10}$ — 0.2 $\frac{3}{10}$ — 0.3 $\frac{5}{10}$ — 0.5 $\frac{6}{10}$ — 0.6 $\frac{9}{10}$ — 0.9

Write each number in its decimal form.

$1\frac{1}{2}$ — 1.5 $7\frac{1}{2}$ — 7.5 $4\frac{1}{5}$ — 4.2 $7\frac{2}{5}$ — 7.4 $9\frac{1}{4}$ — 9.25

$6\frac{1}{5}$ — 6.2 $9\frac{3}{10}$ — 9.3 $2\frac{9}{10}$ — 2.9 $12\frac{1}{5}$ — 12.2 $15\frac{2}{5}$ — 15.4

$8\frac{4}{5}$ — 8.8 $5\frac{3}{4}$ — 5.75 $7\frac{8}{10}$ — 7.8 $15\frac{3}{5}$ — 15.6 $2\frac{4}{10}$ — 2.4

$14\frac{2}{5}$ — 14.4 $18\frac{3}{4}$ — 18.75 $12\frac{3}{4}$ — 12.75 $2\frac{1}{2}$ — 2.5 $15\frac{6}{10}$ — 15.6

Join the shaded fraction to its decimal form with a line.

$\frac{3}{10}$ 0.4
$\frac{4}{5}$ 0.75
$\frac{9}{10}$ 0.2
$\frac{1}{5}$ 0.3
$\frac{3}{4}$ 0.9
$\frac{2}{5}$ 0.8

168

Children should know the simpler conversions by now. Although $\frac{1}{3}$ is shown as 0.33 and $\frac{2}{3}$ as 0.66, the decimal actually continues to infinity and is known as "repeating."

Percentages and conversions ★

Change each fraction to its percentage equivalent.

$\frac{1}{2}$ = 50% $\frac{1}{4}$ = 25% $\frac{3}{4}$ = 75% $\frac{1}{5}$ = 20%

$\frac{2}{5}$ = 40% $\frac{3}{5}$ = 60% $\frac{4}{5}$ = 80% $\frac{1}{10}$ = 10%

$\frac{2}{10}$ = 20% $\frac{3}{10}$ = 30% $\frac{4}{10}$ = 40% $\frac{5}{10}$ = 50%

$\frac{6}{10}$ = 60% $\frac{7}{10}$ = 70% $\frac{8}{10}$ = 80% $\frac{9}{10}$ = 90%

$\frac{50}{100}$ = 50% $\frac{80}{100}$ = 80% $\frac{10}{100}$ = 10% $\frac{20}{100}$ = 20%

$\frac{90}{100}$ = 90% $\frac{40}{100}$ = 40% $\frac{70}{100}$ = 70% $\frac{30}{100}$ = 30%

$\frac{60}{100}$ = 60% $\frac{25}{100}$ = 25% $\frac{75}{100}$ = 75% $\frac{5}{100}$ = 5%

$\frac{17}{100}$ = 17% $\frac{28}{100}$ = 28% $\frac{35}{100}$ = 35% $\frac{46}{100}$ = 46%

$\frac{52}{100}$ = 52% $\frac{63}{100}$ = 63% $\frac{76}{100}$ = 76% $\frac{83}{100}$ = 83%

Write each amount in dollars.

27 ¢ — $0.27   35 ¢ — $0.35   60 ¢ — $0.60   90 ¢ — $0.90

41 ¢ — $0.41   12 ¢ — $0.12   42 ¢ — $0.42   79 ¢ — $0.79

75 ¢ — $0.75   56 ¢ — $0.56   30 ¢ — $0.30   80 ¢ — $0.80

Write each amount in cents.

$2.00 — 200 ¢ $5.00 — 500 ¢ $10.00 — 1000 ¢ $40.00 — 4000 ¢

169

Children should become used to converting between fractions and percentages. It is also good practice to convert cents to dollars and dollars to cents.

★ Keeping skills sharp

Ten people win a lottery prize of $345 270. The prize is shared equally between them. How much will they each receive?　$34 527

A scientist has to put some animals on display in order of their length. The smallest animal must go first. Below are the lengths of some animals. Put these lengths in order, starting with the shortest.

| 27 m | 3750 cm | 18.25 m | 99 mm | 0.87 m |

| 99 mm | 0.87 m | 18.25 m | 27 m | 3750 cm |

A child reduces each of these amounts by 8 units every minute. What will the amounts be after 5 minutes?

	After 1 min	After 2 min	After 3 min	After 4 min	After 5 min
62 g	54 g	46 g	38 g	30 g	22 g
79 cm	71 cm	63 cm	55 cm	47 cm	39 cm
102 mL	94 mL	86 mL	78 mL	70 mL	62 mL

The temperature in a freezer drops steadily by 3°C per hour. If the freezer starts at 0°C, what will the temperature be after six hours?　-18°C

Put each row in order, starting with the smallest number.

| 7.5 | 5.7 | 7.05 | 5.07 | 5.55 | 5.75 |
| 5.07 | 5.55 | 5.7 | 5.75 | 7.05 | 7.5 |

| 12.8 | 1.28 | 0.12 | 0.28 | 2.18 | 1.82 |
| 0.12 | 0.28 | 1.28 | 1.82 | 2.18 | 12.8 |

| 34.06 | 30.46 | 36.4 | 36.04 | 30.64 | 34.6 |
| 30.46 | 30.64 | 34.06 | 34.6 | 36.04 | 36.4 |

The 10 questions on this page and the following are intended to act as a small test of the preceding work. It is up to you to decide if a time limit should be set but something like 10 minutes would be about right.

Keeping skills sharp ★

Circle the fractions that are equivalent to $\frac{3}{4}$.

(30/40)　9/10　4/6　(12/16)　(300/400)　18/30

Boris has five children. Each child has a certain amount of money.

Annie $12.00　Billy $20.00　Carol $18.00　Doris $24.00　David $8.00

Boris tells each child they must give one-fifth of their money to charity. How much will each child give?

Annie	Billy	Carol	Doris	David
$2.40	$4	$3.60	$4.80	$1.60

Write the answers.

$\frac{4}{5}$ of $14 = $11.20　　$\frac{3}{4}$ of 80 cm = 60 cm　　$\frac{3}{10}$ of 2 m = 0.6 m

$\frac{2}{5}$ of 4 m = 1.6 m　　$\frac{2}{3}$ of 60 km = 40 km　　$\frac{9}{10}$ of 800 g = 720 g

Circle the fractions that are equivalent to 0.4.

$\frac{3}{4}$　(2/5)　$\frac{1}{2}$　$\frac{1}{3}$　(4/10)　$\frac{4}{8}$

What is $\frac{2}{3}$ of each amount?

$9　$6　　3 m　2 m　　150 cm　100 cm

$21　$14　　60 mL　40 mL　　$210　$140

Clearly it would be important to go over any questions that may be wrong but give plenty of encouragement for those that are correct.

★ Adding lists

Find the sum.

265 m	482 km	359 cm
177 m	209 km	423 cm
564 m	788 km	630 cm
+ 443 m	+ 734 km	+ 823 cm
1449 m	2213 km	2235 cm

894 g	412 g	4530 g
653 g	745 g	523 g
506 g	211 g	9 g
+ 789 g	+ 295 g	+ 3423 g
2842 g	1663 g	8485 g

7564 m	8675 km	5321 cm
7345 m	4173 km	3123 cm
6445 m	8347 km	5264 cm
+ 9673 m	+ 2331 km	+ 5234 cm
31 027 m	23 526 km	18 942 cm

2756 mm	9678 mm	675 g
452 mm	4500 mm	8 g
174 mm	657 mm	56 g
+ 1894 mm	+ 4336 mm	+ 3445 g
5276 mm	19 171 mm	4184 g

These questions require accuracy and concentration but should not be difficult. Just watch out for little mistakes in addition, which may lead to an incorrect total.

Subtracting ★

Find the difference.

5565	6723	9786
− 4331	− 5694	− 7564
1234	1029	2222

7407	3321	8564
− 2321	− 1665	− 3423
5086	1656	5141

7008	4505	3202
− 1745	− 1534	− 1332
5263	2971	1870

2000	5000	7000
− 1500	− 1320	− 2312
500	3680	4688

6500	6200	7800
− 2310	− 5300	− 4305
4190	900	3495

6578	4312	4560
− 789	− 656	− 206
5789	3656	4354

Schools teach subtraction in different ways but by now your child should have his or her own preferred method. It may not be the same as the one you know so be careful of trying to change what your child is doing.

★ Recognizing multiples

Circle the multiples of 12.

50   (24)   (60)   (144)

38   70   80   100   90

(36)   (120)   56   94

Circle the multiples of 15.

(45)   10   (60)   130

80   70   (75)   100   (90)

1   (150)   50   65

Circle the multiples of 20.

15   (20)   310   110

(60)   90   70   (100)   (400)

(500)   130   (200)   30

Circle the multiples of 50.

(50)   20   (350)   (500)

(750)   (1000)   70   (100)   (400)

(300)   130   240   470

Children should understand what the word "multiple" means and be able to work out some of the more usual ones such as 12 or 20.

Factors of numbers ★

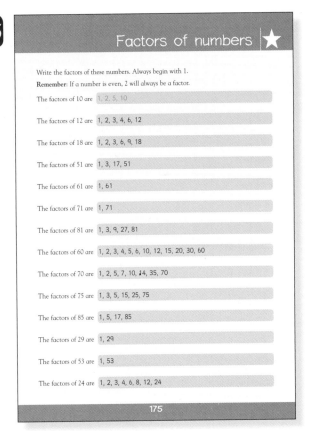

Write the factors of these numbers. Always begin with 1.
Remember: If a number is even, 2 will always be a factor.

The factors of 10 are 1, 2, 5, 10

The factors of 12 are 1, 2, 3, 4, 6, 12

The factors of 18 are 1, 2, 3, 6, 9, 18

The factors of 51 are 1, 3, 17, 51

The factors of 61 are 1, 61

The factors of 71 are 1, 71

The factors of 81 are 1, 3, 9, 27, 81

The factors of 60 are 1, 2, 3, 4, 5, 6, 10, 12, 15, 20, 30, 60

The factors of 70 are 1, 2, 5, 7, 10, 14, 35, 70

The factors of 75 are 1, 3, 5, 15, 25, 75

The factors of 85 are 1, 5, 17, 85

The factors of 29 are 1, 29

The factors of 53 are 1, 53

The factors of 24 are 1, 2, 3, 4, 6, 8, 12, 24

Encourage children to work through the possibilities for factors of large numbers logically. Children should know 2 is a factor of all even numbers. Be careful they don't assume small numbers are not factors of larger ones.

★ Times tables

By now you should know up to the 12-times tables very well.

Write the products.

Be quick and accurate!

6 x 12 = 72	5 x 9 = 45	4 x 10 = 40	3 x 8 = 24
2 x 7 = 14	5 x 12 = 60	6 x 9 = 54	7 x 10 = 70
8 x 8 = 64	3 x 7 = 21	4 x 12 = 48	7 x 9 = 63
8 x 10 = 80	7 x 8 = 56	4 x 7 = 28	3 x 12 = 36
9 x 8 = 72	10 x 10 = 100	12 x 12 = 144	11 x 9 = 99
6 x 8 = 48	6 x 7 = 42	4 x 11 = 44	3 x 9 = 27
5 x 6 = 30	7 x 5 = 35	8 x 4 = 32	9 x 7 = 63
1 x 7 = 7	3 x 6 = 18	4 x 9 = 36	7 x 6 = 42

When a number is multiplied by itself, the answer is a square number or perfect square.

Write the answers.

1 x 1 = 1	2 x 2 = 4	3 x 3 = 9	4 x 4 = 16
5 x 5 = 25	6 x 6 = 36	7 x 7 = 49	8 x 8 = 64
9 x 9 = 81	10 x 10 = 100	11 x 11 = 121	12 x 12 = 144

As with all times tables at this age, children should be accurate and fast. If they are not, give more practice. It is vital they have very good knowledge, which is speedily recalled.

Multiplying in columns ★

Work out these multiplication problems, using the method you prefer.

```
      48          67          79          54
    x 11        x 12        x 13        x 14
      48         134         237         216
+   480      +  670      +  790      +  540
     528         804        1027         756


      23          85          35          46
    x 15        x 16        x 17        x 18
     115         510         245         368
+   230      +  850      +  350      +  460
     345        1360         595         828


      59         123          68         154
    x 19        x 21        x 23        x 25
     531         123         204         770
+   590      + 2460      + 1360      + 3080
    1121        2583        1564        3850


     143         135         214         167
    x 27        x 13        x 15        x 16
    1001         405        1070        1002
+  2860      + 1350      + 2140      + 1670
    3861        1755        3210        2672
```

The questions on this page have been laid out in the traditional column style. If your child has been taught another method, check to see how it works. Be careful about trying to change the method the school has taught as this could cause confusion.

178

You may have been shown different ways to work out these problems.
Use the method you prefer to find the quotient and remainders.

47 r1	22 r1	26	20 r4
3)142	4)89	5)130	6)124
−12	−88	−10	−12
22	1	30	4
−21		−30	−0
1		0	4

18 r4	9 r6	16 r6	83 r1
7)130	8)78	9)150	2)167
−7	−72	−9	−16
60	6	60	7
−56		−54	−6
4		6	1

25 r1	26 r2	35 r3	21
3)76	4)106	5)178	6)126
−6	−8	−15	−12
16	26	28	6
−15	−24	−25	−6
1	2	3	0

26 r2	20 r6	21 r1	24 r1
7)184	8)166	9)190	2)49
−14	−16	−18	−4
44	6	10	9
−42	−0	−9	−8
2	6	1	1

30 r2	25 r1	14 r4	18 r3
3)92	4)101	5)74	6)111
−9	−8	−5	−6
2	21	24	51
−0	−20	−20	−48
2	1	4	3

The division problems on this page are shown in the traditional format but parents should be aware, as with multiplication, that schools may teach other methods. Success with this work depends greatly on good times tables knowledge.

179

Find the quotient and remainders.

15 r6	18 r9	13	4 r6
10)156	10)189	10)130	10)46
−10	−10	−10	−40
56	89	30	6
−50	−80	−30	
6	9	0	

23 r2	17 r8	8	11
10)232	10)178	10)80	10)110
−20	−10	−80	−10
32	78	0	10
−30	−70		−10
2	8		0

15	1 r4	18 r6	20
10)150	10)14	10)186	10)200
−10	−10	−10	−200
50	4	86	0
−50		−80	
0		6	

17 r2	10	12	14 r3
10)172	10)100	10)120	10)143
−10	−100	−10	−10
72	0	20	43
−70		−20	−40
2		0	3

15 r5	17 r9	18	20 r1
10)155	10)179	10)180	10)201
−10	−10	−10	−20
55	79	80	01
−50	−70	−80	−0
5	9	0	1

This page continues to reinforce children's confidence on division with remainders.

180

Write the operation (+, −, x, ÷) that makes each question true.

12 x 8 = 96   50 ÷ 6 = 8 r2   15 + 3 = 18

15 x 3 = 45   6 x 20 = 120   42 − 12 = 30

11 − 8 = 3   100 ÷ 12 = 8 r4   12 − 4 = 8

29 − 8 = 21   50 ÷ 7 = 7 r1   12 − 6 = 6

7 x 9 = 63   14 x 5 = 70   15 ÷ 3 = 5

50 − 20 = 30   21 x 3 = 63   35 ÷ 7 = 5

10 x 9 = 90   100 ÷ 8 = 12 r4   24 ÷ 3 = 8

20 − 9 = 11   40 x 8 = 320   22 x 3 = 66

50 ÷ 2 = 25   62 + 17 = 79   16 ÷ 3 = 5 r1

Children just need to look carefully at the number "sentence" and then choose the operation that will make the sentence true.

181

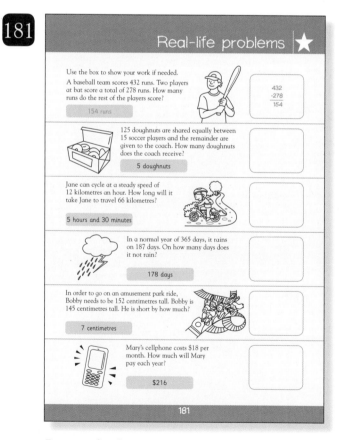

Use the box to show your work if needed.
A baseball team scores 432 runs. Two players at bat score a total of 278 runs. How many runs do the rest of the players score?
154 runs

432
−278
154

125 doughnuts are shared equally between 15 soccer players and the remainder are given to the coach. How many doughnuts does the coach receive?
5 doughnuts

Jane can cycle at a steady speed of 12 kilometres an hour. How long will it take Jane to travel 66 kilometres?
5 hours and 30 minutes

In a normal year of 365 days, it rains on 187 days. On how many days does it not rain?
178 days

In order to go on an amusement park ride, Bobby needs to be 152 centimetres tall. Bobby is 145 centimetres tall. He is short by how much?
7 centimetres

Mary's cellphone costs $18 per month. How much will Mary pay each year?
$216

Putting the four operations into use is most important and something schools don't always do because of lack of time. Children need to work out which is the right operation to use that will produce the correct answer.

★ Adding decimals

Write the answers.

3.84 + 1.39 = **5.23**	4.29 + 2.66 = **6.95**	3.91 + 4.22 = **8.13**	5.16 + 3.45 = **8.61**
7.43 + 2.66 = **10.09**	2.33 + 9.17 = **11.50**	8.92 + 3.17 = **12.09**	5.26 + 3.75 = **9.01**
11.46 + 6.56 = **18.02**	19.32 + 3.84 = **23.16**	16.67 + 4.21 = **20.88**	18.74 + 6.06 = **24.80**
15.03 + 18.78 = **33.81**	14.92 + 2.37 = **17.29**	10.45 + 5.93 = **16.38**	12.67 + 18.06 = **30.73**
32.08 + 7.92 = **40.00**	46.02 + 19.12 = **65.14**	15.01 + 14.99 = **30.00**	17.84 + 2.16 = **20.00**
423.97 + 67.94 = **491.91**	301.75 + 19.12 = **320.87**	412.85 + 56.73 = **469.58**	213.52 + 68.08 = **281.60**

182

Children need to be careful to add each column carefully and then "carry" if necessary. Remind them to place the decimal point in the correct place as some children forget to put it in the answer.

Subtracting decimals ★

Write the answers.

4.78 − 1.44 = **3.34**	9.52 − 4.56 = **4.96**	8.74 − 3.11 = **5.63**	3.97 − 1.84 = **2.13**
7.82 − 3.49 = **4.33**	6.13 − 2.08 = **4.05**	3.27 − 1.45 = **1.82**	5.24 − 4.01 = **1.23**
9.04 − 2.53 = **6.51**	6.01 − 2.67 = **3.34**	8.06 − 3.57 = **4.49**	4.79 − 1.32 = **3.47**
16.05 − 11.45 = **4.60**	12.42 − 8.67 = **3.75**	18.67 − 12.37 = **6.30**	10.23 − 3.78 = **6.45**
413.65 − 213.65 = **200.00**	215.07 − 180.01 = **35.06**	312.56 − 121.65 = **190.91**	569.72 − 236.09 = **333.63**
500.05 − 1.06 = **498.99**	150.06 − 100.09 = **49.97**	200.01 − 99.99 = **100.02**	420.69 − 89.43 = **331.26**

183

Care is needed especially when it becomes necessary to "steal" from the next column. The phrase "borrow" is incorrect because the amount is never given back. As with other operations, the school may teach a different method.

★ Money problems

Use the box to show your work if needed.

Dave delivers free magazines to houses and is paid 5 ¢ per magazine. Dave delivers 600 magazines. How much will Dave earn? **$30**

Sean wins some money on a game at the fair. He wins 79 ¢, $1.38, $0.37, and 66 ¢. How much has Sean won in total? **$3.20**

Harris is a used car dealer and on a good day he sells three cars—a Honda for $7850, a Ford for $5999, and a Toyota for $8499. What was the total value of the cars Harris sold that day? **$22 348**

Emmie is given $20 for a birthday present and spends $18.12 on clothes. How much does Emmie have left? **$1.88**

A house on Middle Brook Street costs $285 000. The house next door is smaller and costs $228 000. What is the difference in the costs? **$57 000**

A large sack of potatoes costs $12.56. A smaller sack is half the price of the large sack. How much does the smaller sack cost? **$6.28**

184

The main object here is for children to select which operation to use and then work the calculation carefully, quickly, and correctly.

Real-life problems ★

Use the box to show your work if needed.

Gas costs $1.30 per litre. Donny's dad puts 20 litres of gas in the car. How much will Donny's dad have to pay for the gas? **$26.00**

The highway route between Fredericton and Moncton is 170 kilometres. A route avoiding the highway is 196.8 kilometres. How much shorter is the highway route? **26.8 kilometres**

Rashid discovers that one-fifth of the strawberries in a pack are rotten. The pack contains 75 strawberries. How many strawberries are not rotten? **60 strawberries**

Mary measures the growth of a tomato plant. The plant grows 8 centimetres every week. How many weeks will it take for the plant to grow to 104 centimetres? **13 weeks**

Nadia measures the distance she has to walk to school. She walks 950 metres to school. How many metres will Nadia walk in five days? **4750 metres**

A doctor sees one patient every seven minutes. How long will it take for the doctor to see 25 patients? (Give your answer in hours and minutes.) **2 hours 55 minutes**

185

Putting the four operations into practical use is most important. Children need to work out which is the right operation to use to produce the correct answer.

★ Keeping skills sharp

These are the amounts collected at a church in one month.

$213.78 $197.56 $202.67 $184.26

What was the total amount collected in the month? $798.27

At the end of the year, each person owes $1250 in taxes to the government.
Each person has the following amounts in their savings.

Sean has $12 600   Darius has $9423   Emmie has $10 571

How much will each person have left after paying taxes?

Sean $11 350   Darius $8173   Emmie $9321

Write the factors of each number.

32   1, 2, 4, 8, 16, 32

64   1, 2, 4, 8, 16, 32, 64

Circle the numbers that are multiples of 12.   21   78
(24)   50   (60)   90
110   (120)   20   (132)

These are times tables questions given to Jonas in a test. Jonas has written his answers.
Put a smiley face (☺) if Jonas has written the correct answer.
If the answer is wrong, then put a (✗).

6 x 8 = 48 ☺   3 x 12 =36 ☺   5 x 9 = 54 ✗   7 x 8 = 54 ✗

6 x 7 = 42 ☺   9 x 6 = 45 ✗   8 x 9 = 72 ☺   12 x 7 = 77 ✗

This test covers the work undertaken in the previous pages and will act as a reminder and as a way of judging how well learning has taken place.

Keeping skills sharp ★

John thinks of a number and then multiplies it by 3.
He adds 6 to the new number and the result is 21.
What number did John start with?   5

What is the remainder in each division problem?

27 divided by 2   1   32 divided by 3   2

60 divided by 8   4   75 divided by 10   5

40 divided by 6   4   49 divided by 9   4

9 walkers each travelled 777 kilometres. What is the total distance the 9 walkers travelled?   6993 kilometres

Write the answers.

8.67	12.45	9.78
+ 4.88	+ 17.97	+ 12.06
13.55	30.42	21.84

A storekeeper makes $1312.86 in one day and then pays his assistant $219.90 for his wages.
How much will the storekeeper have left after he pays his assistant? $1092.96

★ Reading schedules

Look at this school schedule.

	Period 1	Period 2	Period 3	Lunch	Period 4	Period 5	Period 6
Monday	Math	Math	Science		English	PE	Social Studies
Tuesday	English	English	Social Studies		Music	Art	Art
Wednesday	Math	Science	Science		PE	English	English
Thursday	Math	English	English		Computer Projects	Computer Projects	Social Studies
Friday	Math	Math	Science		English	Library	Library

Write the answers.

On which days is Science taught?

Monday, Wednesday, and Friday

On which days is PE?

Monday and Wednesday

How many periods of Math are taught during the week?

Six

Only one subject takes place every day. What subject is that?

English

How many different subjects are taught during the week?

Nine

Which subject is taught for only one period during the week?

Music

On which day are both Social Studies and Science taught?

Monday

Which lessons take place during the 6th period?

Social Studies, Art, English, and Library

Reading schedules is an important skill and children usually enjoy it. If children are unsure about anything, suggest they simply use their finger to run along rows or columns.

Time problems ★

Use the box to show your work if needed.

A plane journey between London, England and Halifax takes 6 hours 35 minutes. If the plane leaves London at 9:35 a.m., what time will it arrive in Halifax?   4:10 p.m.

Sophie has to go shopping with her mother. They go shopping at 11:15 a.m. and return at 3:45 p.m. How long did the shopping take?   4 hours 30 minutes

A railway station clock says the time is 3:07 p.m. The clock is 10 minutes fast. What is the actual time?   2:57 p.m.

A bricklayer can lay 180 bricks in one hour. How many bricks will the bricklayer lay in eight hours?   1440 bricks

Rashid takes 35 minutes to complete a quarter of his exercises. How long will it take Rashid to complete all his exercises? (Give the answer in hours and minutes.)   2 hours 20 minutes

Lucy and Darius go on a boat trip around Georgian Bay. The trip lasts one and a half hours. If the trip begins at 2:45 p.m., what time will it finish?   4:15 p.m.

By this age children should be very familiar with analog and digital time displays and be able to change between them. Have a clock or watch nearby to demonstrate any problems if necessary.

★ | Coordinates

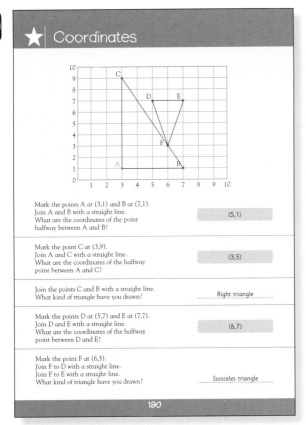

Mark the points A at (3,1) and B at (7,1).
Join A and B with a straight line.
What are the coordinates of the point
halfway between A and B?

(5,1)

Mark the point C at (3,9).
Join A and C with a straight line.
What are the coordinates of the halfway
point between A and C?

(3,5)

Join the points C and B with a straight line.
What kind of triangle have you drawn?

Right triangle

Mark the points D at (5,7) and E at (7,7).
Join D and E with a straight line.
What are the coordinates of the halfway
point between D and E?

(6,7)

Mark the point F at (6,3).
Join F to D with a straight line.
Join F to E with a straight line.
What kind of triangle have you drawn?

Isosceles triangle

The answer to the last question may prove interesting. The isosceles triangle is "upside down" compared to the one children usually see, and they may fail to recognize it without the page being turned upside down.

Graphs | ★

Temperature in a house

Look at the graph and then answer these questions.

What is the coldest temperature
in the house?

19°C

What is the range of the temperatures?

6°C

What is the warmest temperature
in the house?

25°C

For how long is the temperature
at the maximum?

3 hours

Between which hours does the
temperature drop by 2°C?

2:00 p.m. and 4:00 p.m.

7:00 p.m. and 8:00 p.m.

Between which hours does the
temperature rise the quickest?

9:00 a.m. and 10:00 a.m.

What is the temperature difference
between 8 a.m. and 8 p.m.?

2°C

How much does the temperature rise
between 10 a.m. and 11 a.m.?

1°C

Reading the graph should be done carefully but should not present too many problems. Encourage children to touch the graph with their finger if they are unsure.

★ | Using data

Children from three grades were asked to vote for their favourite breakfast cereal.

Breakfast cereals	Frequency	Total
Maple Loops	⼞⼞⼞ II	17
Weetynuts	⼞⼞⼞⼞⼞ I	26
Corndunks	⼞⼞⼞⼞ IIII	24
Grainygrit	⼞ III	8
Coconutty	⼞⼞⼞	15

The frequency table shows the results. Look at the frequency table and then answer the questions. Complete the total column.

Which was the most popular breakfast cereal?

Weetynuts

What was the mean number of votes?
(**Hint**: Mean means the average.)

18

What is the median amount of votes?
(**Hint**: Median means the middle number.)

17

How many more votes did Weetynuts have than Maple Loops?

9

What was the range of the votes?
(**Hint**: Range means the difference between the most
and the least.)

18

What is the mode of each row?
(**Hint**: Mode means the number used most.)

| 7 | 28 | 14 | 35 | 7 | 28 | 28 | 35 | 28 |

| $\frac{1}{2}$ | $\frac{1}{3}$ | $\frac{1}{2}$ | $\frac{1}{3}$ | $\frac{1}{4}$ | $\frac{1}{3}$ | $\frac{1}{3}$ | $\frac{1}{4}$ | $\frac{1}{3}$ |

Some schools will not teach these concepts until 6th grade. Mode is the number that occurs most often and median is the middle number when the numbers are arranged in order. The range is the difference between the lowest and highest value.

Perimeters | ★

Calculate the perimeter of each shape.

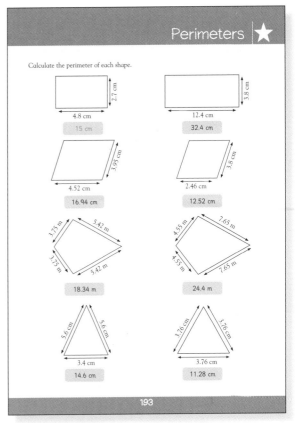

4.8 cm, 2.7 cm — 15 cm

12.4 cm, 3.8 cm — 32.4 cm

4.52 cm, 3.95 cm — 16.94 cm

2.46 cm, 3.8 cm — 12.52 cm

3.75 m, 5.42 m, 3.75 m, 5.42 m — 18.34 m

4.55 m, 7.65 m, 4.55 m, 7.65 m — 24.4 m

5.6 cm, 5.6 cm, 3.4 cm — 14.6 cm

3.76 cm, 3.76 cm, 3.76 cm — 11.28 cm

Children should know "perimeter" means the distance around the outside of a shape. With these perimeters they need to be careful about adding the decimal amounts.

★ Square numbers

Calculate the area of each square. You may use a calculator.
Round your answers to the nearest hundredth place.

4.65 cm × 4.65 cm × 4.65 cm × 4.65 cm → 21.62 cm²

5.96 m × 5.96 m × 5.96 m × 5.96 m → 35.52 m²

3.81 cm × 3.81 cm × 3.81 cm × 3.81 cm → 14.52 cm²

7.5 m × 7.5 m × 7.5 m × 7.5 m → 56.25 m²

4.8 cm × 4.8 cm × 4.8 cm × 4.8 cm → 23.04 cm²

17.5 m × 17.5 m × 17.5 m × 17.5 m → 306.25 m²

Work out each of these.

15 x 15 = 225   13 x 13 = 169   14 x 14 = 196

16 x 16 = 256   20 x 20 = 400   25 x 25 = 625

The idea of "area" should be understood by now as the amount of space inside a shape. Using a calculator to work out the answer is reasonable, but you may want your child to complete the answer with long multiplication.

Areas ★

Find the area of each shape.

5 cm × 4 cm → 20 cm²

10 m × 7 m → 70 m²

3 m × 3 m → 9 m²

9 m × 9 m → 81 m²

12 m × 10 m → 120 m²

6 cm × 3 cm → 18 cm²

15 cm × 15 cm → 225 cm²

13 m × 13 m → 169 m²

The answers can be written as "square metre" or "metres squared" but are usually written in the m² style.

★ Recognizing angles

Write whether these angles are acute, right, obtuse, or reflex.
(**Hint**: Reflex angles are larger than 180° but less than 360°).

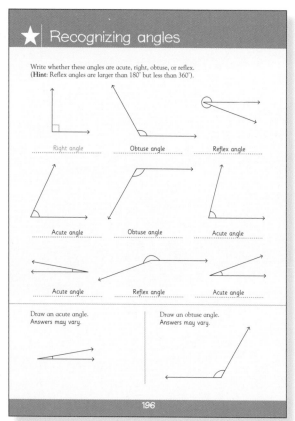

Right angle   Obtuse angle   Reflex angle

Acute angle   Obtuse angle   Acute angle

Acute angle   Reflex angle   Acute angle

Draw an acute angle.
Answers may vary.

Draw an obtuse angle.
Answers may vary.

Children must be careful to look out for the arc that indicates which part of the angle is being considered. The right angle has its own form of recognition, which children should know.

Measuring angles ★

Use a protractor to measure each angle.

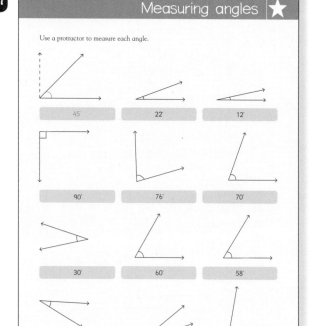

45°   22°   12°

90°   76°   70°

30°   60°   58°

28°   39°   80°

Although students in Grade 5 usually measure and construct angles up to 90°, encouage them to try constructing angles larger than 90°.

★ 3-D shapes

Name each shape and give the information.

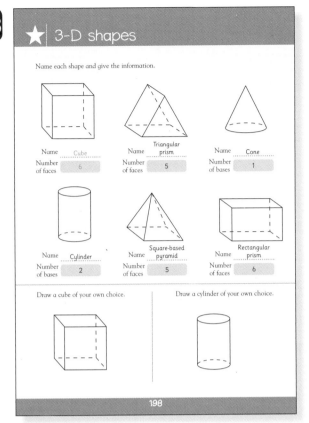

Name Cube	Name Triangular prism	Name Cone
Number of faces 6	Number of faces 5	Number of bases 1
Name Cylinder	Name Square-based pyramid	Name Rectangular prism
Number of bases 2	Number of faces 5	Number of faces 6

Draw a cube of your own choice.

Draw a cylinder of your own choice.

Children should be confident with knowing the names of the common 3-D shapes and their attributes such as flat or curved surfaces and number of edges.

Sorting 3-D shapes ★

Draw the 3-D shape in the box.

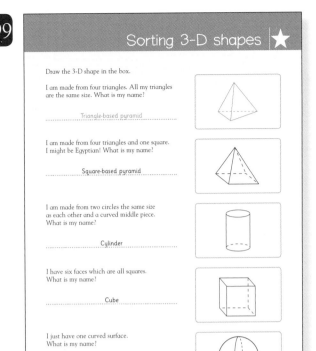

I am made from four triangles. All my triangles are the same size. What is my name?

Triangle-based pyramid

I am made from four triangles and one square. I might be Egyptian! What is my name?

Square-based pyramid

I am made from two circles the same size as each other and a curved middle piece. What is my name?

Cylinder

I have six faces which are all squares. What is my name?

Cube

I just have one curved surface. What is my name?

Sphere

It can be tricky to draw shapes such as cubes, so offer help but don't expect complete accuracy. Drawing and showing a sphere can be especially difficult and may turn out to look like a circle so be encouraging.

Keeping skills sharp

These two clocks show times in the morning. What is the difference between them?

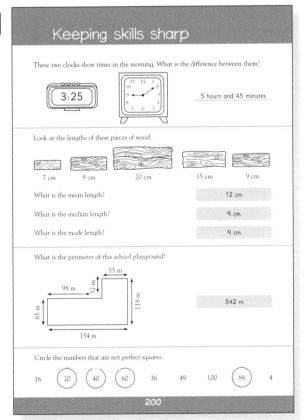

3:25

5 hours and 45 minutes

Look at the lengths of these pieces of wood.

7 cm   9 cm   20 cm   15 cm   9 cm

What is the mean length?   12 cm

What is the median length?   9 cm

What is the mode length?   9 cm

What is the perimeter of this school playground?

55 m, 52 m, 98 m, 118 m, 65 m, 154 m

542 m

Circle the numbers that are not perfect squares.

16   ⟨20⟩   ⟨40⟩   ⟨60⟩   36   49   100   ⟨88⟩   4

The final test covers the work of the previous pages. Encourage children to seek advice if an answer is wrong and then go through it very carefully until they gain confidence.

Keeping skills sharp

Draw one of each type of angle. You do not need to use a protractor but make sure you mark the angle correctly. Answers may vary.

Right angle   Acute angle   Obtuse angle   Reflex angle

Use a protractor to carefully measure each angle.

a.   38°   b.   54°

Use a protractor to carefully draw these angles.

67°   45°

Mark the points on this grid.

A = (3,5)   B = (5,0)

C = $(4, 1\frac{1}{2})$ D = $(0, 5\frac{1}{2})$

DK
Senior Editor Deborah Lock
Art Director Martin Wilson
Publishing Director Sophie Mitchell
Pre-production Francesca Wardell
Jacket Designer Martin Wilson
Canadian Editor Barbara Campbell
Canadian Math Consultant Marilyn Wilson

DK Delhi
Editorial Monica Saigal, Tanya Desai
Design Pallavi Narain, Dheeraj Arora,
Tanvi Nathyal, Jyotsna Khosla
DTP Designer Anita Yadav

Expanded Canadian Edition, 2013
DK Publishing is represented in Canada by
Tourmaline Editions Inc.
662 King Street West, Suite 304
Toronto, Ontario M5V 1M7

Published in Great Britain in 2013
by Dorling Kindersley Limited
Copyright © 2005, 2013 Dorling Kindersley Limited
A Penguin Company
13 14 15 10 9 8 7 6 5 4 3 2 1
001-187486-August 2013

Library and Archives Canada Cataloguing in Publication
Math made easy : grade 5, ages 10-11 /
Canadian math consultant,
Marilyn Wilson. -- Expanded Canadian ed.
ISBN 978-1-55363-206-1
1. Mathematics--Problems, exercises, etc.
2. Mathematics--Study and teaching (Elementary).
I. Wilson, Marilyn
QA107.2.M3886 2013   510.76   C2012-908198-1

DK books are available at special discounts when
purchased in bulk for corporate sales, sales promotions,
premiums, fund-raising, or educational use.
For details, please contact specialmarkets@tourmaline.ca.

Printed and bound in China by L. Rex Printing Co., Ltd.

All images © Dorling Kindersley.
For further information see: www.dkimages.com
Discover more at
www.dk.com